Advance

THE BOY FROM BUZWAH

"This book chronicles the life and times of Cecil King from his humble beginnings on an Indian reserve to the giant of a man who paved the way for Indigenous control of education in Canada. Cecil's story is one of perseverance, strength, and resiliency. This is a must-read for everyone." —MANLEY A. BEGAY, JR., Applied Indigenous Studies, Northern Arizona University

"Indigenizing the academy begins here with Cecil's vivid memoirs of a life lived Indigenizing the academies." —MARIE BATTISTE, author of *Decolonizing Education* and Honorary Officer of the Order of Canada

"Dr. Cecil King's memoir is a fascinating account of his childhood on Manitoulin Island during a time of transition where education controlled by residential schools run by religious orders was ending and his own education led him to becoming a warrior for the 1973 goal of Indian Control of Indian Education and the right to self-determination to include Indigenous languages, cultures, histories, and values into pedagogies and curriculums in training institutions he helped create. We owe him much thanks for his contributions in the continuing quest for Indigenous Control of Indigenous Education!" —RUSS DIABO, Senior Indigenous Policy Analyst

"Cecil King's book…presents an important perspective in the debate on educational change in the past half-century. His personal perspective and his use of Ojibwe as part of this history introduces a new qualitative dimension to this debate." —KEITH GOULET, former Minister of Northern Affairs for Saskatchewan

"Cecil King's memoir is an important contribution to Indigenous literature, documenting early life on the Wikwemikong Unceded Indian Reserve, disclosing the enduring roots of Odawa tradition, chronicling the re-emergence of Anishnawbe culture and the rise of Indigenous activism, particularly in the important area of Indigenous education." —THE HONOURABLE LEONARD S. (TONY) MANDAMIN

"The teacher, respected community leader, and post-secondary professor and administrator argues most convincingly for a system of First Nations education that incorporates fully Indigenous history, culture, and present-day realities. I love Cecil's book!" —DON SMITH, Professor Emeritus of History, University of Calgary

"An essential account of an Indigenous scholar's trailblazing and sweeping contributions towards restoring and inspiring Indigenous control of Indigenous education." —VERNA ST DENIS, Professor and Special Advisor to the President on Anti-Racism/Anti-Oppression, College of Education, University of Saskatchewan

"Miigwetch Cecil King, for sharing your remarkable journey and life in this essential book, which educators and learners will treasure. This is a book of extraordinary generosity and humility, and one that provides both context and direction for the future of Indigenous education." —JESSE WENTE, Chair, Canada Council of the Arts

"[Dr. Cecil King] laid the grounds for the birth of what we now relish; namely Indigenous Education from [an] Indigenous perspective; a mindset that saw everything and everyone of great importance in his presence, not at all effaced by the colonial attitude nor structure put in place to do away with 'Indians.'" —KARLA JESSEN WILLIAMSON, College of Education, University of Saskatchewan

University of Regina Press designates one title each year that best exemplifies the guiding editorial and manuscript production principles of long-time senior editor Donna Grant.

THE BOY
FROM BUZWAH

A Life in Indian Education

CECIL KING

 University of Regina Press

COVER PHOTO: "Cecil in a Mountie jacket taken from rummage provided by Garnier Residential School." Courtesy the author.

COVER AND BOOK DESIGN: Duncan Campbell, University of Regina Press
COPY EDITOR: Marionne Cronin
PROOFREADER: Kendra Ward
INDEXER: Trish Furdek
MAP: Weldon Hiebert

Library and Archives Canada Cataloguing in Publication

TITLE: The boy from Buzwah : a life in Indian education / Cecil King.

NAMES: King, Cecil O., 1932- author.

DESCRIPTION: Includes index.

IDENTIFIERS: Canadiana (print) 20210360100 | Canadiana (ebook) 20210360178 | ISBN 9780889778504 (softcover) | ISBN 9780889778535 (hardcover) | ISBN 9780889778511 (PDF) | ISBN 9780889778528 (EPUB)

SUBJECTS: LCSH: King, Cecil O., 1932- | LCSH: Teachers,—Canada,—Biography. | LCSH: Language teachers,—Canada,—Biography. | CSH: First Nations,— Canada,—Biography. | CSH: First Nations,—Education,—Canada. | CSH: First Nations,—Canada,—Residential schools. | LCSH: Wikwemikong Unceded Indian Reserve (Ont.),—Biography. | LCGFT: Autobiographies.

CLASSIFICATION: LCC E99.O9 K56 2022 | DDC 371.10092,—dc23

University of Regina Press, University of Regina
Regina, Saskatchewan, Canada, s4s 0a2
tel: (306) 585-4758 fax: (306) 585-4699
web: www.uofrpress.ca

U OF R PRESS

We acknowledge the support of the Canada Council for the Arts for our publishing program. We acknowledge the financial support of the Government of Canada. / Nous reconnaissons l'appui financier du gouvernement du Canada. This publication was made possible with support from Creative Saskatchewan's Book Publishing Production Grant Program.

To the Ancestors

CONTENTS

ACKNOWLEDGEMENTS

ahow!! Maatchta dah—Wenesh wok gah shkih keek mitt wah zin towgiyan?

Okay!! Let's start. Who was first in telling me about growing up? I wish to acknowledge all who have had something to do with my horizons and my life itself. I'll attempt to thank the many. I do owe you all special thank-yous.

As I launch into this I am awed as I see the scope of this undertaking and view you all to whom I owe your priceless time, patience, and visions of my prospects for success, as it is you, the individuals who undertook the hammering and shaping of one hapless Indian into what you may have believed was needed in this case. You have all been superheroes yourselves and again a *kitchi miigwetch* to all of you.

I acknowledge, firstly, my three septuagenarians, as they did set my beginnings and, of course, it has counted. Then I must acknowledge the four Ojibwe teachers of Buzwah Indian Day School and how significant life can be under such tutelage. These First Nations teachers mattered. So, thank you Christine, Clara, Rita, and Liza Jane. Life with you four was a slice through my elementary school years. You successfully entered me into the helter-skelter world of academe and the culture of my people.

The trail has been long and I suppose arduous, but as I think now it has been a happy trail. Thanks to you, John Sugden, for keeping me on track. Then, I have an army of stalwarts without whose interventions this day would not be. Thanks, Rodney Soonias, Smith Atimoyoo, Danny Umpherville, Art Blue, Adam Cuthand, Stan Cuthand, Danny Musqua, Ken Goodwill, Audie Dyer, Robert Surtees, Jerry Hammersmith, and Murray Scarf. No doubt there are many others equally deserving my thanks, such as Helen Hornbeck Tanner, Evelyn Moore-Eyman, Don Smith, and of course the Kirk (Dean Kirkpatrick).

I wish to honour my first born, a daughter, Denise, who now dwells in the land of spirits. Denise showed me the meaning of life for, while she struggled with it in her own world, she showed me how precious life can be and what a privilege life really is. Denise left us as she entered what should have been her midlife and when she was about to make a difference for us all. The beauty of Candace's and Feather's mother's spirit is reflected in their accomplishments and would make her proud. Thank you, Denise, your life lives with us.

I am most indebted to my son Daryl. He is a good researcher and historian who will carry on teaching our community its story. I want to thank Anna-Leah. She became a teacher who worked with kids and families in the inner city. She is now a professor at the University of Regina. She and I have had high-powered discussions on educational theory and the intricacies of Ojibwe words.

Alanis is the creative one. She has the gift of telling a story in a gentle way so that the audience realizes the hard realities of Indigenous lives in Canada without feeling hatred or rancour. Tanya has assisted me with the new technology. She is efficient with organizational skills that I could never hope to acquire. Thank you Shoo-Shoo.

Also I would like to say *miigwetch* to Sharon Thomas, Canada Council for the Arts, University of Regina Press, Shingwauk Archive Photo Collection, Gladys Wakegejig, Shoo-Shoo King-Maracle, B'Elanna Maracle, Elizabeth Bateman, Tony Mandamin, and all who helped along the way towards publication.

And finally, in conclusion, I must acknowledge a very special person and, to me, a loving mate for over forty years who patiently corrected all the academic faults and shortcomings of a blossoming author. Catherine, you have been a real soldier for my memoirs. *Kitchi miigwetch*.

Many thanks.
Cecil King

A NOTE ON OJIBWE ORTHOGRAPHY

Our language is not meant to be written. For generations it has always been passed down, has always been taught as a part of our oral tradition, and it makes us who we are. Ever since I became an educator utilizing our language in the classroom in the 1950s, there have been many orthographies that have come and gone. I've used the one that was developed by Frederic Baraga (1797–1868), a missionary priest from Slovenia who worked among our people in the middle of the nineteenth century. I also tried that developed by the linguist Charles Fiero, but felt it didn't quite work for me. I have observed much debate about orthography over the years and have learned that it can take up a lot of time and energy, when what is really important is speaking our language and passing it on. So, yes, I spell Ojibwe in my own way, but I am confident I will be understood by my community and the wider base of fluent speakers who might have a different dialect.

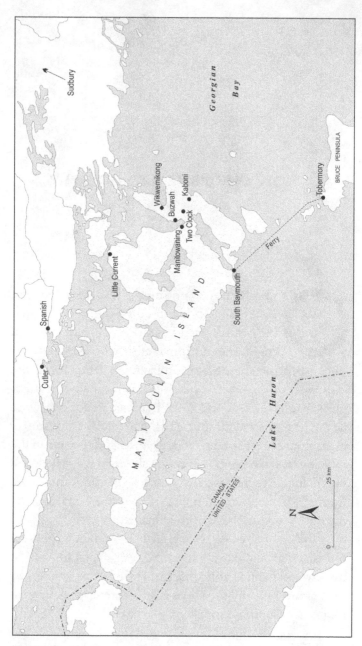

Manitoulin Island.

1. GROWING UP WITH PA, MAMA, AND KOHKWEHNS

Miigwetch, n'dikit, Wekomehyek Nongo
Monpe Wenassamigabowitonegok—behmi
Peetchi Zeetahyahn Dush N'ge Bigossenmah
Wo Kina-gego Nehtahatod Wewedgeewid,
Wee Moshkineshkawid Nebwakahwin Onje
N'dahkodowinan Djeminokagoyeg . . .

This was the prayer of my grandfather, John King. Before he spoke to a gathering, he would ask the Master of Life to make his mere words a good medicine to those who heard them.

The purpose of this writing is to finally set to paper the story of my life. This work represents that story and perhaps, more arrogantly, can be referred to as my memoirs. My name is Cecil King and I originate from a household prominent in an area known locally as Two Clock. There I began my life's saga.

I am *Odawa*. My grandfather maintained that, in the beginning, there were three biological brothers—*Odawa*, *Pottawatomii*, and *Ojibwe*. Together, they were the *Anishnabek*. Over many years, they went their separate ways and, as a result, three separate nations were formed—the *Ojibwek*, the *Odawak*, and the *Potawatamiik*. In the old stories, we are remembered as *Niswi Shkoden Wiikanendowin* (the Three Fires Confederacy). We, the Odawak, were the younger brothers, the Ojibwek, the eldest brothers, and the Potawatamiik, the middle brothers. To this day, we of the *Niswi Shkoden Wiikanendowin* speak the same language, reminding us that we are descended from the same ancestors.

We call ourselves Anishnabek. I am *Anishnabe,* which literally means "I am a person of good intent" or "I am a person of worth." Our people believe that we and other human beings are all fundamentally "good." While we take pride in being Anishnabe, we see ourselves as part of the larger human community. We recognize all of humankind as the creations of *Kizhe-Manito* (Great Benevolent Spirit).

My ancestors inhabited the lands adjacent to all the lakes and rivers in the middle of the continent in the area referred to as the eastern Great Lakes Basin. In the centre of this region, on the north shore of Lake Huron, the part called Georgian Bay, is *Manito-miniss,* Isle of Manito—or "Island of God." The Old Ones say that Manito-miniss is a gift from the Creator to the Odawak and has been the traditional homeland of my people since time immemorial. We did not come from some faraway place; Manitoulin has always been our home. Our elders tell us this.

In many stories, our Old Ones have told us about our beginnings, and this is my attempt to share what I have learned. It is said that the Odawak travelled from our island all over this vast land in the four directions, from the Atlantic coast in the east, then westward to where the great Mississippi River divides the continent, and then northward to the height of land, from where the rivers all flow the other way, then southward to the Florida Gulf Coast. We lived and thrived, exercising our sovereignty over this vast land, living by the Laws of the Orders and respecting our reasons to be.

In the Odawa worldview there is only one law, and that is *Enendagwad*, the Law of the Orders, prescribed by the Maker of all Things. Creation came about from the union of the Maker and the physical world. Out of this union came the natural children, the Plants, nurtured from the physical world—Earth, their mother. To follow were the Animalkind—the two-legged, the four-legged, the winged, those who swim, and those who crawl, all dependent on the plant world and Mother Earth for succour.

Finally, last in the Orders comes Humankind, the most dependent and least necessary of all the Orders. Human beings, of all the Maker's creatures, are totally dependent. Our existence in the order of things is dependent upon the benevolence of those with whom we coexist. Aware of this interdependency, our people looked on the other Orders as our parents, siblings, and kin.

The Odawa worldview, then, is established on the belief that, in the order of things, human beings are last. We are acutely aware of our interdependency on all the other Orders. The Odawak respected the physical world, the plant world, and the animal world, for without them there would be no life or meaning. Meaning exists in the interrelationships of things, in the way in which things happen together. We see that only together do things have meaning and become whole.

As stated, I am from Two Clock, a suburb of Buzwah, on the Wikwemikong Unceded Indian Reserve, Manitoulin Island, Ontario. Joe Jocko built a store. He felt there should be a name and that's when he came up with Two Clock.

I lived on the bottom corner of Manitowaning Bay. It is there that I began my first walk in life, over ninety years ago. I grew up in a household with my grandfather, John King (Pa), my grandmother, Harriet King (Mama), and an elder my brother and sisters and I called *Kohkwehns*. Over the years there were many other people who joined our household for different periods. My parents and siblings lived with us until I was about five, when they moved to their own place. I was left behind. I figure it was to keep my grandparents company given their own early loss of a child. At times, a hired man lived with us. I don't remember his name. A family friend of Ma's, *Getaykwe*, also lived with us in winters to have warmth and not to be alone. She stayed in the little shack behind the house until she died. She ate with us, and Pa kept the fire going at her place.

Pa, according to family history, was the grandson of David Madjig, who was not considered one of the "owners" at Wikwemikong because he had arrived as a refugee in the 1840s from Beausoleil Island at the southeast end of Georgian Bay. Not being descendants of what were believed to be the five original families at Wiwemikong, his family were still considered "outsiders" by the original Odawa or "owners." Mama, on the other hand, was Odawa, the great-great-granddaughter of Jean-Baptiste (J.B.) Assiginack, spokesperson for the Odawak. I'll have more to say about him later.

As a child, I knew I was Odawa, but by the time I came along, the priests and the white government agents had told our elders that it was more important for children to learn English than Ojibwe (as our language was called) and that we should not know our stories, our songs, our ceremonies, or pray to *Kizhe-Manito* in our traditional way. We were to become like all other Canadians. My grandmother was trained as a teacher and she brought me up in the style of a very strict Victorian schoolmarm. She was determined to teach me to be a good person and a productive citizen.

Mama believed that I would need English to get along in the world. I was raised speaking English under Mama's watchful eye, but Kohkwehns was a very traditional person and she taught me many traditional things. I learned Ojibwe expressions from her when we would go together to pick medicines and berries or do the many other things that she wanted to teach me. She was determined that I would be a good human being who lived in harmony with the Orders. Kohkwehns was midwife for my brother, Don, and me but was replaced by another woman for the birthing of my sisters, Liz and Loretta.

Kohkwehns was tall and seemed to tower over us. She was strong. She had silver-coloured hair, which was braided, and she was about seventy years old. She wasn't really my grandmother; in fact, she wasn't anybody's grandmother. She was the teacher that stands out from all the others. Kohkwehns always made my world so important. No matter how simple or childlike my world was, she had a way of making it the most important thing of the moment. We always walked places. She always had things that needed to be done at a certain time. She knew where to go, and on the way she would find things to occupy our minds. When we were alone together, she talked to me like an equal. I was the important person. The whole trip would turn out as if I had organized it myself. We'd go for water, pick strawberries, pick medicines, or gather birchbark.

And once a year, we would go on a pilgrimage to her old house. We'd just sit in it and always have a treat. When we went to her house, she'd find things to look at. There was an old Bible and old catalogues. When we got home, she'd relate stories about things I had done that were very simple, but she made them very important. She'd say, "*N'gee-kitchi-bapah nongo maba*" (I really laughed at this one today). She had a pipe, and I would steal matches from my grandfather for her. At night, she'd sit out in the shed and smoke her pipe and braid her hair. I remember trying to get a stump for her to stand on to cut bark higher up the tree. I could hardly budge it and she had to help me, but afterwards she made me feel that it was my strength that moved the stump.

Mama King was the one who named us all. Where she came up with my name has always been a mystery. "Cecil" was a very English name in our community in the midst of all the French names, a legacy of the fur trade and the influence of French Jesuit missionaries. My friends, all who were growing up in Ojibwe-speaking homes, found a way to change my strange-sounding English name into something they knew. They called me *Cheesan,* which means "Turnip." No other Ojibwe word came close.

I went through life thinking that I had only one name, and it was a shock, to say the least, to receive my baptismal record when I was planning a trip to Mexico in 1975 and to find that I did indeed have a second name. The baptismal record read: "Cecil Oraza King." What does one do with a name like Oraza? And what would my initials have been? Thank goodness my schoolmates never learned of this!

As mentioned, I grew up in a household of senior citizens, as they would be called today. My parents and siblings lived down the road. We had all lived with my grandparents when I came into the world on February 22, 1932, but when my parents moved away to their own place, I stayed at Two Clock with the septuagenarians.

When my parents moved away, I remember Mama saying to me, "So you're going to leave us?" I ended up staying.

I guess Pa and Mama liked kids. I didn't know much about them. Like most kids, I didn't question what their younger lives were like. I was aware of the picture of Rose in an old alarm clock housed high up in Mama's room. I somehow knew that she was a child of Pa and Mama's who had died. That is as far as it went. As a student, working on our genealogy, I found reference in the 1911 census to Alfred, a child living in the household of Harriet and John King. This may have been a brother of my father that we were never told about. So I may have been more precious to two people who had a history of lost children than I had any way of knowing. However it happened, I became like a son to the Old Ones.

Kohkwehns was the resident nanny. I was always left with her when Pa and Mama went somewhere. Kohkwehns always had things for us to do as soon as Pa and Mama drove off. We picked roots, went for birchbark, dug up different plants that she needed, or picked berries. In those times alone together, we used to talk. I could ask her any question that was on my mind and she'd stop what she was doing and make it a very important occasion to respond. It was in these sessions with Kohkwehns that I must have learned Ojibwe. My grandmother, as an old teacher, believed that it was her responsibility to teach me to speak English and so it was the language of the household when I was being addressed. But in those times when Kohkwehns and I were alone, we were in an Ojibwe world—Kohkwehns's world.

The Ojibwe language was spoken in our household, too, but only on certain topics. Mama spoke Ojibwe quite easily, but as certain events took place, the language would swing into English. Kohkwehns, as I understand now, was a fluent Ojibwe speaker until she joined in at the supper table, where she would enter into the world of English. Mama spoke only English at mealtimes but seemed quite comfortable in a conversation in Ojibwe. Pa spoke only English at the table, but when he needed to emphasize his topic or give it some import, he would come charging in in Ojibwe. He was never stuck for an Ojibwe word. So I might as well say that English was the language at the table, but other times, other places, Ojibwe would take over.

We had a comfortable home. Our house was large compared to other dwellings in the Two Clock area, made of logs and stuccoed walls. It was two levels, with the bedrooms all on the upper level, and I slept upstairs. It is my impression that Pa built this home himself. Everyone built their own houses when I was growing up in Buzwah.

My first awareness certainly starts here. We were comfortable—Pa, Mama, Kohkwehns, and I. We all united as a family unit, each with his or her own role, and each played the role well. Pa farmed, so we ate our own pork and mutton and drank milk from our own cows. Pa provided a good living for us. He seemed to always be cutting wood with my brother Don and Dad, who cut firewood for their place as Pa did for ours. The house was warm and we were all cozy.

I had no alternative but to have a role in that, too. The wood had to be carried into the house and piled in a strategic corner, a practice that never varied, and I knew, should I have tried something else, the fire in the house would have gone out. So one of my commandments was never to be late, otherwise Mama would soon be looking for me and I would endure a fitting punishment for my negligence. Kohkwehns was always my salvation, for she would cover for me one way or another. If Mama was particularly tyrannical, Kohkwehns would speak very quietly to Mama and try to tell her something amusing about me to make Mama at least smile.

This was routine life at home—never varied and always expected. I was content as long as Kohkwehns was there and I was comfortable—except when I started school. Things seemed upsetting to Kohkwehns and she had difficulties maintaining her roles in protecting me and appeasing Mama. Pa was always outside and never noticed the tyranny of Mama, though his involvement would seem futile, as she kept out of his road to avoid crossing him.

Our lives had daily rituals. Pa would get up first and light the fire in the kitchen stove. He would sit beside it until it got going. Then he would fill the kettle with water dipped from the pail kept near the stove on the cupboard he made for it. He made coffee, when we could afford it, with the hot water. But tea was always ready. The teapot stayed on the stove, and in the morning what remained in the pot only needed a dash of hot water to be made ready again.

Pa kept a small cast-iron black pot in the cupboard where the water pails sat. He would put just enough water in the little pot and put it on the stove. When the water was boiling, he got the bag of *ne-nah-be-gahn* (rolled oats) from its place on the shelf in the pantry cupboard. Pa measured the *ne-nah-be-gahn* by putting his hand into the bag and bringing out a precise amount for the boiling pot. He then stirred the porridge until it was ready for breakfast.

Life in Wikwemikong First Nation centred on the water. Growing up on Manitowaning Bay, my view always included water. Many teachings about the water came to me as a youngster. I did not learn to swim. Swimming was not a traditional activity. Our people feared the water and the water spirits who lived beneath. Kohkwehns cautioned me about the power of the water spirits. She said, "*Gi de be ne gwun midinahn.*" She said that the powers in the water would lure you into the deep water and you would drown. The spirit of the water would catch you walking near the shore, put a spell on you, and the waves would suck you back into the deeper water.

I remember one afternoon when Mother and the rest of us were playing on shore. This was laundry day for Mother, and Don, Liz, Loretta, and I were playing in the water. We were swimming when, all of a sudden, Elizabeth disappeared into the deeper water. She was terrified and called for Mother. Mother flew into the water and saved Liz, but this was an example of the water spirit getting at us. We never went swimming there again. The water spirit became annoyed because we were making too much noise and disrespecting the water spirit.

Kohkwehns said that *Kwa shi* was the term for shipwreck or the "winds breaking the boat." Sailboats were *be mos igin.* The sail was the *mos. Dagowogda gi be boshkiiwuk* meant the "big waves would have crested" and would then enter the boat itself. If this happened a number of times, the boat would *gin dah un* (swamp). These were scary moments, as it was felt that *Mishepeshu* (Spirit of the Sea) was determined to sink your boat. Mishepeshu was a scary monster—it drowned people. This was in the minds of my seafaring people. Kohkwehns made sure I knew this and these stories.

Kohkwehns knew of shipwrecks. She had stories, some sad, but these tales were always told as a lesson. I had to know something from them. It seemed that Kohkwehns had arrived here by sea, though she was never clear where she had sailed from before settling in with Mama and Pa. This part of her life was private and she kept it to herself.

I never knew exactly who she was or how she happened to be in our world. Small hints came out about her life, and it may be that she was, in fact, Mama's sister-in-law, the widow of Mama's brother who we only spoke of as *Shoehn*. This would make her my great-aunt by marriage in English terminology, but this was never explained to me.

It seemed Pa had no problem with the arrangement. For Mama it was another thing; she always seemed to boss Kohkwehns. Mama scolded her at every opportunity, but Kohkwehns never seemed to mind. In my growing-up years I watched this often, and Kohkwehns never said anything. Pa and Kohkwehns got along, it seemed, and he used to tease her; they would laugh. She was always helpful in whatever Pa happened to be doing. I used to feel good when the two of them were together. Mama just totally ignored them.

Kohkwehns was a strong woman who could work with men on any task. She could chop wood and carry huge bundles from the boat when loading and unloading. Kohkwehns was there to help and, in fact, the loading or unloading never started until she was there in her place. She instructed me about work. There was an art to it, she used to say. She told me that some men never learned this and so they ended up hating work itself. This made the work harder to do, Kohkwehns would tell me. She taught me to like work. She used to tell me that if I saw someone working, I should edge my way in to help with the strength I already had. She said, "Never wait until you are invited to help. Just help! If the person doesn't want your help, he will tell you, but you will know that he recognized that you know how to work." This was Kohkwehns's always-ready lesson. Some people just loved working and Kohkwehns understood what had to be done;

usually I'd be there somewhere, busy at something she had set aside for me to do. And so, in my very early years, I knew a lot about what work was about. In fact, everyone learned this from Kohkwehns.

Mama tended the house. She seemed to like decorating, putting up fancy things like starched curtains on the windows. She would scrub the floor, although this was definitely one of Kohkwehns's jobs. Mama would be there to criticize and stand over her. Scrubbing, I suppose, was an art that only Mama knew and she was convinced Kohkwehns wouldn't know. So it was up to her to show Kohkwehns how to do it. Our house was not exactly modern. Most of the walls were wallpapered, an art of Mama's, though with the help of Kohkwehns. Some walls were wallpapered with basic newspapers. This would be Mama's decision and that was all there was to it.

I found what I can only call *peace* in the atmosphere of our household after Mama had hung up a new set of starched cheesecloth curtains. I never knew how or where she got all the cheesecloth. This practice seemed to coincide with the festive seasons like Christmas or Easter. I knew our windows would be decorated and I knew it was Mama who would do this. This seemed to add to making a happy household. Pa and Kohkwehns never touched these curtains. I think this was out of respect for Mama—it was a silent thing. In the summer and spring months these curtains were pulled aside and tied and lids with fly disinfectant now appeared. In the summertime we had to contend with the houseflies, as they were numerous. We never quite figured out the use of window and door screens. So swatting flies was a constant activity and an endless battle. Furthermore, refrigeration had not reached our household (although I did know what an icebox was), adding to the fly invasion.

Cool storage places like the basement or cellar of a home were used for preserving food.

Mama liked flowers and she would make bouquets for the house. She had what she called a tea rose in her flowerbed. I didn't learn until much later in life that a tea rose was a special kind of rose not likely to end up in a flowerbed at Two Clock. I never thought to ask her where it came from; I guess I just thought that all plants were always there, but now I wonder where they came from. Her rosebush was in the bed beside the irises. When there were no flowers in her flowerbed, Mama would go into the fields and pick wildflowers for her bouquets.

Next to the house, which was Mama's domain, was the *Wigwamehnsing* (place where a workshop is), which was Pa's domain. I would venture into this place that Pa kept so well organized that he knew immediately if anything was missing. He had put evenly spaced nails in the wall and hung a leather loop on each through which he could secure each of his tools in its own special place. I was a curious young man and wanted to know how everything worked. The workshop had a fascinating collection of levers, things to hit things with, things to fasten things with, and things to demolish things with. I wanted to try them all. There was a vice, perfect for holding things, on a workbench. When things were broken in the house, they had to be fixed. Everything that was broken could be fixed. First, you had to take it to the *Wigwamehnsing* and clamp it to the vice. You had to look at it and decide how it could be fixed. If it was made of wood, you always had wood around to fix it. If it was tin, there were always rattail files on the wall in the leather loops where the tools were hung. I would use things to fix things and experiment with how things worked. I would fiddle around with tin and make something.

With Pa busy doing jobs to bring cash into the household, sometimes things that needed fixing around the place had to wait for him to attend to them. I remember that, when I got big enough, I would sometimes decide to do the fixing myself. I built a wide gate once. I dug out the old posts and found enough lumber to make the gate itself. I had to attach chunks of iron to it. I got the bolts out that were there and placed them onto my creation.

I went into the bush, cut down a cedar tree, delimbed it, and skinned it. I took our horse, Queen, into the bush with me. I wrapped a chain around the log and Queen dragged it home for me. When I had dug out the old posts, I had made a nice hole. I decided to use Queen to put the new post in the hole. I blocked the hole and tied the small end of the log to the horse and pulled it up to a certain place where I could slip it into the hole. I pushed it different ways to make sure it was straight. I added gravel and stones to make it firm. Then I had to measure the bottom hinge into position. I put one in and then calculated the right distance for the other one. I remember I had to fuss and jiggle the gate until it slid into place.

It swung. I was so proud. I just sat all afternoon and watched the gate swing back and forth. Pa would never have taken the time to make another gate!

Mama, Kohkwehns, Pa, and I bonded in every way that happens in a household. There were never any indecisions or ill feelings. Sometimes, approaching mealtime, I would get tired—like little ones are apt to do. At times, supper seemed to drag and never end. Kohkwehns liked to make scones, which she did quite easily. Mama tended to do baking, something from the cookbook created especially for the meal. This baking was special and every one of us had to eat it. Mama would then speak to us all about the virtue of food and the respect we owed it and how lucky we were to have a plate loaded with food in front of us. This would go on for some minutes until Mama felt she had gone through everyone at the table. This happened many times and Mama left no one out. Everyone knew that each of us had a place in Mama's weekly tirade.

Mama tended to complain constantly and about everything—the weather, the neighbours, and her aches and pains. Pa would just listen. Kohkwehns always stayed in the kitchen. She kept an eye on the kitchen stove, keeping it going. She kept the kitchen clean, scrubbing everything. Kohkwehns never had an opinion, as Mama would nip that in the bud, so she just kept quiet. She certainly looked after me. I knew she loved me. We used to have quiet visits and talk of many things. Kohkwehns knew a lot and had such wonderful stories.

Life at Two Clock in those days was uncomplicated. Nothing too chaotic ever happened and we were completely governed by the seasons and the weather, each month basically the same month over again. Nothing changed in the way we related to each other, even though each month had a different name.

Sunday meant two things—church and the Sunday papers. Every Sunday I was marched to church for confession because that's what the catechism said—you had to go whether you had sins or not. I remember one Sunday when Mama and Kohkwehns were trying to beat each other into the confessional so we could get out of church first. I was in the line and couldn't get ahead of the person in front of me. Then Henreh Pelletier jumped in front of me, but Kohkwehns came out of nowhere and dragged Henreh back so I could get ahead of him into the confessional!

There were stories of priests who had come to the community long before I was born. There was one who was called *Behbahminwajimut* (Bringer of Good News). Another called *Gizhigunung* (Day Star) was remembered for the way that he berated our people. My mother's mother was insulted that he called Indians "dogs." And he didn't stop at that. He went on to refer to us as "dog vomit." He lectured us on how despicable Indians were. He thought we were the lowest of the low. Even so, I was not allowed to analyze the behaviour of the priests. In my household, they were considered to be holy men, beyond reproach. My parents and grandparents did not allow me to question the priests' views.

Grandpa David Corbiere, my mother's father, was known for being a very hard man. My memory of him is not as a hard man but as a man who was very different from Pa. One of his characteristics was to yawn in church so loudly that everyone would stop and look at him.

After lunch on Sundays, Pa stoked up the fire in the other room and pulled out the reading material he had acquired during the week. I never knew where the newspapers came from or even whether they were current. I only knew that they appeared magically after lunch and were part of Sunday at my home. Pa read them and passed them on to Mama. She wanted to read them, too. So, Sunday afternoons, Pa and Mama passed the papers back and forth and discussed the events of the day. Occasionally I was dragged into their exchanges. I grew up in a household where the written word was enjoyed, savoured, explored, and shared. Sundays were boring—and the only excitement was the turning of the pages of the newspapers.

My experience growing up was bilingual and bicultural. I was aware that there were two patterns of speaking, two sets of behaviours, and two ways of being. Most First Nations people grow up in a dual reality. For my generation, the two worlds were very distinct. You either stayed on the reserve or you left. If you stayed, your options were very limited. You could have a small farm with a cow, a pig, and a small garden.

Pa had chosen to stay. Wabaginees, Pa's brother Charlie, had stayed too, but he became the postmaster and ran a small store. We had a small farm and small garden and we ate well. I remember in the summer Mama made green pea soup with the first harvest. The peas were shelled and put into a broth made from salt pork. At the very last moment, Mama thickened the soup with a paste of flour and water. Later in the season, Mama made soup with a bone and whatever garden vegetables were available. New potatoes were a treat and fresh yellow beans made a very tasty soup. And when corn came, the old family recipes for corn soup came out. Mama would cut the corn off the cob when it was very immature. In our part of the country, we had a very short growing season, so Mama didn't take any chances with the corn freezing. In soup, these young kernels were very tender and tasted good. Mama had her own vegetable soup recipe. It always began with salt pork and onion, then diced potatoes, green beans, and the corn. Oh, how we loved it! *Nijeemnabow* (dried pea soup) was a special treat in the wintertime. It seemed we had it as a celebration.

Our fruit garden had a few apple trees and some plum trees. We picked wild plums; only some of them were sweet, but we knew exactly which plants yielded the sweetest fruit. Kohkwehns was the one we turned to for the secrets of

Cecil and Kohkwehns.

the plant world. She had a source of knowledge that the rest of us didn't understand. But she knew things! Pa would prune them and they always bore fruit. Mama used to make applesauce, apple preserves, and apple pies. Mama and I had a little game we played when she was preparing the apples for cooking. She would peel the apple so that the whole peeling was in a long spiral. She knew that I was just waiting to see how much of the spiral I could get into my mouth at one time.

We planted tomatoes and beets. Mama made chow chow (a kind of relish) from green tomatoes for us to eat during the winter. Cucumbers grew profusely but, as I remember, Mama never made pickles. We ate them fresh as they became big enough to eat. Our turnips were magnificent as long as Pa put King Bug Killer on the leaves.

Mowizoh (berry picking) went on all summer. It began in June when we were still at school. We used to crawl around on our hands and knees in the field next to the school and eat the *conjeeshun* (unripe strawberries). Nothing was left after a few recesses. *Puskominuk* (wild raspberries) came next and were picked all over the territory. *Pishkiigominan* (highbush cranberries) grew around Buzwah and Mama would boil them and squeeze the pulp through a piece of cheesecloth, usually one of the curtains. The resulting pulp was called *muskkiig mini pashkimin sigan*. As children we called it "toe jam" because that's what it smelled like!

Boze is a special word used to express all the things involved in picking blueberries. The word literally refers to getting into a boat (embarking), and because blueberry picking entailed going by boat to the berry-picking grounds, *boze* was used exclusively in that context. It encompassed all the preparation for the excursion—getting the food ready for the trip, packing the tents and bed rolls, the berry-picking pails and other paraphernalia for storage, the cooking utensils, and on and on. It is true to say that blueberry-picking time was a time of great anticipation and excitement for a little boy from Buzwah!

In the fall, we had *cusmonun* (pumpkins), which Pa would cut into pie-sized slices and cook in the oven. Then it was called *skaapkidehn*. The slow oven drying made the pumpkin sweet. We all looked forward to this treat.

The land was not fit to grow any saleable crops. Being on limestone, the topsoil could not sustain much beyond what you could grow for yourself. In fact, the soil didn't grow certain things like carrots.

We had animals on our farm. We had three horses: Tony, Queen, and Mikons. They were our horsepower for hauling wood in the winter and for planting and haying. In winter, they took us over the snow-covered roads and tramped the snow down so we had a road to walk on.

We had milking cows. So, like every farmer, Pa got up early every morning to milk the cows. He milked again in the evening, part of the natural rhythm of the household. Our lives were governed by such routines. It was good! It was almost as if the cows were part of the family. The same cows were there when I left the farm as had been there when I became aware of their presence. You might say we grew up together, and Pa never butchered one. A relative, Jeannie Wakegejig, had cows, too, and she was always worried about brucellosis.

The pigs were not so lucky; we ate them. If it was a sow, it bore little pigs that were not allowed to get too big because Pa didn't think he could look after them properly. He seemed to know the optimum size to keep the herd of all the animals so that we were self-sufficient and the animals had a reasonably contented life. Pa felt that when you got too many of anything, the quality of life went down for all the animals. So, even though we ate pork, the number of pigs and cows stayed the same. We butchered the pigs and smoked the meat in our own smokehouse, which Mama managed with her usual tyrannical reign. Pa did all the butchering himself and I was his unwilling helper.

Pa experimented in anything he did, like *zeetaginigokosh* (salt pork making). He would acquire a large oaken barrel from a grocery store in Manitowaning. The barrel had been a container for molasses (treacle), and when it was emptied, the barrel was normally discarded. This barrel would still have its walls painted with a coat of the *kitchi jiwagamisiggan* (semi-sweet molasses) that added a sweet flavour to the pork. Pa would butcher the pig carcass into kitchen-stove-sized pieces and pile it into the molasses barrel with handfuls of salt and a splash of warm water. This gave us our ham, side pork slices, bacon, and roast parts. Nothing was wasted.

Headcheese was made out of the head. The pork skin was baked and used in baked beans. Bacon was made in the smokehouse beside the house that had been made before my time. It was closed in and covered with tin. I think my cousin, Eli King, made the smokehouse, but it had become Mama's over time. The ceiling of the smokehouse had poles used for drying and smoking fish. The fish were hung over the poles, but if we were out picking blueberries or camping we would dry fish on a frame in the sun.

Kohkwehns and Pa would save the intestines and inner organs and start what was called *nugish* (blood sausage). The first step was to stab the pig and let it bleed out into a receptacle; literally, the pig would simply bleed to death. The blood was caught and saved and set aside. The organs—lungs, kidneys, heart, and pancreas—were removed from the body cavity and placed in a large cast-iron pot with hot water and then boiled until thoroughly cooked. Strips of side pork were placed in another pan to be roasted in the oven. The biggest part of this operation, of course, was the emptying of the intestines and turning them inside out, thereby emptying the undigested food, and washing them carefully to remove any remnants of feces. Meanwhile, Kohkwehns and Mama peeled dozens of onions. Mama said that she had found a way to peel onions without crying. They cleaned heads of celery previously acquired for this occasion and diced the vegetables. Now Mama took on the big job of grinding the cooked meat in the food chopper along with the onions and celery pieces. The roast meat was important to the sausage for flavour and the roasted fat. The collected blood, now in a large pan, was salted down and peppered and the finely chopped up meat was mixed into the blood, along with flour for thickening. The intestines, having been carefully cleaned, were now ready for filling with the mixture of meats and salt and pepper using a funnel specifically for this purpose. Mama measured these intestines into two- to three-foot lengths and filled them with the mixture. They were secured and placed in a big pot of boiling water. This finished the *nugish*. The intestines were watched and tested for firmness before they were removed from the pot and set aside.

Pa and Dad were grub farmers. A team of horses, a plow, a disc, and a mower were the extent of the farm equipment and with these instruments we tilled the soil. A farm, of course, is influenced by seasons and so one can see which implements pertained to a particular season. I do not think that either Pa or Dad was the absolute farmer-type, but they worked as committed farmers, as everyone else in the area. I did not like farming and swore I would leave the land as soon as I could. Very early in life, I could manage the farm. Driving horses, while interesting, had no appeal, and since Pa could not afford a tractor, in spite of all his proclamations, I'm not sure if even a tractor could have enticed me to farm life.

I was not cut out to be a farmer; my boyish impression of farming was that you shovelled manure all winter and then your feet were muddy or dirty the other seasons. I'm sure that my lack of suitability for a career in farming was perfectly clear to Pa. Just as my dad had escaped the drudgery of farming to "work out," it must have been abundantly clear to Pa, Mama, and Kohkwehns that I was going to run as fast as I could from the farm when the opportunity presented itself. But, as long as I lived on the farm, I was the resident helping hand for just about everything.

We had our own flock of chickens, the ones that were known as good layers. Pa favoured White Leghorns and Rhode Island Reds. I guess he got his knowledge of the gifts of different chickens from the industrial school or the Wikwemikong Agricultural Society and his trips to the Royal Agricultural Winter Fair in Toronto. If he happened to get a chicken that grew into one of the breeds that he didn't like, that chicken was destined for Mama's stewpot or roasting pan. We ate eggs from our own chickens and I used to pick them up. There is nothing that feels as good as a warm chicken egg!

Easter breakfast was always special. Mama would colour the eggs when she cooked them. She had onion skins to dye the eggs yellow, raspberry preserve juice to make the eggs red, and dyes from the store to make other coloured eggs. We had boiled eggs as the main course; even though boiled eggs were eaten on other occasions, somehow the coloured boiled eggs of Easter were extra special.

We had another poultry enterprise: we grew turkeys to sell. We never had the problems that I have heard of turkey breeders these days, who talk of overcrowding or the turkeys smothering each other when they are frightened. I remember our turkeys as sturdy, strong, and healthy birds. We had one hen, and our flock consisted of as many chicks as she nurtured. There was a time that I didn't have a dog; my dog died and Mama chose a turkey to be my new pet. So, perhaps I have a soft spot for turkeys!

Pa got about twenty poults in the summer to be raised and sold for Christmas. A buyer came to Mastin's Store in Manitowaning about a week before Christmas. Pa hitched up the horses and delivered our crop, all cleaned and plucked, and was paid immediately. The money came in handy to buy the extras for Christmas dinner.

We had sheep, not just for their meat, but for their wool as well. Pa would shear them and Mama had a *beemtaygun* (spinning wheel) where I learned how to spin wool. I remember that I made one ball of yarn one winter. I had a real feeling of satisfaction in being able to take wool and make it into yarn and then watch my grandmother knit woollen socks for Pa. It was so good to be able to see the whole process from sheep to socks.

Fall brought the harvest, and threshing time was exciting. Bob McMullen and Mr. Little had an itinerant threshing machine that circulated around the reserve, and when our turn finally came, it was a big bee and all the neighbour men came to help. Our crew were all good workers: Eli King and his brother Blaise, John Bearfoot, Ben Kanasawe, and Dad when he wasn't away working somewhere. One time the threshing machine went through the floor of the barn. When the grain was in the barn it was a big occasion. The men loved it and there was a big feed.

In our household, Mama kept her strict schedule as soon as the fall fair was over. Anything that needed to be "put up" just sat and piled up until the canning pot appeared. It was scoured and made ready for whatever fruit or vegetable was available. Mama would start with plums. First, she would measure the amount of white sugar to be mixed in with the fruit. As the sugar and the water boiled down, the plums were washed and sorted for maturity to eliminate the possibility of missing rotten plums this early in the canning process. The plums were added immediately to the pot of boiling syrup, and while they were cooking, Mama scoured a number of fruit jars, perhaps thirty at first, to make them ready for the canning that was now in full swing. The jars would be taken downstairs and arranged on shelves along the wall that Pa had long ago been ordered to build. Pa was never amenable to building shelves and I think Mama knew this and forced him to do it each year anyway. Once the plums were finished and safely in their respective bottles, strawberries were next. Then, perhaps she would preserve a run of peaches, depending on the harvests of southern Ontario. Mama would can all fall and we would eat preserves for many meals; this mushy fruit was a tasty diversion from our usual fare. This preserving for the winter lasted about three weeks before Mama would say the cellar was full and it was time to stop for the year.

We always had lots of tomatoes. Pa planted seeds in cans and the plants would be about six inches high by the time that the ground was warm enough in the back of the garden where Mama created her tomato patch. At the end of the growing season, if tomatoes on the plants were still green, they were picked and packed in boxes with brown paper to ripen. In midwinter, Mama would surprise us with a ripe red tomato and make a wonderful omelette for breakfast.

In the winter, Pa supplemented our larder with fish. Ice fishing was an art. First, you had to chop a square hole about a length and a half of the axe handle when laid on its side. You'd have to cut several holes in a row the length of your net. Then, you had to get your new cord, which you would tie to a pole a little longer than the distance between the holes. You tied your line to the stick and shoved it through the hole. Someone would catch the stick through the other holes to send the net to the end of the holes. This was called *ziibasigoge*, which merely means passing from one hole to another under the ice. This stick was pushed with another crotched stick to move the net along in the water until the whole length of the pole reached the end of the holes, which was the length of the net. When Pa found the pole at the other end, he had to raise it out of the water so that he could get the twine. After he caught the pole and pulled it out, he tied it across the hole. Pa would go back to the first hole to tie the twine at the first end. This meant that the person at one end pulled the net along with the twine to the end of the holes. Then that person tied the net to another pole across the hole. After that, Pa and I only needed two holes to lift the net, although you needed perhaps five holes in a straight line. Every Saturday we went and cut a hole in the ice at one end where the net began and another where the net ended and then in the same manner as when the net was set, it was pulled along by the twine to raise it. If a fish was in the net you *geetanamegwe* (disentangled the fish from the net). Once that was done, the net would be set again and the hole covered with balsam branches as a warning marker for others. The fish would be put in the fishnet box with slanted sides. The box was used for storing the net, but when we caught lots of fish it was also used to carry the fish home. Mama would be so excited that she would immediately grab one fish, clean it, cut it into pieces, and heat up the frying pan. When suppertime arrived, we would have a meal of beautifully fried fresh fish. In the winter this was a delicacy. The rest of the fish were gutted, scaled, salted, and placed in a barrel to be eaten later.

Winter, a season of virtually six months from November to April, was a quiet time when people seemed to hibernate. In our household, a simple outing to Manitowaning was an invigorating experience. We met new acquaintances and strengthened old relationships. At the end of this one day, everyone would return to their individual isolation, as was done every winter. When there was a church service at Buzwah Church, the winter tranquility would be broken by the forlorn pealing of the church bell signalling the gathering of the flock. This seemed to be more of an occasion for gossiping than for one's salvation because it was one of the few times during the winter when all the neighbours came together. Pa was a very important member of the church choir as he knew the Latin liturgy and led the laic participation in the service. Mama was there, too; she sang in the choir or played the organ. Many of our extended family were good singers and musicians. My cousins, Stella, Josephine, Rose, and Stan, were always in the choir. They were my Uncle Charlie's, Pa's brother's, children. While my uncle's name was Charlie King, everyone in the community knew him as Waabiginees. As we shall see, he was a man of many talents. His wife, my Aunt Elizabeth (aka Aunt Bessie) was also always involved in church activities. When it was needed, Stella could play the organ. I particularly remember us all performing in the Mass in G. We didn't have a director and more or less taught ourselves. As I got older, I could sing with the tenors or the basses, depending on the piece and the attendance.

The church was heated by a huge box stove that Ben Kanasawe would have stoked up long before the priest arrived. I do not recall ever missing Sunday Mass. I suppose this was because Mama, Pa, and I were well inculcated with Catholicism and believed that missing Sunday Mass was, in fact, a mortal sin. Pa and Mama had both spent part of their younger years at the Wikwemikong Indian Industrial School and, under the religious order of the Jesuits and Daughters of Mary, that experience had a permanent effect on Pa and Mama, so much so they were "dyed-in-the-wool" Catholics.

In those days, winters were winters and snowdrifts were expected, and someone to *dwaage* (our colloquial way of saying "to clear snow") was also expected—it just happened winter after winter. Things were done the same way every winter. When people stayed indoors, a box stove provided warmth, but the stove required firewood, which meant having a trail to the bush to transport a load of wood back home. Firewood in our household was made every day, enough for that day only. Pa went into the bush, selected an old tree, cut it down, loaded it on the bobsleigh, and hauled it home, where it was sawed into stove-length pieces. Some splitting was done with the splitting axe, and when all this had happened, all that remained was to carry the wood into the house where it was piled in the same place every day to feed the box stove and the kitchen stove for cooking and a bit more heat.

Home in the wintertime was very cozy. Generally, we stayed in to watch the winter blizzard outside as it created snowdrifts, burying our trails. This never changed. Winter after winter, someone would *dewaagaanege* (the formal term for clearing the snow). Since we lived on a farm, we had farm animals to winter, which required animal shelters. Pa had pigs, sheep, some cows, and, of course, the horses. This required daily chores. In the morning, we had to let the animals out, put feed outside and prepare a drinking trough with fresh water. The horses and cows were punctual about getting a drink. The pigs survived on kitchen slop. At the end of the day, we did the reverse of the morning chores. When we opened the barn doors, the animals would immediately file in and go into their individual stalls. Pa would then feed them hay that had been cut the summer before and stored in the barn hayloft. Nothing varied. Each day was the same day all over again. We had milking cows and someone had to milk them. The milk was collected, brought into the house, and separated. The cream was set aside for making butter.

The one chore that bothered me most in the keeping and feeding of animals was dealing with the manure. The amount that was manufactured required a particular day, every week, dedicated to shovelling it. Pa had two wheel-barrows that he used and one for me to haul the manure to a pile just outside the barn door. As I remember, this thankless chore happened Saturday morning and every Saturday morning was like every other Saturday morning.

In the winter, when there were the usual blizzards, there were times I could not get to school. Where we lived was a bit of a distance from the school and the road was impassable after each storm so I had to wait for the *dewaagaanege* to break a trail. Since this, too, was expected, staying home was not a big deal. I suppose the teacher simply made allowances for this, and there were times I could go nowhere, winter day after winter day.

All Saints' Day broke the monotony of early winter. November 1 was the day we honoured the dead. Actually, it was a day of visiting and eating. Kohkwehns used to say, "You never get overfull," even though you were fed at every house.

Christmas also broke the winter monotony. My first awareness of Christmas was quite early in the scheme of things. Mama had a calendar from the church and had a general knowledge of the Christmas story. The old priest at church for that Sunday opened with that story and implied that Christmas Day be observed like a Sunday and then told us a bit about the practices in other northern communities. These were customs practised the world over. Mama had the knowledge in our household and could tell the customs of Christians; she more or less told us it was a good time and people agreed to be good to each other. Even the whole idea of gift giving was described to us.

Christmas was about having a household feast and we got ready for it—cooking and decorating. The Christmas bird, a goose, was very exactly prepared for the Christmas table. There was Christmas cake served with dumplings and icing, an extra-special treat made only once a year.

Christmas became even more special when a day was set aside to go decorate the church before the Sunday of Christmas. Mama was very handy and had a taste for decorating. Kohkwehns was not so Christmassy, because she would not have known the images and colours of Christmas. But Mama knew all the history of Christmas and missed no occasion to instruct someone about it.

One particular Christmas, I remember a taxi arriving at the house from Little Current and the passenger was a woman called Rose Lewis. Mama was elated. Rose was her cousin and she had not seen her for a long time. The visiting began immediately. Cooking was forgotten as visiting was too important—to catch up on relatives, those who were still living and those already gone. Rose herself was a historian of some import and she knew everyone Mama talked about. The gossip was rampant and Rose was as grateful for it as Mama was. Kohkwehns moved into the corner, as she had no knowledge of the people that Mama and Rose Lewis were talking about. Kohkwehns didn't mind, as she knew an opportunity would come along when she would be a source to verify Rose Lewis's stories. Mama just let this go by and Kohkwehns remained on the outside of that gossip session. However, Rose never missed a beat and could almost keep up with Mama and add to the milieu. Pa stayed in the barn and created odd jobs for himself. This was the beginning of Christmas in the King household. With the days becoming shorter, darkness would descend early.

That first night after Rose's arrival, the visiting drifted to many topics, until Mama said she wished it was possible to visit her remaining relatives—if only there was some form of transportation. It was Rose that opened with, "Well, you have horses in the barn. We could hitch them up and maybe have Cecil drive them." That is what happened. Pa didn't want to go anywhere, but was in favour of lending his team of horses, as long as there was someone to drive them, and that's how I ended up hitching up the horses and driving to Wikwemikong from Two Clock. Mama was thrilled with the idea, as she, more than anyone, never went anywhere—according to her, of course.

It was dark when we took off on our journey—and it was a dark, dark night. Since I did not know anything about driving horses any distance, I did not know to take enough hay to feed the horses upon our arrival in Wikwemikong and during the next day. I had no way of knowing at whose place we would wind up—and, of course, Mama had no idea either, but we were convinced this would resolve itself when we arrived in Wikwemikong, which is kind of what happened. Mama and Rose seemed to know a few places, so we struck out for them. The first place, as it turned out, was the residence of Joe Atchitawens, Mama's first cousin. We rapped on the door, and when Joe answered, he was dumbfounded when he discovered Mama and then Rose Lewis. He was elated, stoked up the fires in the house, and the visiting started immediately. Joe was just as glad to see Mama as Mama was to see him. Rose had not seen him for a year, so there was some catching up to be done and Joe had lots of stories to tell his guests. A trip of this kind certainly meant an overnighter. Some bedding was borrowed from next door as this topic became clarified. Joe was very hospitable and knew fully what had to be done on these occasions. The arrival of guests was an unusual event and proper respect was taken for granted. No one ever left hungry, especially at Christmas.

Joe had stoked his stoves so his home was nice and warm. Mama and Rose chose the bedroom upstairs where there was lots of room. It was only then that Joe asked me about the horses, which were still outside where I had left them tied to his gate. I had no idea what I was going to do for the horses, although Pa had always insisted that your first concern upon arriving at your destination had to be the horses. I talked to Joe and he understood what I needed and suggested his small wooden barn, where I could unharness the horses and feed them. Fortunately, I had brought an armful of hay—hardly enough for a team all night. But for now, this would have to do. Since Joe did not have any hay himself, he suggested that we go to his brother Jerry's place the next day and use his hay, as he had lots. Jerry was Mama's first cousin, as well, and Mama ordered that someone go to Jerry's house and inform them of her arrival. My horses were fed and we bedded down for another night's stay and another night's lodging was resolved. The gossiping never stopped.

This was my first excursion with a team of horses. I had a lot to learn. Mama caught up on all her relatives and, of course, Rose Lewis learned of her distant relatives. By now, food was mentioned (I suppose since the horses had been fed) and the cooking began.

We left Wikwemikong to go back to Two Clock with a good feeling and made some sort of arrangement for Rose to get back to Little Current, as the visiting was now over. I felt somewhat fulfilled and realized what was expected when you were in charge of a team of horses and took them from their barn. You have a responsibility. I will always remember Pa meeting me on our return from Wikwemikong. The first thing he wanted to know was, "Did you feed the horses?" and I had to explain. Rose Lewis phoned for her cab to return to Little Current. Mama's Christmas was over and she was satisfied with Rose's visit as, in her own terms, this was the icing on the cake.

That was the year I was inculcated with the mystique of horse sense. It wasn't enough to assume my horses would be all right after I had gotten them to another area of our farm. I arrived. I unhitched, watered, and fed them. The horses knew their own comfort and they reminded me that there were some duties when the horses knew the day was ending and the driving was over. Every day was the same and the horses knew that. Horses are affectionate animals and believe in their master, but only if the master is in sync and the farm is run under his direction.

I remember the first Christmas that I convinced my grandmother to have a Christmas tree in the house. I went out into the bush just behind the house and found just the right tree. It was a little fir and I cut it down and brought it home. This was where Santa left my presents—under the tree. On Christmas morning when I got up, I found a little bag tied at the top. It was a bag of pennies. Next to it, Santa had left a long flat box. It turned out to be a game of Parcheesi.

Santa Claus was a tradition very strong among my grandparents. Christmas presents for the kids would be prepared and put under the tree and the house would be decorated. The children knew that Santa Claus would not come unless they were all asleep. When the crowd came home in the middle of the night, I could hear them laughing and talking, but I had to get up early to go to Christmas Day service at Buzwah Church so I didn't get up. I had my responsibilities on Christmas morning, along with other village boys Herman, Napo, and Gawgee: I was a server at Buzwah Church services.

Christmas Day began with getting the turkey or goose ready for the big Christmas dinner, the main event. We would all dress up in new or semi-new clothing, special

The four King siblings, Elizabeth (Liz), Don, Cecil, and Loretta.

for the occasion. A new tablecloth materialized from somewhere and the best silverware was selected for the table. Pa sat at the head of the table and carved the roasted turkey or goose. My, how our mouths watered as the meal was being served. Pa just loved that. Everyone had to eat and no one was left out. Those who were too shy to eat, Pa would give them hell right at the table. We ate this meal together, filling the table with twice as many eaters as we were used to—my brother, Don, Dad, Mom, and my sisters, Liz and Loretta, Kohkwehns, and any other relatives that happened to be around. The meal was a spectacular event that I remember very well. We really celebrated the Christmas holiday.

By now, the winter season would be in full swing. There would be lots of snow to contend with, and Pa shovelled from the main door of the house out to the barn. If he wanted me to do this job, he usually gave me the order and I was obligated to do this chore. I had no difficulty shovelling; it was easy.

As the winter progressed, snow piled up and footprints of wild animals were everywhere. It was then that Dad went trapping, a skill I did not know he had. However, he had a trapline in the forest behind our house and I followed Dad's tracks on the trail to see how to set traps and studied the art of trapping. Pa had never taught me; neither had Kohkwehns, even though she also knew how to run a trapline. I discovered Dad had an assortment of metal traps that he boiled in the household soup pot with sweetgrass before they would be strategically set in spots in the bush where animal tracks seemed plentiful, especially in places where they ate. That seemed to be all that was required. Dad was an intriguing individual and treated his trapline the same way. Animals were trapped and then the carcasses had to be skinned. Each skin was stretched out on its own frame and hung to dry. I learned the skills of skinning from Dad and Kohkwehns taught me about making the frames to stretch the skins. At some time in the winter, Pa would tell Dad to tie up his fur skins and send them to Winnipeg. This was an important occasion, and Dad would send his fur bundle out from Manitowaning Post Office and wait for a cheque to come, signifying the value of his fur trapping. I never knew whether this was good or bad, but it was a skill I learned from my Dad.

I had learned how to snare rabbits; Kohkwehns taught me how to make snares. By this time, I had learned what snare wire is and that it was rather cheap to buy. I remember borrowing twenty-five cents from Kohkwehns to buy some from Charlie Hind's store in Manitowaning. That winter, Pa gave me a sharp-bladed jackknife, and only Pa and Dad owned ones like it. It was a genuine Joseph Rodgers that Charlie Hind sold. When it was sharpened on the household grindstone, you owned a very sharp jackknife.

I never forgot the brand name and that it was bought in Manitowaning; it was the only type that would do.

The same winter of trapping, I learned how to fashion my own slingshot. My friend Gawgee had one, a precise instrument used only for hunting, made by John Bearfoot. Napo, his brother, would take it from the house near Two Clock. I remember when I first saw it—Napo showed it to me right after he had taken it from John Bearfoot's house. This was a masterpiece both in carving and the cutting of rubber straps. And we would use it to hunt and hit things. Thus began the world of the slingshot. I understood how to make one and soon became very proficient in how to use it, as well. This opened a new world for the boys at Buzwah School, since now every boy of some worth owned his own slingshot and we used them to kill rabbits, squirrels, and certain birds. Our skills were infamous—around Buzwah, at least. It was during this time that I opened a fur-buying project. I bought squirrel pelts, traded rabbit skins, and even traded ducks from the Two Clock stream. I would always be asked, "How did you do your kill?" and I would say, "By myself with my slingshot." As the fur trader, I paid up to twenty-five cents a pelt. I had some money and could pay for my pelts, but it was always the slingshot that settled any deal. I became famous for acquiring squirrel pelts. This was fairly easy, but my skills increased.

I could fashion a slingshot in one afternoon, even when I was still in Buzwah School. For crafting a slingshot, you had to find a white ash tree with a symmetrically crotched limb—that is, having a yoke-branched limb. I used to walk much of our hardwood bush to find the right white ash tree with the proper limb formation and I was pretty good at spotting these. All that was left was to cut the branch, take it home, peel it, and hang it from the rafters of the house. This "Y" branch needed to be symmetrical, which required some strategic tying across the two prongs of the stick and letting it dry that way. Some carving would be required, and then the rubber bands had to be obtained. I found you needed a genuine rubber tube from the car to make these straps that you then tied, with store twine, in a loop on each branch of the dried, forked branch. I found tying a leather pocket at the centre of the rubber straps attached to the crotched limb could become a detonation chamber and had to be made very precisely for overall accuracy. After this, all that was necessary was to take the completed mechanism to the bush with a pocket full of stones—half-inch projectiles found in river bottoms, the ones we found most accurate for our weapon. At fifty feet, these slingshots were deadly. I found that with the right attitude, I could drop a squirrel or rabbit with one stone. Kohkwehns was good with a slingshot, too, and she used to help when we had treed a squirrel. We rarely lost one. Kohkwehns used to cook the squirrel carcasses for me and my buddies Herman Kanasawe and Joe and Albert Whiteloon. We'd have a feast after she had cooked our prey. I always ate with them.

In the winter, the snowdrifts and the cold weather wended their way, day after day, month after month. Pa and Dad chopped wood for our house fires and Kohkwehns launched into her craftwork with birchbark. Kohkwehns used the scraps and trimmings from the birchbark left from the building of a large canoe. Then, she made eight-inch souvenir canoes for the tourist trade. She made them to order for Ed Cummings at Manitowaning Lodge. It never was a rate where she could get wealthy, but Kohkwehns was humble and proud to be able to supply groceries for the household. Beyond having to shovel snow, tend the cattle, and plow the roads, our lives settled into a form of hibernation and we lived a very calm, slow life. I hung snares for rabbits and occasionally caught a partridge and even a deer once. Pa had shown me how to do this. This was an exciting occasion, one to remind the household of some cultural practices as well as to be thankful for the Creator's bounty.

For Pa and our household, the first exceptional day in the winter was March 10. While the month of March would have already established whether it came in like a lion or a lamb and foretelling its prediction for the end of the month, March 10 was the first reminder that spring was on its way and winter was perhaps over. Pa declared it as the day that the crows came back. He would scan the horizons in search of the first crow sighting. Based on his obvious belief in the date, Pa would announce at the supper table that he had, indeed, seen the first crow. I was never sure if he had actually seen one, but with his declaration, we were all certain that spring had come. It was unthinkable that March 10 would not bring a crow to Two Clock.

Things now began to change. We could speculate on when to start *Sisibaktokaying* (sugar-making season). *Manakiking* (the maple trees) would have to be tapped and *wiigwas naganun* (birchbark dishes) or tin cans made ready to collect *sisibakwatabo* (sap, literally sugar water) dripping from the spile. Pa would go to Manitowaning to buy some new spiles as he did every year. Since money was scarce, Pa could only buy a few of them, not more than he needed. Rust ruined the spiles, which had to be replaced after a single season it seemed.

Pa used a half-inch wood auger bit that he had among his pile of tools for tapping maple trees in a bush right next to the house. By the time I left home, Pa had started to cut down the maple trees, one by one, for firewood for the house.

The maple sugar-making season began as the days got warmer. Firewood had to be chopped for the fires that would heat the cauldrons or evaporators that would make *kijiga ininatigon* (the sap, literally that which leaks from the maple tree) into *jiwagamisigan* (syrup). We would be involved in the *Zhigigewin*, the art of tapping maple trees. Since Pa was a *kikohnsekowinini* (tinsmith), he had acquired the old fireboxes and other furnace parts from the band schools that he fashioned together to make an evaporator. Originally, the furnaces would have burned coal, and they had grates in them that made very good heaters for evaporators. Pa would make evaporator pans for anyone who had something to make fire in that he could attach the pans to. Pa created a large, low pan from sheets of tin that he then set on top of the furnace fireboxes. As soon as the sap began to run, a wood fire was started and the collected sap was poured into this pan. Basically, the whole process involved the daily collecting of sap and keeping a good fire going in Pa's furnace contraption.

Pa tapped about fifty trees in our maple grove, some with two spiles. Everyone who collected sap had a carrier like a yoke on their shoulders to carry two pails at once. A trail was made, no matter how deep the snow was. Pa and I would go from tree to tree. I was the official helper to carry the tools, the spiles, and the birchbark dishes or tin cans. Kohkwehns would make the *wiigwas naganun* to be placed on the ground at the root of a tree, supported by a pile of flat stones. She was the expert on *naganun* placement and she called herself *Iskigamisigekwe* (sugar-making woman). I had to find the stones for her. When I was helping the

Old Ones, we were in a transition between the old way and the modern way. Tin cans, the modern receptacles, hung from the spiles after we poked holes through the tins so that they could attach to the metal hooks on the bottom of the spiles.

On a good day's run, we had to collect the sap every two or three hours. I can remember the first maple sugar seasons when I was very young but old enough to know what tree tapping was. Pa shaped an iron chisel in his blacksmith forge and then ground it sharp. This was the tool he used to notch the maple trees. In the notch was stuck a short twelve- to eighteen-inch length of cedar that directed the flow of sap into the *nagan*. This predated the era of spiles. The split piece of cedar was flat and about two inches wide. Pa hit it hard enough to wedge it in a notch. The cedar was already sloped, and when he made the notch, the cedar length was hammered into the tree on an angle. After he collected the sap, he boiled it in four cauldrons that he had made himself. He made maple syrup equipment for whoever needed it. When he got enough tin cut, he would get his muriatic acid, his blowtorch, and his soldering iron. He would steal a zinc ring from Mama's fruit sealers and put it in the muriatic acid, make a paste, and rub that on the edges to be soldered with lead, sealing all the seams. It's a wonder we weren't all poisoned!

When the sap was running, Pa would boil all day and into the night. So the wood and sap had to keep coming. That's where I came in. I would take the horse and drag a log out of the bush to where Pa was boiling. He would chop it up for the fire that was essential to the whole operation. I had to run home from school to go to collect more sap.

I grew up in the time of transition from wooden spiles to metal ones, from collecting in birchbark dishes to collecting

Pa and Cecil boiling sap.

in tin cans, and from boiling in cauldrons to boiling in an evaporator. I had time to hate boiling sap in cauldrons, as this system took too much wood—and guess who had to haul it! Pa's evaporator contraption was a godsend to me as it didn't burn so much.

To convince ourselves that a boil was finished, the maple syrup was tested numerous times. One method was to take a teaspoon of the syrup and drip it into a glass of cold water to see if it would make a ball. When it made a ball it was done. Although this was the final test that told us that the syrup was ready, the preferred method was to taste the syrup with a slice of scone!

When the syrup was ready, it was bailed out of the evaporator pan until there was just a little left and then the evaporator was tipped and the syrup poured out of one corner into a big brass cauldron. At one time, these pots had been government-issue, and the only time you could tell they were brass was when Mama cleaned them with a stone and they shone a yellow colour! This pot, known as the *zekwekik* (boiling-down pot), was used for the final boil.

Meanwhile, back at the house, Mama would have been scouring fruit sealers for storing the syrup. She would have supervised the final boiling down of liquid from the evaporator and the brass pot would have been carried to the house. Mama bottled the syrup after determining the exact moment to take it off the stove. Only she knew this!

There were at least two other processes that took place at least once during the maple sugar season. A portion of the syrup was boiled down in a cast iron frying pan until it became taffy. To make this an occasion, there had to be some clean, fresh snow around. The taffy mixture was poured on the snow, where it instantly hardened. Oh what a grand time—a once-a-year treat for us all! Another day, a batch of the taffy would be pulled to make candy.

A small amount of *sisibaskwat* (maple sugar) would be made using the *mucukonson* (little birchbark boxes) that Kohkwehns made for us. The syrup was cooked until just the right moment before it *n'sesin* (crystallized). It was removed from the heat and immediately poured into the *mucukons*. It cooled to a sugar consistency in the little boxes. This was another real treat, and I can't forget Mama's sugar pie, a favourite of the season.

Pa was the one who determined when the sugar-making process ended. In the morning at breakfast, he would say, "*Ishkwaga!*" and we knew it was time to remove the spiles, gather the cans, dismantle the evaporator pan, and stand it upright by the stove. It was the end of another season and everyone knew it would be the very same next year.

Spring brought *namehbinak* (suckers) to the river at Two Clock. The sucker run was an exciting time. We didn't even need to use a hook or fishing rod; all we needed was a stick and our arm to harvest fresh fish for our suppers. Later, the *geegohnsuk* (smelts) also ran and we caught them in scoop-nets. They were so good to eat!

Spring also brought spring-cleaning. Kohkwehns made a new broom out of supple new tree limbs tied together. Spring also began medicine gathering. Kohkwehns picked *Nahmeshkohns* (Penny Royal; wild mint) to make tea. She picked *Weengushk* (sweetgrass), which she sewed with, and wrapped it in a cloth until she needed it. She made mats for the table and used it to decorate the little birchbark canoes that she made. She would harvest *Wahbahgahg* (sage) if she came upon it by accident on our walks; we never deliberately went out to look for it. Mama used *Wahbahgahg* in cooking turkey or chicken. Kohkwehns looked for *sema*, which could be smoked as a herbal substitute for tobacco or mixed with store-bought tobacco to increase the quantity or quality.

Pa taught me that there was a right way to do everything; if something needed to be done, then it was done, but it had to be done right or left alone if you couldn't handle it. That was the way with everything. Growing up at Two Clock, this order was easily followed. I don't think my brother had this luck, though Dad did things the way Pa taught him. The girls—Liz and Loretta—were hounded as well. Mama and Kohkwehns reigned over them on virtually everything—washing dishes, cooking, doing laundry, sweeping floors, and forever tidying up, making beds and assisting in the endless sewing or remaking of old garments. I used to kind of feel sorry for them, but I had to be careful, or their task would fall into my hands with Mama or Kohkwehns in charge. This was never too bad, as Kohkwehns usually took over relatively early in the process. I've always felt that my brother, Don, had it easier. He was always treated calmly on any task and took advantage of this by being extra good and very watchful on what to do next. By being extra gracious to Kohkwehns or Mama, he avoided their wrath. I guess Don learned early how to charm the ladies!

Where we lived was right across the bay from Manitowaning. Our life was scheduled by days. Saturdays were for going to Manitowaning. Sundays were for going to church. Mondays and Tuesdays seemed to be for chopping wood for the fireboxes in the house. Chopping wood was not automated; we chopped it up outside the house after we had drawn it there from the forest. Chopping wood was everybody's job, including Kohkwehns's. She taught me lessons about wood chopping that set my pattern of thinking about it and generally set an attitude of the importance of developing the art. The chopped wood had to be sawed into stove-length pieces and some of them had to be split. This routine was always the same; everyone knew what to do. Pa showed me how to sharpen the axe and he had made a grinding stone for this purpose. It worked very well, but it was totally handmade and had to be cranked by hand.

Kohkwehns was determined that I would learn how to be a good Anishnabe. It was she who would comfort me if I wanted to cry. Mama didn't think little boys should cry, but Kohkwehns knew that sometimes little boys got their hearts broken and it was right that they learned to express their feelings. She was a tall woman who always wore an apron and it was very reassuring for me to nuzzle into her apron and let my feelings out. This had to be done out of sight of Mama. When I was upset, Kohkwehns was always right around the corner.

The 1928 Chevy Touring Car was Pa's pride and joy. Sometimes it was a car, sometimes it was a truck. It used to be a convertible, but the canvas had been ruined in a rollover and Pa had replaced it with two-by-fours. It would have been a nice car if he hadn't rolled it. I owned the back seat, except when it was time to take the ram to service the neighbour's ewes. Then, I had to share the back seat with the ram!

When we went visiting, Pa drove and Mama sat poker straight in the passenger's seat. One person my grandparents visited was Waabiginees. Pa and Waabiginees would get together in a corner and talk and talk. The women conversed in another part of the house. I circulated. As a result, I never did get the whole story in either gathering. I now realize that Waabiginees was one of our more traditional people, a real historian of our people. Unfortunately, by the time I came along, the traditional people were discouraged from talking Indian to the children and we missed out on the traditional teachings as a result.

I remember the time when Pa hung lanterns at the front of the car so we could travel at night. If the fuse in the lights was faulty, Pa could fix that. He would take the aluminum foil out of his tobacco and wrap it around the fuse. *Voila!* We would have lights again. But, when the bulbs burned out, there was no easy fix, so out came the lanterns and we were on our way!

We used to visit John Bearfoot. Behind his stove, he had marionettes that danced when the stove fan came on. Mr. Bearfoot made these playthings to amuse himself, but when company came he would take them down and show us what they could do.

My grandparents played cards when I was a kid. Cards were *Tadowinuk*. The state of playing cards was *Tadowin*. They each had their own deck of cards. They would play *Tadowinke* (solitaire) and when company came to the house, they would play euchre. This was *Tadoinuk* (playing together with cards). There was a whole Ojibwe vocabulary around playing cards. Gambling at cards was referred to as *Shoonya tadowuk* (they are playing for money). *Tadowin* was a card, *Gima* (*Gimak,* pl.; king), *Gimakwe* (*Gimakwek,* pl.; queen), *Jacquook* (jack), *Medas wegun* (ten), *beshigik go beegun* (one), *mekadewzid* (black one), and *meskozid* (red one).

When we visited Shehn Koplahñ (John Wemigwans), he would give us heck. He lived in bed and had developed his own form of *Tadowinke*. He made four sets and displayed the remaining cards in sets of three. He would take the card that matched. If he could not find a card to match, he would move the first card from the pile to the bottom of the pile.

My elders had high expectations for me. It was taken for granted that I would go to school and do well. It was taken for granted that I would be a responsible human being, able to take care of my family and make an honest living. For Mama, that meant learning English and the manners and behaviours that were acceptable in white society. To Pa, it meant learning how to work hard, becoming independent, being accomplished at something useful, and being able to sell my skills. To Kohkwehns, it meant seeing myself as part of the Creator's plan, respecting all the Creator's creations, and living within the space that the Creator had meant for me.

It was taken for granted that I would work away from the reserve. I was expected to do whatever I did not only well but in the way it should be done. This was a very strong precept in the King household and in my Odawa culture. We said, "*Enendagwad.*" This assumes that there is a right way to do everything, the way it should be done, in other words, the successful way of doing things.

Our people had to be successful at what they did. If my ancestors had not been successful hunters, fishermen, warriors, medicine people, and traders, I would not be here. In our traditional society, our youth went on what was called the vision quest. During a time in isolation and fasting, our youth received a dream that, when interpreted by the spiritual leaders, foretold the young person's future life in the community. When the youth's future journey was told to the community members, from then on, the whole community supported the young person's journey through life. The young person had a purpose in the community and the community respected and supported that purpose. Individuals spent their lives "living their visions." Through this process, our communities had the specialists needed. The training followed the vision and the conditions for success for each individual were set in place.

In my world, with my three old people, no one told me that I was not capable of doing anything. Each in her or his own way supported me, providing the foundation for me to learn my strengths and to become the person I could be. Mama used discipline to encourage correct behaviour. Pa showed me how something should be done, and Kohkwehns listened to me. Mama worked on my head, Pa worked on my hands, and Kohkwehns worked on my heart. Together they strengthened me. They developed my confidence, skills, and ability to respond to the world with my head, hands, and heart.

From my grandparents, I learned that success depends on high expectations; deliberate, direct teaching of the elements that develop capabilities into abilities; working on all aspects of the child's being (heart, mind, and spirit); finding out who the child is and what he or she needs; providing unconditional support; giving a clear description of what constitutes "appropriate" behaviour and being fair and firm in administering the predetermined discipline for "bad" behaviour; and above all else, convincing the child that it matters to you that he/she is successful.

2. SCHOOLING AT BUZWAH

My schooling began in a small Indian day school when I was seven. In grade one, only Moses Lavallee and I could speak English. The other kids spoke only Ojibwe, which I could not speak very well. Most of my fellow students lived in very traditional Ojibwe homes, so their language and culture were the foundation of their learning. There was resentment against speaking English among the members of the community because English was the language of the school. Moses and I were buddies, but we soon had to learn "Schoolyard Ojibwe" to be able to play with the other students. As mentioned, we lived a bilingual–bicultural experience. We were influenced by the Ontario Department of Education's expectations at school and our traditional Anishnabe parents' values and beliefs at home.

The goal of the school was to "de-Indianize" us. However, that goal was never fully realized at Buzwah Indian Day School because over the time we attended, we had four different qualified First Nations teachers—Christine Wakegejig, Clara (TchiClara) Trudeau, Rita Corbiere (Mrs.

Adam), and Mrs. Lawrence Pelletier. Miz Wakegejig was the first to go. So, for a few days we did not have a teacher, but another was soon appointed. Clara Trudeau, a retired teacher of Buzwah School, took over. Pa seemed to admire her teaching wisdom and she did carry the school program. There certainly were no problems and Miss Clara was a good teacher; she taught the importance of saving our language, industrial arts, and certain sports. She was indeed an active person. Clara just finished the year at Buzwah and then retired, and once again we were without a teacher.

Indian Affairs was very efficient in finding the replacement so that we did not lose any school days and our programs continued or survived. However, this wasn't the end either. This meant still another new teacher, Yvonne, who also did not last, and then Liza Jane Pelletier, who was married to a Lawrence Pelletier from Kaboni. They had a young family and both were very musical. Lawrence was a musical prodigy who could play the violin, piano, saxophone, and trumpet. Their son, Herman, seemed to have acquired the same talents as his father. As a teacher, Liza Jane was astounding. She wanted all of us to finish grade school and move on, get a life, graduate, and this is what happened.

The First Nations teachers were all unique, but they stuck closely to the Ontario Department of Education curriculum. At the same time, they were very Anishnabe. Even though we learned the ABCs and read the great stories of the world, they never devalued our Indianness, because that would be devaluing themselves. They were, in fact, role models that it was possible to teach in the English world and still be Anishnabe.

We learned the three Rs and lots more. At school we learned and communicated in English, and although what we read was foreign to us, we learned. We, the little boys and girls from Buzwah, learned about the adventures of Marco Polo, the atrocities of Kublai Khan, and the romance of Camelot. We knew of Robin Hood and his merry men at Buzwah Conservatory of Higher Learning. We didn't read about First Nations history or heroes, but we lived among First Nations people and learned that part of our education from them.

I knew how to write the name of my grandfather, John King, before I went to Buzwah School. I imagine it was because, when he worked for someone, he signed that he would do the work and signed for the materials for the job. I remember it was a long time after I got to Buzwah School that I was able to write my own name!

I was a bit of a hero because I had the longest way to walk to school—most of it uphill. Remembering back, I realize that in the beginning, I wasn't alone on that long walk. Each day, Kohkwehns would come out on the road, and at the end of the school day she would walk almost halfway to the school just to meet me and walk home with me. I wasn't frightened, but I had never walked that path alone, and the first time was kind of a terrifying thought. Having Kohkwehns near, or knowing that she was somewhere along the road and we would meet up soon, gave me a sense of comfort and made me brave.

Going to school at Buzwah Indian Day School had its special aura. It was a one-roomed school, but our teachers were professionals in every sense of the word. The first teacher was new, a first-year teacher. She was young, but she meant business from the start and she was a good teacher. The next woman who taught was different, but conscientious just the same, and she was almost family. She and my uncle were courting (they did get married later) and they were very much in love. When she taught, she was different from our first teacher, who was long gone now. It seemed easier to learn from this teacher, but what did it matter—the learning process went on whether you were in tune or not. Our teachers were there to teach and the school was run efficiently, with each day sliding into the next. Because of the one-room school, the teacher included everyone in each lesson, and since we saw no difference in each other, we were just all there, even though the system divided us up into groups, in grades.

I was in grade two for a long time, I think, but since that was where all the boys were, we all enjoyed ourselves and even got into trouble. That was easy for us. All of us were punished together and no one was favoured—we were all guilty. One of the things that got us in trouble was when we would play "God Save the King" with our armpits. Our teachers did not seem to appreciate our orchestra as much as we did.

There were some responsibilities in our school; the most critical one was maintaining heat in our stove. It was a big cast-iron box stove acquired from one of the government houses. In those days, there were the usual retired Indian Affairs houses, vacant but suitable for other purposes, as the necessity arose. These big stoves were in the basement of the school, requiring a more or less stalwart student to go down there and stoke the fire each day. *Boo dah weh* was a duty. We not only had to keep the school heated, we also had to bring in enough wood for the teacher's apartment, which was in the same building. The teacher's quarters at Buzwah School were something we had to contend with—what with making kindling a four o'clock task or perhaps a minute before.

The teacher was able to buy wood, leaving us out of that duty. Chopping wood in the bush in the back of the school was a dangerous activity when boys were there unsupervised. Having only one axe made it difficult to take turns when each of us was convinced of our superb axe skills. Napo would have actually chopped Gawgee's foot off one afternoon when he felt it was his turn to use the axe to make the kindling. We were all ready to look on and witness the spectacle of someone bleeding, and Gawgee and Napo were quite adamant in carrying out one of the necessary actions that was now needed for a proper event to happen. Gawgee and Napo were both trepidatious about following through to carry this bloody event out. I could tell by how they stared at each other. Napo was ready to swing the axe down, holding it high above his head with both arms, plus we needed fresh wood in the school. Fortunately, the school bell rang calling us all back to classes. This was all that saved Gawgee that day!

Some of us knew to go to the back door of the school to pick up the water pail since the school did not have running water. We knew our responsibility and hauled water or kindling by the pailful to keep the teacher comfortable. We knew Miz Wakegejig's generosity was boundless and we, the boys of the school, were always at the back of the school, where she or her mother would give us a treat for the lovely cold water we would dip from the side-of-the-hill water fountain. There was also the weekly garbage run, which would involve packing the items neatly in cardboard boxes and carrying them into the bush behind the school. They would reward us with gifts like candies or chocolates and they were always appreciated.

Besides Gawgee and Napo, there were other stalwarts that we could count on to make wood. They might have been slow but they were steady, and because they had bobsleighs, it was always better to allow them to have the axe in the first place. Having a bobsleigh was quite a status symbol around Buzwah Indian Day School. Each bobsleigh was graded by speed, and at four each day, an Olympic-type race would get underway. Everyone in the school had a chance at the experience of sliding down the hill if they were able to barter something in trade for a ride. Some of us were Odawak, the traders of the Anishnabek. Trading was in our genes! Everyone knew the best trade. The economics were not that difficult! If you had a scone, you were guaranteed a seat on anyone's sleigh. The owners, mind you, would become selective, based on which scone they preferred.

There were many kinds of sleds in the community. As little kids we started out in *zhobaginigun*. These were bentwood runner sleighs for parents to transport little kids. Narrow pieces of ironwood or ash were heated and bent. A piece of wood was put on top of the runner and another on top of the other runner. These pieces were made of split cedar. Three crosspieces formed the place to sit. A half-inch auger made two holes that connected the runners to the wood on top. When we got older, we used our *zhobaginigun* to slide with.

Another kind of sled was the *onkosehn* or bobsleigh. The runners were whole pieces of lumber eight inches wide. We cut a curve at one end—*beopkododehn*—and found some iron to edge the runner. The best iron was if you could get a wheel rim from a buggy. You had to look around because people weren't driving buggies by the time we came along. The runners were absolutely no use unless they had something like iron on them.

We all had homemade bobsleighs. The place to be Saturday afternoons was Manitowaning Hill. I remember using Herman Kanasawe's sled, which could hold six of us. Two sleighs were coupled together and we had to steer with our feet and have two little ones riding in front. One time when I had insisted on being the steersman, coming down Manitowaning Hill I hit a man coming up the hill and carried him back down the hill on the sled. I was annoyed at the man for putting me off course, as I did try to avoid him, and the man was equally mad at me. He said, "Couldn't you miss me." I replied, "I couldn't miss you when you kept jumping every which way in front of my sled."

The bobsleighs, especially if any forging was needed, were all made at Willie's Corner. It was an obvious asset if your sleigh was shoed properly to maintain speed on the hill. Every sleigh was tested to see that it slid down the hill in the expected fashion. Every sleigh that hit the icy coastline first was studied to determine the mechanical fixture that must have come into play to give this particular sleigh its obvious advantage on the hill. Julius Gaiashk, Herman Kanasawe, and Tommy Taikwagewan had sleighs and they all knew the latest intricacies of their runners and why one went faster than another. We were like a society, and the best bobsleigh was the best for our society. Henreh always had the fastest and most efficient sleigh because he could get his father to fix it for him. Every once in a while, Pa would ask me what I was doing to fix my sleigh. I'd ask him how my sleigh could be fixed to go faster, but Pa never helped me; I think he hated my sleigh.

Sliding on Buzwah Hill was an art that only certain boys managed. Sliding down from the top—or near the top—of Buzwah Hill was not so scary in itself, but for one without a sleigh it could be quite scary. You needed a sleigh and you had to figure out the building of it. I always believed that boys were more adept at this trade; girls just could never manage the intricate task of building a bobsleigh, or even if they could, would it slide down the hill? Furthermore, you needed to steer the sleighs, guiding the loaded-down vehicle to stay on the path as it gained momentum, plummeting down Buzwah Hill. I don't think I knew any of our girls who could steer a sleigh down Buzwah Hill, although many tried and many owned the traditional sleighs fit for only Buzwah Hill. But girls tended to be a different class of intelligence themselves who did not enter the sanctimonious domains of boys, so we just left the situation for wiser Buzwah thinkers!

I remember when I learned to skate. It was an exhilarating feeling discovering something on my own. I had quite a time getting skates. Since spending money on something as impractical as a pair of skates was unthinkable in the King household, I had to devise another method to get my own skates. One winter, at my cousin Blaise King's place, I found boots equipped with skate blades. Someone had filed the blades off. I needed wood screws to attach the blades to the boots. So I went to see Charlie Heinz in Manitowaning. Charlie gave me eight screws for a dime, which was not enough. I had to beg more from Charlie to have enough screws for both skates. I remember he reluctantly lent me eight more screws, which I promised to pay for later if I could acquire five cents from somewhere. I assembled them, and now I had my own skates. I put the skates on and headed for Manitowaning Bay to try them out. For the longest time, my skate blades wouldn't stay on; one of the blades would come off and go ahead of me. I would look for the screws and blade and go back home and put them together again. Finally, I got the right combination of screws and they held. What a feeling!

To think back, in school I was never aware of the fact that some of us were maybe just a bit slow. In Buzwah we were all the same. It was kind of hard to tell who were the smart ones and who the dummies were. We accepted each other without any evaluation of academic difference or any sense of it. Until one year when one of the teachers divided us up. Each group was named for different birds. There were the blue birds, the red birds, and the yellow birds. The whole idea was that we would not be labelled by academic ability, but it didn't take us long to figure the system out! I was a yellow bird because I could read. We soon figured out who the red birds were and none of us wanted to be thrown in with that group, even though they were our buddies and outside school they were often the ones we counted on.

Outside school, the red birds were the ones with imaginations who could create or build things. There was one guy I will always remember. His name was Julius. He was able to make things out of just about anything that he picked up around the place—lumber, pieces of boards, and things. He would make different kinds of toys for the rest of us to try. He was, I suppose, amusing himself, but we were certainly envious of his ability to make things. None of us were able to do that and we could hardly wait to see what he would create next.

He made the fastest sleigh ever to go down Buzwah Hill. Julius knew how to build a sleigh from scrap, but usually it would fall apart by the time it reached the bottom of the hill. It was only good for one slide at a time, so he would have to rebuild the whole thing every time he used it. But, he knew how to build one. He was the one that also realized that you had to put steel runners on a sleigh. I don't know where he got the steel and he didn't have tools of any kind but he used to be able to make holes in the iron. He knew he could make iron bend by just heating it until it was red hot and then he'd pound it. He had figured all that out by himself. None of us, the yellow birds or blue birds, could have thought of that without Julius having shown us how. Yet he was a red bird at school—but we all knew he was smarter than the rest of us.

One year, a sandbox was introduced. Someone was allowed to work in the sandbox while the rest of us had to do our reading or arithmetic. It seemed a lot of students spent a lot of time in the sandbox. I knew one guy who spent all year there. We were all very jealous of him but we couldn't join him. Now that I have learned about teaching technique, I guess that the sandbox had something to do with discipline, but at the time it just seemed like a great way to get out of doing school work!

Actually, we all had our talents and special heroic characteristics. Julius Gaiashk excelled in dancing on one foot and made the biggest bobsleighs from the scrap he found at the Manitowaning dump. Moses Lavallee was a skilled arbitrator.

One of the most exciting times of the year at Buzwah Indian Day School was the annual Christmas Concert. I'll try to describe it in the following way:

Buzwah School Christmas Concert
by Cecil King (Apologies to Dylan Thomas)

One Christmas was, I suppose, pretty much like all the
    others,
In those years around the Buzwah corner, at Willie's.
No snow yet, Wah-jen, the wise one, wisely would say:
"Mii-go, Bah-mah-pii school concert tem-guk dgi-zoke-pok."
He was always wise like that—we all just took his word.
But then, there was not a whole lot else one needed to
    take—at Willie's Corner.

To be with the Buzwahyans, at Willie's Corner, at any
    time,
Wah-jen, was basically wise; in fact he never had to go
    to school—
Even to Buzwah School—like the rest of us, Wah-jen
    was just naturally wise.
In times when it was necessary to look more wise, Wah-
    jen wore a Capt'n's cap,
An acquisition of significance from his seafaring days in
    the summer months,
On that famous lake steamer, known as *The Caribou*.

I can't quite remember whether it snowed for six days
    and six nights when I was twelve,
Or whether it snowed for twelve days and twelve nights
    when I was six.
Gill-butt was pretty sure it snowed one of those days as
    well as one of those nights
Because the ground was white in the morning and stayed
    like that all day.

Of course, Wah-jen, always wise about such matters,
    wisely nodded at Gill-butt,
For figuring all this out for himself.
In the Buzwah School classroom, Gill-butt was a member
    of the Bluebirds,
In reading and then in pretty much everything else,
And we all just knew what that meant!

The Buzwah School concert came as it always did, and
    the snow
Came as it always did, with the Buzwah School concert.
Nobody knows really when the Buzwah School concerts
    began.
Napo, always the Willie's Corner historian, felt pretty sure
Jesus was born in a stable somewhere near Kahnuk-o-nong,
Which then made Christmas an obvious Buzwah holiday.
Tommy Grull, of course, did not agree, and since he
Was so strong, we more or less just let him think we
    believed him.

Tommy Med-we-yahsh, who lived somewhere near
    Kahnuk's—
As did Tommy Grull, for that matter—felt that he had
    never heard of the famous birth,
Which then would be dangerously close to the consid-
    eration that
Obviously, it just could never have happened—the birth
    that is . . .
Napo, undaunted, maintained staunchly, "Why would
    there be the Buzwah School concert then,
"If Jesus was not born at Kahnuk's?" With such irrefutable
    logic,
In true Buzwah fashion, who could possibly disagree.

Napo, of course, knew he had now gained the high
    ground—for as far as anyone knew
There had always been Buzwah School Christmas concerts.
Gill-butt, naturally supported Napo, which was a given,
    I suppose.
And furthermore, Gill-butt said, he always thought that
    Jesus was born in Buzwah.
Or why would we have a Buzwah School Christmas
    concert?

Tommy Med-we-yahsh, who Donald called Tommy
    Med-we-wehns,
Had to believe Tommy Grull, for sure,
Because Tommy Grull was as strong as a horse around
    Kahnuk-o-nong.
Tommy Med-we-yahsh (Med-we-wehns), on the other
    hand,
Used to beat up on the rest of us, just as a matter of
    principle, and so,
We were afraid of him too. But anyways, the Buzwah
    School Christmas concert
Did come year after year, and I don't think I can remem-
    ber a year
That it did not come, nor could anyone else at Buzwah
    corner—at Willie's—I suppose.

It may have been the winter of '32 or it may have been
    the winter of '22,
Our authority on such matters in Buzwah, Julius Gaiashk,
    though better known as *Ah-zhi-deh-gowan*
To those brave enough to call him that,
Expressed that he pretty much remembered when . . . .
The very first Christmas concert came to Buzwah—

And that was the winter of '22—in spite of the fact that
we all knew that Julius wasn't really completely born
until the winter of '32,

The winter when virtually everybody else in Buzwah
was born.

Thirty-two, I was born too, so everybody else just said
that, too,

But none of us could say when the first Christmas concert
came to Buzwah—

We did say we were not in Buzwah School yet—

And we did say we were not in Buzwah School's first
Christmas concert.

On this matter we all seemed pretty much to agree with
Napo

Even if some of us, at least, had happened to be in the
first Christmas concert.

Miz Wakegejig, the teacher in the Buzwah School, our
school, maintained

The Buzwah School Christmas Concert would happen,
snow or no snow,

And on this we all wondered. How could Buzwah School
Christmas Concert, in Buzwah, be any good without
snow?

Wah-jen, the wise one, of course, continued to reassure
us—as long as there was a possibility of a Christmas
concert at Buzwah School, it would snow and this
be for sure.

Gill-butt, but then again it could have been Alla-butt
who kept our spirits up

Undaunted by the "no snow" they wore their new winter
mittens—just in case

It snows like, before the Buzwah School Christmas
　　Concert,
And we waited,
And waited,
We checked for snow clouds,
And we hoped.

Miz Wakegejig was a nice teacher, crabby of course, but
　　a good teacher.
December was Christmas concert month at Buzwah
　　School.
Preparing for the concert was an exciting time, our school
　　completely changed.
Miz Wakegejig would have long since ordered us to put
　　all our books away.
Gone was the drudgery of classroom learnin'.
Miz Wakegejig would have ordered us to keep out our
　　scribblers and pencils though,
And then she would write words on the blackboard
That Mary Cooper would have brushed extra clean for
　　the occasion.

On those extra-clean boards, then, would be the numbers,
　　one by one, we had to learn for the Christmas concert.
Probably we learned these same numbers every year,
　　but what of it.
This was different, though some of us could actually hum
　　some of the numbers.
These were exciting times and Buzwah School took on
　　a Christmas air,
The more we copied from the blackboard, the more
　　Christmas it seemed to get—

Until the time came when we would have to start the
    singing part of preparing for the Buzwah School
    Christmas Concert.

First came the copying from the blackboard into our
    scribblers.
Basically we copied, because copying machines had not
    yet reached Buzwah School.
The impressive songs of Christmas came first:
"Old Black Joe" was one song to be learned,
Then high on the list, "Santa Claus is Comin' To Town."
We copied. When "We Three Kings of Orient Are"
    was copied,
Napo asked out loud where "Orient-are" was.
Miz Wakegejig was not amused—
And of course, she scolded us all. But we knew she was
    just jokes.

And so the bustle in Buzwah School continued,
Our desks, usually in rows, moved to one side of the
    room, adding to the bedlam,
Fresh sheets of bristol board appeared, red and green,
All to be cut up into poinsettia leaves and Lord knows
    what, to decorate our school room;
Glue, which was a concoction cooked on our classroom
    stove,
Materialized and was liberally smeared
On virtually everything that could be glued as well as
    not glued—

Julius and Jos-zup could dance on one foot—
We all knew they were a shoo-in for a number in the
    Buzwah School Christmas Concert.

Napo tried to dance too—but since he used two feet, this
    matter alone tended to confuse his dancing style and,
He would be sadly rejected, as it was deemed he could
    not dance at all.
We all admired Napo, though, as he was fearless at
    Christmastime at Buzwah School.
He wanted to sing solo—but his gravelly or one might
    say buzz-saw-like voice was devastating
For even the most straightforward numbers like the
    alphabet song—
Which wasn't too difficult a number to begin with,
But Napo's voice would drown out the rest of us, 'specially
When Napo felt he could emphasize the letters "F" and
    "N,"
The initials for "Napo Farmer"—he felt some emphasizing
    would be novel.
However, as a polite measure, to keep Napo quiet, he
    was appointed classroom monitor,
And to see to it everyone was where they should be, even
    himself, at any given time.

Perhaps the single most exciting event in preparing for
    Buzwah School Christmas Concert,
Even more exciting than the event itself, was the antic-
    ipated moving of Miz Wakegejig's desk.
It sat on a raised platform at the front of the room—but
    when we removed it,
The raised floor now became our stage for the Buzwah
    School Christmas Concert.
What anticipation!
What excitement!
What agonizing over when that desk happening, would
    happen. We could hardly wait.

Finally, the day came—we had copied down many numbers, and the singing was ready to start.

Tommy Grull, Arponse, Henreh, and of course, Napo had long since figured out that they would be the logical ones to move the teacher's desk.

Mind you, Miz Wakegejig's desk wasn't that big and certainly not heavy, but to Grull, Arponse, Henreh, and Napo, it was a herculean task of mammoth proportion, a fact, I suppose,

Pretty common in eight-year-old boys.

Grull, of course, was known by everyone in Buzwah for his horse-like strength, a fact he demonstrated when he pulled his homemade bobsleigh of stove wood.

Arponse and Henreh were strong too, stronger than anyone else,

And then of course, came Napo.

Napo prepared himself by flexing his biceps every morning and having a select few

Touch the muscle to feel its strength. Napo was serious about being prepared.

Finally, Miz Wakegejig, on still another day of total excitement, announced,

"Our four strongest guys—

Come forward please, and, move my desk"—Oh! What excitement. The moment had come.

Our four heroes rose—and were ready . . .

Grull, Arponse, Henreh, and, of course, Napo. Our esteem was overflowing—

unequalled, unparalleled, and all-engulfing . . .

For our four undaunted Buzwah heroes of Buzwah School.

Nothing could be more unceremonious than our four uncoordinated boys

Attempting to hog-tie an unwilling doggy at a rodeo.

Miz Wakegejig's desk was most unceremoniously lifted, then kind of half dragged

To the farthest side of the room,

Perhaps as a precaution more to keep Miz Wakegejig from teaching,

Should she happen to forget its Buzwah Christmas Concert time.

On getting it there, our four stalwarts stood up straight, and Napo, of course, clapped his hands together in a vertical motion of up and down as if to dust off the extra power he still had left after moving the desk.

There was now no doubt that the Buzwah Christmas Concert was about to happen—

Even if there was no snow.

Now the singing could begin, in full force—we all had been waiting.

The eighteen of us comfortably fit on our teacher's stage, and

We were ready. We were herded into four almost straight lines by Napo—

The youngest and shortest at the front—the oldest and tallest in the back three rows. This would be our choir arrangement—as well as Napo's management, no doubt.

Whatever row you were in, you sang hard, the harder the better, that was the criterion and, of course, Napo said so.

Miz Wakegejig could sing, too, and she sang so sweetly— that all of us attempted to sing just like Miz Wakegejig, too.

And so the Buzwah School Christmas Concert gestated to
become born, for that fateful night of the Christmas
concert of Buzwah School.

While the heroic moving of Miz Wakegejig's throne,
well, desk, was now accomplished, the total doin's
for the Buzwah School Christmas Concert were not,
other doin's became evident,

As Napo and Grull now indicated, in a most audacious
heated encounter with higher level Ojibwe,

There was obviously a problem—

To make a legitimate Buzwah School Christmas Concert,
and to honour the sanctity (whatever that word
means),

Grull was adamant, especially since the teacher's desk
had been moved,

Some other image sort of had to take its place.

However, Napo was already satisfied, the teacher's desk
had been moved, that was well enough.

Grull became insistent, as he indeed could very well be,

And he was not about to cave in to Napo, who was now
taking his manager role ever more seriously,

Even though the fact that he could only dance on two feet
disqualified him by Julius's and Jos-zup's marvellous
one foot dancing . . .

Even though Napo was also eased out of the singing
portion of the concert,

Napo took his managerial role promotion more seriously
than anyone else in Buzwah and that was for sure—

He now had authority over the concert, and even authority over us—

How we envied Napo.

It now dawned on us all, yes, of course, we needed a
    Christmas tree.
Buzwah School Concert was never without a Christmas
    tree
To fill the place Miz Wakegejig's desk used to be.
Tommy Grull, his bobsleigh ready, nodded to Arponse
    and Henreh,
And, of course, Napo, who had caught the mysterious
    repartee,
"We'll get the Buzwah School Concert Christmas Tree."
An argument of which way to go was nipped in the
    bud by Napo
In his proclamation that he knew which way to find a tree.
The fact that there was no snow yet mattered not,
Grull had religiously dragged his winter bobsleigh to
    Buzwah School already—
Just to be the first to slide down Buzwah Hill.
Should snow happen to come during the school day,
To be the first to slide would be an egotistical thrill.
Miz Wakegejig's permission had to be sought first—even
    Napo knows the rule about that—
Four little boys, outside the school fence, free,
On a legal school day, certainly was not the policy of
    Buzwah's school law.
Permission, permission. Where? Who???
Who would it be?

Even, to ask Miz Wakegejig to get the Christmas tree?
Of course, it was Napo, who stalwartly stepped forth,
Even when it was Grull who caused this fiasco.
Miz Wakegejig became serious, very serious indeed,
To ponder the request from Napo, no less to proceed,
    while

The Buzwah School Christmas Concert was so ready
  to proceed,
Miz Wakegejig pondered on, "Could we ask Wah-jen,
  just across the road—
Or Willie, down at the corner—or Eli Dugwahjiwan,
  from Kahnuk o-nong—
Eli, was an annual servant, when he would bring the
  Christmas trees,
For the Buzwah Church Nativity event"—but Miz
  Wakegejig hesitated,
No we need another way, "No money in our bingo jar."

Then Miz Wakegejig pondered a little bit more, but now
  the timely solution,
Really the only solution, leaving, of course, the obvious
  resolution,
"Arponse, Henreh, Grull, and no less than Napo, you four
  will represent Buzwah School Christmas Concert
  Committee, to go outside the school yard into the
  bush
And select a suitable Christmas tree."
O joy, now our concert can legally go on, and maybe it
  will start tomorrow as a final closing of our dilemma.
Indeed we knew what was to follow, where to go now,
  with total permission.
A tree will be obtained and now the Buzwah School
  Christmas Concert could go on with all its
  accoutrements—parts.

Napo, Henreh, Arponse, Grull, Tomah, to mention a few,
Were now gathered outside the Buzwah School classroom,
Miz Wakegejig's desk had been moved,
Napo was now satisfied

But Grull felt that the Christmas tree had been left out
　　by the entire class.
The reasons were quite legitimate—as the project was
　　indeed complicated.
Buzwah School had no funds to hire someone from the
　　village of Buzwah,
So Miz Wakegejig decided—yes decided—to remedy
　　the situation
With the solution in mind, to obtain a Christmas tree
　　for the Buzwah Christmas concert.

The solution seemed very straightforward—
Miz Wakegejig rounded up her students and addressed
　　the entire classroom—
"We have a problem that needs a resolution."
(This was because there are laws and acts that govern
　　our school.)
"And since most of you old ones know them already,
"Then the laws must be respected.
"You know you can't just shut the school down,
　Even when it's to get a Christmas tree for the Christmas
　　concert.
"It is in the law and I can get fired if I break the law.
"But now our strongest boys are ready to go to the bush
　　for a Christmas tree
　For the Christmas Concert."
"Napo has told me that he knows where there's a respect-
　　able Christmas tree
　Awaiting our action even now.
"All we have to do is go and chop the tree down and drag
　　it to the classroom for our concert."

And so Grull, who had been ready all week, now spoke
    up and said, "We are taking too long. Let's go!!"
And that's what happened, on that fateful day.

Napo knew the forest
And where the Christmas trees grew.
We ran to get to Napo's tree, though it was not far away.
Napo knew which way to go!
Advancing to where there was a stand of Christmas trees
    was no big deal.
Napo knew where the trees grew.
Upon arriving at the stand in the bush, only one thing
    remained.
Who would chop the tree down?
Napo refused! He did not like the axe.
Another argument ensued but was soon settled by the
    other boys who did not fear using an axe.

It did not take long to chop down the special tree.
In like fashion, we captured Napo's tree, chopped it
    down, and dragged it to the school
And the boys were on their way back.
Napo was indeed pleased,
So much so that he visited with Grull all the way back
    on his bobsleigh.

Arriving at Buzwah School door,
All that remained was to drag the tree into the classroom
    and try and make it stand up
Where Miz Wakegejig's desk had stood.
Such was the excitement!!!
With all the bigger boys ready,
They all took charge

And soon the tree was standing in the corner.
Miz Wakegejig was indeed pleased.
The girls were prepared with shiny tinfoil
To make decorations for the tree.

Everyone was ready to decorate the tree.
The difficulty remained—to make the tree stand up
A certain skill was needed.
The Buzwah School boys were looking.
Someone suggested we should get Wah-jen at this point
And request his help or maybe Eli Dugwahjiwan with
    all his Christmas tree knowledge.
With all this help, the tree stood up and was steadied.
Of course the eager decorating began. The singing could
    happen and so it did.

The Buzwah School concert,
With the tree safely standing, the kaleidoscope of deco-
    rations started to grow.
Numerous inventions were indeed tried.
A favourite was streamers of different colours in the room,
Strung across the room or from window to window
and from anything that could carry an item of Christmas
    decor.
Burlap stockings materialized filled with nuts, candies,
    and sugar canes.

With that the decorating soon ended
And the Christmas numbers, for which a traditional
    Christmas concert had been noted
From perhaps time immemorial or even before, could
    begin!!

We began with "Old Black Joe," a traditional Christmas concert number. We all assembled on the stage. Napo did some managing stuff and our organizing was quite in order. As the singing of "Old Black Joe" got in tune, most of us singing loudly and in key, the tune did start to be melodious and actually harmonious. The next song, "Santa Claus is Comin' to Town," seemed to show some promise as well. The strongest number to follow was "We Three Kings," and as the singing went on to show some sense of harmony, the concert choir grew louder—even with the disruption of Napo demanding to know where "Orient-are" was. Singing was a steady craft of Buzwah School, as the teacher seemed rather gifted herself.

The decorating continued and an angel at the pinnacle of the tree became an insurmountable issue. Each tree traditionally had an angel mounted at the top, so of course Buzwah School had to have an angel. The older girls seemed to love the older boys as the older boys tended to love the older girls and everyone helped in the outcome of the decorating. Some singing ensued, Christmas parcels had now to be wrapped and ribboned—a parcel for everyone.

The Buzwah School concert was about to happen and excitement was mounting. The children were counting the days until Santa would appear. The practising was going strong, the numbers for the concert were well mastered and Miz Wakegejig seemed to be pleased.

Then it happened! The day had come and everybody was ready. Teams of horses pulling bobsleighs and snow cutters, with elders and an armful of hay on board, started to arrive and were tied up on the school fence. Oh! What excitement! The classroom started to fill up and there were children all over the place. The time to start the concert was almost upon us. The teacher went to the front of the room and invited her students to join her. She asked everyone to find a place to sit as the Buzwah Christmas Concert was about to begin. The children were more concerned as to when Santa would arrive.

Napo was arranging the concert participants on the stage with a minimum of noise and everyone seemed to know where their place was, and very soon the lights were turned off and the concert was in full swing. The opening number was "Old Black Joe," followed by more singing and some tap dancing. Everyone was happy and joyful. Around midnight, a young child ran into Santa Claus outside and warned the entire school that he had arrived. So, now, what anticipation! Santa Claus came bounding into our concert hall carrying his traditional sack of toys and candies, bounced around, did some dances, and got the all the children giggling with "Ho! Ho! Ho!" All the children were now upon him as he handed out his bits of joy. Santa would break into a jig or sing a Christmas song in Ojibwe.

That year, the Buzwah Christmas school Santa Claus was Ben Kanasawe and all the children knew him. Many gifts were given out and no one was missed. The older people received gifts, too, and Santa would do a soft shoe dance with anyone he could get up. The bedlam in the classroom was almost unthinkable. Everyone received candies and toys. Some children received clothes and winter boots, even winter mitts. Finally, it was time for the Buzwah School concert to come to a close for the year and all the moms were busy getting their little ones dressed for the journey home, from wherever they came. Once again, the Buzwah School Christmas Concert had been an annual success. And everyone went home happy.

The school would now be closed for the snow season and everyone knew the next day was the big Christmas dinner and all would eat their fill once again.

Now winter was upon us and snowstorms would be the issue now that we all had to shovel snow. Mama and Kohkwehns were not spared. Winter continued as was expected until finally the weather got warmer and the snow melted. Now a new era was to begin.

The schoolyard was raked and levelled, and at one end, a baseball diamond materialized—we had sports right at the school and we cherished that. It seemed the girls were good hitters as well as good pitchers and fielders. I think all the girls were better than the boys.

Summer offered many financial opportunities and we all settled into jobs. Grandpa Corbiere and his son, my Uncle James, cooked for the crews watering the pulp; it was amazing to see how efficiently they could feed so many men.

It was 1947 and my time at Buzwah School was fast coming to an end. Napo and Gawgee were grumbling that everyone was leaving Buzwah. Miz Wakegejig had been adamant that we would become super-rounded students. The idea of leaving Buzwah School was now going full tilt and we were all in this frame of mind.

I guess what I learned in Buzwah Indian Day School was that we were all capable individuals and that we were okay as we were. Our Indianness was never a problem. We learned what the school had to offer alongside of the education we got at home in our culture. There was a culture of success in our school in Buzwah. We were expected to succeed while we remained little Indian boys and girls on a remote reserve in northern Ontario.

From my Buzwah Indian Day School teachers I learned that a child must be accepted as an individual. Culture is an integral part of a child's being, not an impediment. Teachers need to understand a child's cultural background and use that additional information to bring reality and the child's experience to bear on his/her academic life.

As kids growing up in Buzwah School, we learned to get along together. We went through all the phases of growing up. I remember when it was "cool" to walk around with your arms around one of the other guy's shoulders. Herman was my *nichi*. We walked around with our arms over each other's shoulders. We thought we were very grown up.

Buzwah School was at the top of Buzwah Hill. It was an adventure getting to and from school and we needed a way to get around. Arponse Trudeau had the first bicycle in Buzwah. He would stand on the ground making the loudest *rrrrrrr* sound and pretend that his bike was a bulldozer. It was a powerful bike with a beautiful bell that had a distinctive *ding dong*! Everyone tried to get a bell like Arponse's but couldn't. He didn't have the bike long, but long enough to teach me to ride it. He also taught me the mystique of fixing a bicycle: tension in the bicycle spokes and how to have the straightest wheels, ones that wouldn't wobble.

Henreh finally got a brand new bicycle that had been in the back shed of Ross Burn's house in Manitowaning. His son who had owned it had gone into the Air Force. Willie Pelletier must have spoken to the old ladies who lived in the house. Eli Dagwahjiwan could fix bicycle frames, and I had to depend on what Mama gave me to spend on my bicycle. I was the champion going down Buzwah Hill. We all had to push our bikes up Buzwah

Hill and we could hardly wait until four o'clock when we could shoot back down the hill.

As young boys we played at war. Harvey Pelletier had "war" words and we played games that acted out the words. Harvey used to put drama into our play. He had special skills in imitating sounds. He absorbed sounds and could recreate them. He could make sounds of a repeating rifle, exploding bombs, and the click of the rifle when the trigger was set and the rifle was loaded. *Nushka na de* and *aska dopke noon* described his actions.

Harvey knew what grenades were and he had a sound for them. He understood that grenades were touchy and that they had to be thrown as soon as the pin was pulled. By his actions one could see that there was an urgency in getting rid of the grenade. While Harvey could play with the repeating rifle, the rest of us were equipped only with single-shot rifles. It was no wonder that Harvey was always taking us prisoner. He brought rope with him and would tie us up. Herman discovered how to make a noose and he carried it around with him. Everyone was afraid that he would hang them with it one day.

Most of the boys made their guns out of wood. They carved them just so. I made my gun in my Pa's *Wigwamens* (workshop). It was always on my mind that Pa was very meticulous. As I said, he had all his tools organized and hung on the wall in a specific way. He knew where every tool belonged. I knew that it was best to leave them alone.

My gun was made out of lumber. I would do different things with my guns and once made one that was a little different. A gun needs a barrel. We didn't have a drill long enough to make a hole down the board the length of the barrel so I decided to make the barrel out of two boards. I put them into the vice and looked for just the right chisel. Pa had lots of chisels all over. I had to make a rut in each board. I had used the rip saw to make the boards the right length for the barrel. I had to place the two boards with the ruts together. Then there would be a hole all the way down the length. However, to make my gun work, I needed something to push down the barrel. There were lots of sticks around. If the end of the stick was thick enough, you could tie something to it. I had a strip of rubber on both sides so I had a top, and I used to hook the rubber on the back end of the stick in such a way that I could stop the stick at the end of the barrel.

I would put the gun on my shoulder and look through the double hole and the rubber band would propel the stick forward but could not go far because of the stop in the way. Then the next thing was to figure out how to make a trigger. I carved a trigger and then I had to mount it and I found an auger and a bit small enough. I carved my trigger in such a way that when I pulled the rubber band, the trigger raised and released the projectile.

When we were playing soldier, Herman Kanasawe wanted to capture animals to feed the army. Julius Gaiashk was playing the pig in one of these war dramas when Herman got him down and sat on him. Herman was going to kill the pig, so he pulled out his twelve-inch knife, which may have been a bayonet from the gun of a World War I veteran. He was just about to stick his knife into Julius's neck when someone grabbed his arm and stopped him. Poor Herman! He got so into his part that he really wanted to show how he could kill the pig! Herman's knife was only one of the things that came to Buzwah with the veterans who had returned from World War I. Everyone in school had a webbed belt that the soldiers wore.

By this time I had a new teacher; her name was Liza Jane Pelletier. She lived in Kaboni with her husband, Lawrence, and he used to have to drive her to school. This worked out okay until Lawrence's car "gave up the ghost" and they finally had to buy another old car. Mrs. Pelletier was a good teacher, even better than Miz Wakegejig, who had left us. The school was now on a new tangent. Our First Nations teachers affected us all, and Mrs. Pelletier was determined to get us through grade eight, and it seems it was about this time that we started to think about high school.

We were a lively bunch at Buzwah School. Napo was my friend and he felt a certain obligation in his life—just looking out for me—and he considered himself as pretty good at it. He was always watchful since he was making a big deal about all of us leaving Buzwah. He felt we were abandoning Buzwah Indian Day School and that he alone would have to keep it going, since he was not going anywhere when he graduated, and that is what happened. By this time in the school year, X-rays were done on all the pupils of the school. Napo was the first to know that he had tuberculosis (TB). It seemed the rest of us might be infected, too, but no big deal was made—but Napo did make some protestations over the number of us who had to go on the next truck, a mobile TB testing unit. He seemed by now to be getting sicker, in my estimation, though he was determined not to be TB-stricken. He tried to stay strong and resist the effects of tuberculosis, believing he would be the only one from Buzwah School to beat it. That's the way Napo was; he believed in himself and that he could master any human ailment. As it seemed, the truck to pick up all the TB recruits arrived early and most of us were picked up. Somehow, I kind of felt that I would not see Napo again. Maybe he felt the same way, too, because he took an old favourite jackknife from his jacket pocket and traded it with one of us for something I thought was totally useless. It was determined I was all clear and I was dropped off someplace on the other side of Corbiere's in the main village, leaving me to walk all the way back home. Some of the others were put on a temporary absence, but it was taken for granted that the TB ones were pretty much leaving for a long time. Napo must have been taken to a TB sanatorium; I never did see him again. He tried to defy TB, but in the end, he too was taken by it.

There were other deaths that summer. There was also a tragedy that was of some significance in our household, an accidental death in the Dodge family home at Maple Point. A member of the family, Danny, drowned, much to the consternation of all Manitoulin. Danny had used an explosion of some kind, resulting in him being cast off the dock into deep water. A dragging operation went on for several days in an effort to find the remains of Danny Dodge. This incident became significant in our household when Dad indicated his intention, with Joe N'Dip, to try to find the body and pick up the reward posted for Danny Dodge's return.

We could not stay at Buzwah Indian Day School. It only went as far as grade eight, and at the time, the Ontario Department of Education set entrance exams to standardize the level at which all students went on to high school. This meant that when we got to grade eight at Buzwah Indian Day School, we had to be prepared for the dreaded entrance exams. There were four of us from Buzwah School, and when our turn came, Mrs. Pelletier was adamant that we would pass. The day we were to write the exams, a car came from Manitowaning to take us to the high school in Manitowaning. Herman and I did Mrs. Pelletier proud!!!

I could see my term at Buzwah School was fast ending. I had completed my grade eight and passed my entrance exams with honours, I might say! This now meant I would have to consider the prospect of leaving home. This did not appeal to me, but this was the obvious state of things. What was really evident to me was that Buzwah was changing. It seemed that everyone was moving away. Henreh was moving to Wikwemikong, leaving a big gap in what used to be Buzwah, and all the others who left Buzwah Indian Day School went their separate ways. The curriculum of Buzwah School must have been good, for all of us passed our elementary schooling and then selected which secondary institution to go to and which kind of education to pursue. It seemed we all went on; so, from Buzwah Indian Day School to St. Charles Garnier Residential School—the preferred trail to take. Leaving Buzwah meant leaving home and my cherished elders. I had grown up. Things now would be different; no longer would I face such subjects as spelling or arithmetic.

I guess the prospect of leaving Buzwah seemed possible for us as we were developing a stronger sense of independence. Our independence had been apparent in our abilities with our slingshots and fur-trading project. Yes, the time at Buzwah Indian Day School ended and our slingshots did not prevail. We were moving on. The skills that we had with our slingshots, as with the skills learned at Buzwah Indian Day School, were left behind. We could have considered this collective departure from Buzwah School as traumatic, but as it was, passing on our slingshots was never considered. They just passed into oblivion. We left Buzwah Indian Day School. Our boyhood days passed into oblivion, as did our slingshots, our bicycles, and our sleighs.

3. LIFE ON THE RESERVE

My mother and father got together when my mother was sixteen. She always told me in her later years that I had to take responsibility for things because I wasn't that much younger than she was. My mother was the only girl in a big family of boys, and as she told it, she said, "*Yes!*" to the first man who asked her to get away from all the work of looking after her brothers. My father was the first to ask!

My mother's parents were a part of my life. My grandma, the former Jane Assinewe, was known as a kind, gentle woman. She would leave the house when my grandpa, David Corbiere, was drunk. She was hit and killed by a car. I remember the day that Grandma Corbiere died. I was working as a deckhand on a freighter and doing some painting in Little Current. My mother sent my sister, Liz, and my cousin, Rose Corbiere, to the dock to tell me to come to the hospital because Grandma was dying. After my shift, I left for the hospital, and on the way I met my mother walking on the road. She told me Grandma was gone.

Grandpa Corbiere, on the other hand, was known in the community as a tyrant. Most of his grandkids were afraid of him. He had the ability to read fortunes in cards, and one morning when I was at his place, he was looking at the cards and read that a woman would marry him. This was after he had lost my grandmother. The reaction of his children was really amusing. Mother, Adam, and Ambrose all discussed it and marvelled at how he had laid out his cards and believed that there was a woman about the place who would marry him. They were amazed that the old man was thinking of another woman.

One morning, there was a car parked in front of Grandpa Corbiere's house and they watched as he came out of the house with a suitcase. He got into the car and drove off. The watchers knew whose car it was. Degogwanay, the taxi driver, was away all day, and when he returned, the whole family scurried down to his house to find out where he had been. Degogwanay told them he had taken the old man to Neyaashiinigmiing (Cape Croker). He said, "I think he has a woman there that he is going to marry."

Two or three days later, Grandpa Corbiere was back in Wikwemikong, and not long after that, a woman arrived at Grandpa's place and stayed there. The two had gotten married by a justice of the peace at Neyaashiinigmiing and when the couple returned to Wikwemikong, Mom and Uncle Ambrose "shivareed" them. Grandpa told them to leave them alone and that they would put on a party for the community. And what a party it was—people danced and drank for days. The people who stood up for them lived in West Bay and came to Wikwemikong, and the marriage was blessed by Father Oliver for the church.

The summer of 1951, after I failed grade twelve, I lived in Wikwemikong with Grandpa Corbiere. I was painting the manse for the priest. I had to scrape off the floral-patterned wallpaper in the living room ceiling and paint it. In the evenings, Grandpa Corbiere would lecture me on lessons of life. One lesson was that Indians could be flattered. They would fall for it every time.

Another lesson he taught me was the folly of jealousy. He told the story of *Gaway* (envy). According to this story, the reason that Indians had never won any war was that they were too busy arguing with each other over who would be first to be the leader! He was also very strict about commitments; he believed that when you borrowed something you made a commitment to the person who lent it to you. He expected a fulfillment of that commitment. When a bill was incurred, repayment was to be made according to the agreed date—paying late was not acceptable.

Grandpa Corbiere had money in a can in the basement that he saved from working and he believed that everyone could do the same. He had currency from the first money he had earned, and when people came to him for loans, he would go to his stash in the basement and give them bills. The catch was that Grandpa expected the money that he received in repayment to be the same denominations as the ones he had given out. Since he had currency from different eras, it was often hard for the borrower to replace the exact bills; however, that was what Grandpa Corbiere expected. For this reason and others, he was known as a hard-nosed businessman.

Grandpa Corbiere took sick one day, so I called Dr. Bailey and he told me to get Grandpa to the hospital. I had just gotten a new car and my first trip was to the hospital. Uncle Ambrose was strong, and he wrapped Grandpa in a blanket, carried him to my car, and stuffed him in the back of the station wagon on a foam mattress. Uncle Adam's

Cecil's grandfathers, David Corbiere and John (Pa) King.

wife, Rita, brought tea and sugar. My cousin Eric and my future wife, Virginia Pitawanakwat, went with me to the hospital in Little Current. Grandpa was in a coma and never came home. We were worried about finding Uncle James. He was tobacco picking in southwestern Ontario, but he got to Little Current before Grandpa passed away.

Living as we did on Lake Huron, there were many accidents at sea. Kohkwehns talked about the shipwrecks on the Great Lakes and about *gindawun* (sunken boats). My father seemed to have a special gift for finding those lost at sea; he usually went out on the water at night when it would be calmer. I remember that when my cousin Flossie's brother, Dodge, fell off the barge, Dad found him and placed his smock over his body.

Everyone had a boat, but often something would happen to them, so they would go ahead and build another one. Willie Pelletier was a boat builder. He had a pipe about eight feet long that was heated in the forge. Boards were put in the pipe to heat them so they could be bent to make the sides of the *jimonehns* (small boat; skiff, dory).

We were isolated from the rest of Ontario by distance and lack of experience. However, one thing that we knew about was the Royal Agricultural Winter Fair in Toronto. Pa was the president of the Wikwemikong Agricultural Society for many years and attended regular meetings. I guess they talked about the latest things of interest to farmers. I know that Pa started the meetings with his familiar prayer asking the Creator to make his words as a medicine to those who heard him. I went to the meetings with him as I got old enough to drive. I really don't remember anything that was discussed and my main interest in the meetings was getting a chance to drive the old car. Every year, Pa got the opportunity to catch the train in Espanola and go to Toronto to the Royal Agricultural Winter Fair.

I remember the year I attended the Royal with Uncle Adam Corbiere. I had no idea where we were going until we arrived there. We saw a life-sized cow called Elsie made totally out of butter. Uncle Adam wanted to see the horses and watched the sulky races, disgusted at the way they hopped along. He thought the driver should have whipped the horses to make them run right!

There were so many people to teach us things in the community. Louie Gaiashk was a rotund man, always friendly, whose family lived in a comfortable house next to the school. Mr. Gaiashk was a cobbler who repaired anything of leather in his workshop in the house next to his bed. He fixed shoes for us around the school with tools that none of us understood. I remember he had a funny hammer that I later learned was a shoemaker's instrument. He had a rack of tacks and a whole lot of different kinds of thread. After he threaded his needle, he would run the thread through a bar of soap, which would stiffen it so it would slide through the tough leather more easily.

Bridget Gaiashk, his wife, walked to the hotel at Manitowaning where she worked as a cleaning woman. She was a short woman and carried a cane. I remember the wonderful smell of her baking. She used to make apple upside-down cake that smelled delicious when you walked into the kitchen of their home.

Their son, Julius, was an imaginative being who developed miniature villages with rough houses and many roads in the bushy area behind his home. He invented miniature trucks and other vehicles with wheels from materials he scavenged, and we enjoyed going to his house anytime we had the freedom to do so. However, Julius's mom guarded every piece of the yard—for Julius mostly, and I suppose for Thecla, his sister.

Julius was very tolerant of us clods from the school. He did go to school but he was absent a lot. The teacher did not seem to mind this, though. When she took attendance in the classroom every day, she would recite each one of our names to check them off in the register and when Julius's name came up, Miz Wakegejig would remark, "Julius is, of course, not here."

Thecla was blond and looked very much like a doll. She and Julius were very tolerant of each other, especially when Thecla took her turn to navigate Julius's handmade trails in the bush outside their home. Thecla always took her turn, too. In the Gaiashk household, along with Julius and Thecla, there were other brothers. They would have been Tony and Alphonse, who left home before I had finished my schooling, but I remember the announcement in school, very soon after they left, that they had enlisted and had fallen in war-torn Europe.

Life at Buzwah was spiced by the sports heroes in the community. We had great athletes in all sports. In the old days, hockey games were played on the ice of Wikwemikong Bay. The goals were on each side of the bay. It is said that Jokehn Assinewe was such a good player that he could stick-handle the puck the whole mile and a half across the ice. It is reported that one game went into the evening and the length of the rink was lighted by *bewewatehnan* (lanterns). Jokehn got the puck. He stick-handled brilliantly. He dipped and swerved and escaped the hits of all the opposing players. He skilfully manoeuvred towards the opponent's net. He paused. He prepared to release his powerful shot, when the goal judge turned off the bewewatehn. The shot went in the goal, but according to the goal judge, because the light was out, the goal didn't count.

There was a deadly men's baseball team Miji Wiiyam (Bill Wemigwans) used to talk about when they were finally recognized as a team. They got new uniforms and Miji Wiiyam remembered they were so beautiful they even had flowers on them! He was a good storyteller, or how else would baseball uniforms be described as beautiful?

The team had some good hitters. It is said that Sylvesteh Zack hit the ball so hard that at least eight runners came home!

Dan Pete was a legend on the mound. The story goes that Wikwemikong was in a tight championship playoff game with a rival team. The coach decided to change our pitcher. We had no other pitchers, but we had Dan Pete, a fielder with a powerful arm. The coach asked him if he would pitch and he agreed as long as he could choose his own catcher. He chose Miji Wiiyam. The game began. Dan Pete pitched so hard no one could hit the ball. At the end of the game, the catcher's hand was swollen double its size from the force of catching the blistering fastballs of Dan Pete. Wikwemikong won the championship.

We had much music in our lives. Waabiginees, as I mentioned earlier, carried on many of our traditions and he used to sing old Ojibwe songs as he played a hand drum. He and a number of other men from the community travelled to other First Nations communities to sing and took a group of young dancers dressed in traditional style with them. Pa did not know the old songs, but he wanted me to learn. For some reason or other, I never did learn them. Probably because they were in Ojibwe and, when I was a young man, my grandmother did not want me to speak the language.

The Pelletiers were among those who kept the old songs alive and they had an orchestra called The Bell Boys. The history of the Pelletier orchestra went way back. The music in that family was legendary. Joseph Pelletier (Polke) was the bandleader. Bob played saxophone and Lawrence played the violin. Kohkwehns said a fiddler couldn't play the fiddle unless he tapped his toe and Lawrence could really play the fiddle! He played the piano, too, until his son Herman, whose forte was the piano, came back from the Jesuit-operated school in Spanish. Herman had been sent to residential school with the rest of us, but he was so lonesome he was inconsolable. Lawrence drove up to see him and Herman left with him and never went back.

The other orchestra was made up of Willie Bell (no relation to the Pelletier's Bell Boys above), who played piano and chorded for his father, who was the fiddle player. They came from Kaboni road, where they had a huge farm. Mr. Bell wore a suit every day. Stella Kaboni played piano with them. We had dances; square dancing was a great pastime and we had many callers.

A lot of homes had organs or pianos and we had an organ in our house that Mama played. She was the organist in Buzwah Church. She played hymns at home, too, but she also had a contemporary music repertoire. She knew all the World War I tunes and played and sang these familiar pieces.

House-building in the community was done with a building bee. The house design was determined by how much material was available, and many times construction stopped when the owner ran out of material. However, every house, including ours, was two stories. John Jocko, Joe Jocko, and Dan Pete all had sawmills. Uncle John Corbiere was a carpenter. He would be hired to design a house for the owners and help them to work out how much material they needed. Uncle John had three basic styles of roofs: peaked, pyramid style, and one with a little hole in the roof with scantlings through. The design features were dependent on how much material was around. When I got old enough, I was sent nail scavenging. Although there was usually enough wood around to make some kind of house, nails were always scarce. I would be sent from house to house to find nails sticking out of the walls not serving any useful purpose. It was my job to rescue these nails for the new building.

Dan Pete, in the meantime, had a contraption that he had created over time and that could barely pass for a saw-mill. Dan was very ingenious in his own right and, should anything break down, Dan could fashion a remedy out of hardwood in the shape of the broken part. He had an old bulldozer that ran on diesel fuel and served as a team of horses, and Dan kept the bulldozer running, though I knew that there were periods of the year that the bulldozer sat idle somewhere in the bush where it had been left, simply because the job was over. However, Dan Pete knew this machine was in readiness should Ambrose Kitchikake have a breakdown with his machine. Things could not be better because, as long as Ambrose cut down pine trees, there would be money coming in. Dan and Ambrose were expert schemers, and, as a result of that, my home-building was about to happen. And so all their antique equipment and the combined minds of Dan and Ambrose were now launched on an enterprise that each could easily handle.

Dan's sawmill was created entirely from pieces of scrap lying in abundance everywhere throughout his yard and as far as the eye could see. Dan built his sawmill on a bed of bolted-together timbers upon which the mandrill that held the huge saw blade would turn. This, of course, is the most serious part of the sawmill. Next was the wooden trestle upon which a set of metal tracks were bolted down to serve as tracks for the carriage with wheels guided on the tracks. This carriage was located immediately beside the saw blade. With a log clamped securely to it, it was now ready to feed the fast-turning saw blade capable of cutting the entire length of the log. Dan had long before resolved the positioning of the log when he had rigged up a device that would shift the log in controlled measures after each time it had been sawed.

Dan needed sources of power, one to turn the blade and another to draw the carriage, which would feed the log to the saw blade, as well as a sawdust remover. This left Dan with the formidable task of selecting an engine from the numerous antique vehicles in his yard. These vehicles had been scrapped but some still had engines that could serve the sawmill. Dan would choose one, tinker with it, and take it all apart. After fiddling with it, the engine would come to life. Dan would now move it from the old vehicle and somehow trundle it upon a stone boat drawn with Ambrose's tractor and manoeuvre it into position for the saw blade. Unbolting an engine from a vehicle, no matter how old, seemed an easy task, and the reassembling of the engine in a foreign location was not a daunting task for Dan, either, for he had framed in the spot where this heavy engine would sit and from where, with a series of connections, it would be hooked up by a belt to the belt wheel on the saw blade mandrill. When the engine ran, it turned the saw blade, and when the engine ran fast, the saw blade ran fast. There was some control that Dan invented, a lever of some sort lodged securely between his buttocks, that he could move from where he stood.

Dan now needed what he called a power take-off with which to draw the carriage and turn the sawdust conveyor. So, by installing a wide wooden spool affair, upon which would be wound a sizeable rope, it could now pull the carriage along its track when Dan pressed the control lever located between his legs.

This entire contraption of bolted timbers had to be very substantial as upon it was then bolted the huge saw mandrill, the very most critical unit of the entire sawmill. This mandrill was located rusting away in some other used sawmill on some other reserve miles away. Dan accidentally found it and saw its potential should he decide to make his own sawmill someday, which he obviously did. Dragging this heavy unit to his location, Dan built the bolted bed of timbers on a firm, level footing on the bedrock. The saw blade mandrill and the entire business end of the sawmill would be bolted inside a very solid cage, perhaps the size of a large kitchen table (well, not much bigger).

The power take-off assembly, assembled from various mysterious connections entirely formulated by Dan, operated the large sawmill and turned the wooden spool. The coil of rope passed through the pulleys mounted on each of the trestles that held the log carriage in place, pulling the log in that direction, only to return the carriage to the other end again. The power to this sizeable wooden spool was taken off another belt mounted on the saw mandrill axle. Another ingenious contraption was the result of Dan's creativity, using a chain with small blocks of wood extended outward from underneath the saw blade on an arm of lumber. This device entirely removed the gathering sawdust—a characteristic of any sawmill.

When someone was going to build a house, it was critical that they find water. Water witching was and still is a gift that only some people have. Water witchers played an intriguing role in the community. As simple as the act seemed, not everyone could find water. All one had to do was to cut a branch of alder into a Y form, spread the arms of this forked branch and start walking, keeping in mind the four directions. Pa tried this and made me try it out once, too. Nothing would do until Pa was satisfied I, too, had this gift. It did seem to work for me and I did find many wells; Pa was proud of my skill.

Kohkwehns was a *Mashkikew-kwe* (medicine woman) as well as a midwife. The community knew that Kohkwehns was the *Kwe be jig e kwe* (midwife, literally the catcher woman). She always seemed to know when a woman in the community was pregnant and was prepared for them to call on her, ready to go whenever they asked.

When Getaykwe lived with us, although I was very young, I remember that Kohkwehns and Getaykwe were always together and they seemed to teach each other places to find certain plants and would discuss how to make things.

Kohkwehns was known for her cough medicine, in particular. It was made totally from vegetation. I was her constant helper. First, we had to find a *Geesh kon duk* (spruce tree) that reached my wrist when I stood beside it with my arm extended above my head. We skinned the tree of its outside bark, took the bark home, and hung it to dry. Then we went to look for a *Gijik* (cedar tree) and broke off a branch. We rolled it up and tied it with a *Wigob* (basswood) thong. We also needed *Weekehn*, which was the root of the *Tiginaw* (Canadian flag plant), known in Cree country as "rat root." We harvested the roots at the time when it was easiest to dig, usually in spring. The final ingredient was *Okweemij* (pin cherry) bark—the cambia layer. She cut the bark off in strips and took it home to dry.

When the *Geesh kon duk* was dry, Kohkwehns produced the knife that she kept especially for making medicine and cut the bark into about one-inch pieces. She then cut the *Gijik* boughs into little pieces, some green and some brown. The *Okweemij* bark that had been hung to dry was chopped. All of the ingredients were wrapped together in a cloth bag. When you needed to use it, a bunch of the mixture was put in a can with water and boiled as a tea. It was strong and when an expectorant was needed for a *Kitchi sa sad um* (deep chest cough), Kohkwehns said you had to use more *Okweemij*.

Geesh kon duk bark was the active ingredient for chest ailments and its gum was a very good medicine for boils and infections. It was most readily found on a hot summer day when a badly wounded *Geesh kon duk* had been blown down in a storm or was dying; the gum would leak from its wound. Sometimes, I would be sent to look for such a tree when there was a frantic emergency. Many people felt that the remedy really worked well. Mama always pooh-poohed Kohkwehns's knowledge but in the end would try the medicines anyway. And usually they worked!

Kohkwehns was not only the midwife for the community but she was a medicine woman, as I now understand that term. In those days, I was always there to help her. Kohkwehns had many medicines, more than she needed. Many came to her for medicine and at times she would sit by the cot of someone who felt sick and was restricted to stay in bed. Kohkwehns would be there to cheer up the patient and then to try to find out what ailed them. This was always the same. If I was nearby, Kohkwehns would pull me over, especially if I still had my outdoor clothes on. She would talk softly to the patient and interrogate him or her to establish a basic list of symptoms beyond what she had been told. For some who were very sick, Kohkwehns provided painkillers since she knew the right plant for that and she knew which plant had a soothing effect and which plant would put someone to sleep. If the required remedy included a poultice, she usually included me to help her in the production. I would unfold the vegetation and cut it up myself, either into short blocks or long strings.

Pa was the community *Wokahnih messhkiwenini* (veterinarian). People came to him to get advice with animal problems. He had a book on cattle diseases, but beyond that, he had a special sense of how animals felt. He knew when they were not acting normally and he seemed to know just what they needed to make them well again.

My Uncle Charlie King, or Waabiginees, as I mentioned before, was a man of many talents. He was the local optometrist and he travelled all over the reserve on foot or with horse and buggy, testing people's eyesight and selling eyeglasses to those who needed them. He also ran a store in Wikwemikong and he had a large icehouse that was filled in the winter with blocks of ice cut from the bay. Sawdust covered the ice, which often remained frozen until summer. My uncle cut some of the ice to make ice cream for the community's children on Sunday. He also sold bread baked by his family in large ovens, made and sold candy, and butchered and sold fresh meat when most of the community smoked and dried their own. In addition, he planted a large garden of corn, root vegetables, and peas and beans for drying.

Waabiginees also cultivated tobacco. This was not a permanent crop in our territory, but he proved that we could, in fact, grow it! Subsequently, either as a result of this or totally coincidentally, a number of people from our reserve, including me, worked in the tobacco fields of southwestern Ontario.

And as I mentioned before, Waabiginees was a traditional musician who sometimes entertained with traditional dancers. Pa wanted me to become a powwow dancer, but I was too shy to become involved. Years later I realized that when Pa and Waabiginees visited, they talked about the old ways, but I was too young to understand and did not know enough Ojibwe to be able to take part in their conversations. My cousin, Mary Lou Fox, spent a lot of time with Grandfather King and learned a great deal of traditional knowledge that I did not. What I learned, I learned from Kohkwehns.

Kohkwehns, like Waabiginees, also had broad knowledge. In constructing large birchbark canoes, there were very special steps that had to be followed and she understood the principles of them all. First, white birchbark sheets had to be peeled from a sizeable tree and spread out in the sun to dry. Kohkwehns had me gather round stones to be used as weights to hold down the bark. The sheets were no use if they were allowed to curl up in the sun. The dried birchbark sheets were sewn together to make a canoe-sized piece from which the canoe would be constructed.

Since a canoe was a vital mode of travel, it had to function in many conditions and omitting any of the steps invited problems. The most essential element was that it be waterproof. There is nothing that justifies a leaky canoe when it is built right. Kohkwehns understood this condition totally, and in her repertoire of recipes she had one for waterproofing to be applied to the seams as the canoe was being built. Kohkwehns gathered young spruce tree roots and boiled them in a cauldron, usually all day. The roots would boil down into a tarlike substance that was used exclusively as a sealant on all the seams of the canoe. This substance was not spared, and Kohkwehns knew the properties of her tar and lost no opportunity in relating the critical need for this sealant for any water transport. This tar had no substitute and generally was part of a white birchbark canoe throughout the community. Kohkwehns's tar was legendary.

Pa was a creative tinsmith and built things for farmers. He was in high demand because he could fashion stills out of any metal he found. Among Pa's tools was an old torch that he was able to keep going. It was a naphtha gas burner and could be used for melting lead and heating the soldering irons that he used extensively; it seemed that anything could be soldered as long as Pa thought it could! I grew up in this conglomeration of soldered things, which gave me the experience of doing it myself. I knew the art of soldering and I accompanied Pa on all his jobs for the farmers, which meant nearly always climbing up on high

3. LIFE ON THE RESERVE 99

barns to patch broken roofing or put up eaves troughs or patch them by soldering. We were always busy.

Pa taught me a lot during the summer. I remember driving around in our car/truck with eavestroughs sticking out the window. Pa was hired by local farmers to put eaves on their barns. In the winter, he would make them in his workshop, where he had a special piece of hardwood lumber meticulously formed so that when the tin for the eavestroughs was bound to it, a perfectly shaped eavestrough was automatically moulded.

As far as work went, there was a little pulp cutting, a little hauling of materials, and a few odd jobs. My grandfather had most of those sewed up. Pa was a hard-working, disciplined, creative, very busy man. He painted buildings and had definite preferences for certain brands of paint for certain jobs. He was a true professional. The car garage was full of cans with little bits of paint in each. When he got a new job, he would mix paint, and his customers had to come up with the money for it before he began. Pa knew how to calculate the amount of paint that would be needed to finish the job. When the job was completed, Pa would pile the paint cans in the back seat of the car. I was his painter of roofs. Canada Red was Pa's favourite roof colour—not red and not maroon but something in between. Pa had a million paintbrushes and he worked at trying to clean them up. He looked for old brushes because he said the bristles were longer than on newer ones. For indoor painting, Pa had rollers. They were faster. I hated painting window frames.

Mama had unique skills. She made wedding cakes for people for miles around. The thing that I remember about these cakes was that the whole house would be shut down for baking day. The recipe was kept in a special place that was a big secret. Mama maintained that she was the only one who could make a wedding cake and, from the number of people who called on her and the secrecy around its production, there must have been some truth in her claim. We could not make noise nor stamp our feet on cake-baking days. This had something to do with the cake "falling," whatever that meant. Anyway, Mama enforced the rule tyrannically. The finishing touch on the top of the cake was a tiny statue of a man and a woman that she bought at the store in Manitowaning.

As the winter progressed, deep snow would be everywhere and Manitowaning Bay would be frozen solid, so much so as to be a convenient shortcut to Manitowaning. The road circled around the entire bay, but if you could simply cross the bay over the ice, it shortened the travel time. There were a number of ice highways, one from the bottom of Buzwah Hill to the dockyard at Manitowaning and another from Two Clock, sort of on an angle to Manitowaning for those crossing from Kaboni.

Teams of horses hitched to bobsleighs were used to transport people and their effects. This was natural, and anticipation about crossing the ice seemed to be heightened as the winter progressed. It was nothing to see caravans of several teams wending their way across the ice in a day, especially on Saturday. While this mode of transport was expected in wintertime, the danger of breaking through the ice was always there, too, although the ice became stronger as winter progressed.

As spring approached, the ice became weaker and there were the usual accidents with teams of horses falling through ice. Year after year this happened and teams were lost. Grandfather Corbiere had a new team of horses and was very proud of his team, beautiful Belgians for which he had invested in new harnesses. It was March and the day was a warm midwinter thaw when Grandpa set out, with his passengers, from Manitowaning Beach across the ice for Buzwah. Grandpa did not go very far when his team went through the ice. It is told that he tried to save his horses and it is remembered that his reaction almost took Grandpa as he attempted to join them. He had to be restrained. Fortunately for him, after much scrambling, the passengers on the now-floundering bobsleigh were safe and standing on solid ice.

Church was another important activity. I grew up in a time when Christmas midnight mass was at midnight. The Old Ones and any adult guests in the house would go to Wikwemikong for midnight mass, but I was not allowed to go because children didn't go. Pa would hitch up the horses and prepare the bobsleigh with a cushion of hay, all in preparation for the long drive to the church in Wikwemikong, as would most of the people in the area. The church would be all gussied up, with the choir having practised new versions of the liturgy all the month of December. As an adult, I was thrilled by the Christmas music. A rendition of the Wikwemikong Church choir that I will never forget is the Mass in G, a Thomas Costain creation. It was in four parts and there were members of the choir who could sing the parts. I remember there was a solo for a basso profundo and Bobshen did that part like a professional. Being part of the Pelletier musical dynasty, he could read music. Genevieve Pelletier and I sang tenor because we didn't have a tenor for a long time. I was moved from the baritone section when it was discovered that I could cover the tenor part. Genevieve could sing the highest soprano solos as well. Alphonse Shawana could also be counted on for solos.

On Christmas Day the choir involved the school kids, and organization was paramount. But then some of the teachers would help out, so much so that by Christmas even the church choir would have been ready. The choir was usually quite spectacular as I recall, and later I became a wholehearted member as well. The people of Wikwemikong are to be commended as the musical numbers required hours of practice, an exercise that would not have been familiar to them. There were some members who could read music and they would have been the stalwarts of the choir. Each Christmas midnight mass definitely had a spirit to it, making all participants feel truly involved.

In winter, the March blizzards, as expected, blew in the roads, making them impassable. Snowbanks and drifts were too deep for ordinary travel. One person walking was not enough to open the trail. In those times, it was taken for granted that the snow season would do this and everyone just accepted it. People in those days could predict the winter storms and what would happen.

When it snowed, the people just stayed indoors, and when it was over it was time to survey the road and figure out who would break trail. It was *dewaagaanege* time again for someone with a team of horses and a bobsleigh to hitch up his team and make a winter trail. Since the snowdrifts on the main road were too deep for human beings, let alone horses, the new trail would be made in the level fields beside the road. This method required taking down the fences. This trail was automatically done year after year in the same place by whoever broke the trail.

Joe N'dip, or Joe Gete, whichever name you called him, was a household person who usually lived at Mom and Dad's. He set home brew and he and Kitchi Elizabeth imbibed every weekend, usually ending up at Mom and Dad's. Making home brew was an art and only certain homes made it. Up in our corner, it was concocted by Willie at the corner of the highway, and he did it to attract visitors to party with. Then there was Kitchi Elizabeth, who was perhaps the best at it, as she, according to her, knew the art of setting the brew and the principles of how it worked. Pa and Mama made it, too, but Pa also distilled since he knew how and was ingenious enough to create his own still, which worked marvellously, in the shed of the house. I remember those days when half of the house would be shut down and the doors locked, as there was always fear of an ancillary department raid and the inhabitants being charged. As I recall, there was an order to Pa and Mama's home brew parties. You started drinking there, and at some point it would be suggested to walk over to Kitchi Elizabeth's and continue the drinking there. Sometimes we hitched up the horses with hay on the bobsleigh for the comfort of all, but it was wintertime and the deep snow added to the fun of the home brew party. These parties were held regularly at Willie's, Kitchi Elizabeth's, or Mama's and all were attended equally.

Our community knew war. Many men were lost to World War I and more to World War II. I was only seven years old, but I remember the day that World War II started. It was a Sunday. We had gone to Buzwah Church, and after church Grandma Corbiere took me with her. We walked to Grandma and Grandpa Corbiere's house, which was halfway to Wikwemikong. By the time we got there, I knew that something was wrong. When Grandpa Corbiere saw me, he asked Grandma Corbiere why she had brought me there because I was obviously sick. He told Grandma that she had better take me home. She took my hand in hers and we started walking back to Buzwah Church and from there down the hill towards Pa and

Mama's place. On the way, we stopped for a rest at Uncle John's. I remember that his wife, Aunt Victoria, was in a state of great excitement. She told us that she had heard on the radio that we were at war and that it was going to be worse than anything we had ever seen. I didn't know what war was but I knew that the adults in my life were scared of it and so was I. When we got home, I was covered in red spots; I had the measles.

War came to our home in many ways. Mama and Kohkwehns were swept up in knitting socks for the soldiers. Mama was quite indignant that the lady from the Red Cross gave the women explicit instructions on how to knit them. Mama thought there should have been some room for creativity, but creativity was sacrificed for functionality. Mama, in turn, ensured that Kohkwehns followed the instructions to a tee. The women were also involved in fundraising and the proceeds of rummage and bake sales went to the war effort.

We heard about the fighting and news of our soldiers on the radio. We lost men in the war and the family was informed of the death by a man who came from Manitowaning with a yellow paper folded in his pocket. Now I know that that was a telegram announcing that a soldier was missing or dead. At that time, all we knew was that a stranger brought a yellow folded paper and then the community heard that someone we knew was gone. There was no wake, no funeral, and no public mourning like when someone in the community died, which meant that we did not get a chance to perform the ceremonies necessary to say good-bye and help them on their way to the next life. There was just emptiness.

As I realize now, had there been conscription during the Korean War in 1950, I would have been just the right age to be sent. However, since the Korean War was not classified as a "real war" but a police action, boys my age escaped the fate of those our age in 1917. It is a sobering thought that I came so close to being a soldier.

My growing up time was just before and during World War II. I was too young to go to war, and you can bet that Mama would never have let me get away with lying about my age and sneaking off. She would have been right behind me!

Our reserve had a tradition of sending men to join the forces. Many men from our community had been in the First World War. I remember when Clarence Wakegejig quit school. His sister Christine was the teacher. The two of them had words and he left and never came back. Soon after we heard he was in the army. His brother John was already serving his country. I remember the day the telegram came telling the family that Clarence had been killed. He may not have been of age when he signed up, but he was deemed old enough to be sent overseas and to die and be buried in Holland. Alphonse Gaiashk, too, was killed and lies in Belgium.

Harry Jaggard was a local white man who had a farm in Clover Valley and Pa hired him to do the harvesting and he would have supper with us. He would talk to me, and we stayed friends into my adult years. He taught me how to plow and talked to me about politics and the things the government was doing. I remember him telling about the horror of the death camps. He said that the Germans would play loud music just to cover the sounds of the people being tortured or suffering.

Buzwah School did take part in the war effort. There were about twenty kids in the school, and we made our contribution. Miz Wakegejig taught us from her books on

the war and tried to get us worked up for war services—
mostly in Buzwah. Our service was to pick milkweed
pods and collect scrap metal. In the first case, a uniformed
member of the Air Force from the base at North Bay visited
our school. We were in awe of his uniform. He told us
that we could make a great contribution to winning the
war by providing milkweed fluff, which was used in vests
worn by pilots and life preservers for the navy. We found
out that the fluff had been used in Europe to make warm,
lightweight clothing for many years. We were eager to
gather fluff to win the war; even though there wasn't a lot
of milkweed in Buzwah, there was enough to fill a sock for
the Red Cross man who would arrive each Monday with
his truck. We never did know where the truck came from.

Scrap metal was the other thing that the army needed to
win the war. On the reserve there was a lot of scrap metal,
and the boys of Buzwah knew where a lot of abandoned
machinery could be found. We scoured the territory and
lugged our finds back to the school. I detected that the
men who came to pick up the metal judged the quality
of it; they wouldn't take just anything. They would assess
each piece. I remember my two sisters carrying disk plates
to the schoolyard. Every day they would visit a set of
discs in the back field ready to be pulled by the horses in
spring and fall to work the garden. They would remove
the disks and each would carry one to school with their
fingers through the centre hole. Pa did not approve of this
activity as they were ruining his farm implements and Pa
was concerned about his farm equipment, war or no war!
However, Elizabeth and Loretta steadfastly insisted that
they had to contribute to the war effort.

All the pupils of Buzwah Indian Day School understood
their role in the war effort and it changed things. It was

never the same. Gone were all the phonics classes as well as our reading classes. Even the teachers from that day on were different.

Then there was the brass band made up primarily of *Gopskabeejik* (returned soldiers, literally those who came back) from World War II. There was Dominic Odjig, Henry Hill, and other veterans. David Manitowabi played the tuba. They were called *Bodajigainoniwuk*, men who blow horns. They all learned to read music. They marched and played the Sousa marches. They were very impressive. They would stand in a circle outside the church or a house they were going to honour.

Frank Cooper from Two Clock enlisted in the army in World War II and his regimental number was B 27650. On his first furlough, news that he was home really travelled. Parties were held and his mother, Kitchi Elizabeth, being so taken up with herself and her importance, put on feasts in her home when it was felt that he should be honoured by the community. There was a customary supply of home brew to grace the occasion. We were all at her table and kept singing even though Frank was passed out on the bed. He had divested himself of his military accoutrements.

The fun went on with much singing when someone suggested putting on Frank's discarded uniform. This was to honour Frank, who slept pretty well all night, giving the partygoers full permission to devastate the Queen's military issue. Kitchi Elizabeth, caught up in the festivities, zeroed in on me to dress up. She unloaded Frank's packsack, which held all Frank's headgear, as well as a gas mask. We all wondered about each item, but protection from mustard gas became a concern, particularly as the evening wore on. Kitchi Elizabeth was suggesting that one of us don Frank's uniform. She became more and more insistent and wanted me to put the uniform on—all of it! Elizabeth was very powerful in that regard and I felt I had no alternative but to dress up. It seemed that the whole object of this was for me to don the mustard gas mask, and the fact that the mask made me look ridiculous was the whole point. The mask was black with a long snout, making it look like a large pig. Such was my lot, and with the aid of Kitchi Elizabeth, I was harnessed up in the new Private Frank Cooper look. I fit the uniform quite well, but more important was that mask depicting a pig, much to the chagrin of the then-drunk partiers. Kitchi Elizabeth was much pleased with all the changing of clothing and equipment and expressed her gratitude to me for complying with her wishes.

Not all was fun in the community. I remember when returned soldier Ignatius Gabow committed suicide. As a young man, I had no knowledge of the impact of going to war on individual soldiers. To me, his demise seemed uncalled for and caused me to question why anyone would commit suicide—this death seemed so pointless. Suicide was not a thing with which we were familiar. Traditional Anishnabe communities ensured that all members understood and were supported in their life's path, which was revealed in their vision quest, interpreted to the community by the elders. Spirit guides were provided and the individual's contribution to the community was reinforced. Each person understood that he or she was essential to the existence of the community. They knew that they could not die until the task that the Creator had given them was completed. Each person realized that the Creator had given him or her life and he or she did not have a right to take that life. You do not have the right to end the life the Creator has given only to you. Suicide was unthinkable in traditional Anishnabe society. Ignatius's death made me examine, as I had never done before, why anyone would take his or her own life. It made me think about what life meant to me. I concluded I had much to live for!

4. RESIDENTIAL SCHOOL

My days at Buzwah School came to an end. We had done well in Manitowaning in the high-school entrance examinations. Miz Lisa-Jane Pelletier did show pride in us, I suppose. I remember at the time Napo and Gawgee giving the whole incident the usual pooh-pooh treatment. It was pretty much during the first weeks of September that Pa brought home a letter from the post office in Manitowaning. He read it to Mama, Kohkwehns, and me at the supper table. He knew the letter was from Indian Affairs; it looked very official. The letter informed us that I had been accepted at St. Charles Garnier Residential School to begin my secondary education. This was exciting news.

I was ready to go to Spanish, Ontario, where Indian Affairs had worked out a contract with the Jesuits for a new high-school program. My Old Ones had impressed upon me that I had to go because I had learned all that Buzwah could teach me and I had more to learn.

Now my preparation began. I remember looking for a suitcase that Mama had spirited off somewhere in the attic of our home. I eventually found it; it was very old and generally falling apart, but it was good enough as a symbol of my new life. I remember Kohkwehns telling me to be strong and say my prayers and always listen to the priests.

Mama counselled me, reminding me I was about to enter a new world of manhood, that I had to build it myself and my success would depend entirely on how well I performed my studies. Kohkwehns, it seemed, was already lonesome and she would cuddle me whenever I was near her. She would sit with me, or just be with me and say that she'd miss me, tell me to "be good" and that a year wouldn't seem so long. She also told me not to be afraid and to believe in myself. The days now at the King household were changing entirely. Pa seemed to be sick most of the time. Of course, Mama was sick all the time—and the preparation for my departure had begun.

At supper one day, Pa made the announcement that the next day some buses would come. I would have to stand on the road, and when the bus stopped I was to get on. This brought to mind what I knew about those buses. My first knowledge of residential school came when I was still a little tyke. Every September and every June, a procession of wagons and buggies would go by our place. I found out these were the families going to deliver their children to the big black chartered school buses that were lined up in Manitowaning in the fall or they were on their way to Wikwemikong to pick up their children from the big black school buses at the end of the school year. In June, the procession was happy. When they returned, the sound of children's laughter could be heard before the procession could be seen coming around the road at the bottom of Manitowaning Bay. In September, the procession was ominous. It was quiet when it passed on its way to

Manitowaning and there was a sadness about it when it returned, now with all the children gone.

I remember two particular occasions. The first was when one family went to Manitowaning all excited to meet their little girl coming home from residential school. When they got to the buses, she didn't get off. The priest who came with the buses didn't know where she was. Later, we heard the little girl had died. Another time, Julius King was taken away in one of the big black school buses. He was my playmate and we often went to visit at his house, where we played together. He was taken to residential school because it was felt that his parents couldn't take care of him. I was devastated. I cried for days. I didn't understand, or I didn't know what was going on.

So I had mixed feelings about going away to residential school. I will always remember that evening of the night before I was to leave. Kohkwehns was particularly caressing and stayed out of Mama's eyes. Pa seemed rather quiet and didn't talk, even to me. I went to bed that night in a state of emptiness as the thought of my departure began to build up. Kohkwehns sat on my bed for a while, sensing the melancholia of all of us. I guess we all pondered the thought of not seeing each other again.

The next morning came as it always did. Pa got up as he always did, made a fire, and put his iron pot on to boil to make porridge for all of us. The conversation around the breakfast table was mostly about when the buses for Spanish would arrive. Pa was quite sure they would not be on time. We puttered around the kitchen for a while longer.

Then, Pa made the announcement, "Okay, we better head down the road before the buses arrive, as they will be coming any moment." Mama and Pa walked ahead. Kohkwehns took my hand and I walked with her. Down the road we headed. We were all quiet as we walked down to where the buses would arrive. I kind of half hoped the bus would not come or would break down, making it unfit to pick up the young students destined for Spanish. But the big black buses came.

I don't know whether they were deliberately painted black, but they were very foreboding. Everyone understood why they were coming there: to gather the boys and girls that they'd take back to Spanish. The whole idea seemed to be to fill the buses and leave no empty spaces. The priest came to the house and wanted to take my brother and sisters as well, but my mother wouldn't allow them to go, because they were sick. I'm not sure what they were sick from, but they didn't get on the bus.

Kohkwehns kept a strong hold on my hand. Mama spoke to Pa to tell him he must tell the bus driver to drive carefully. Kohkwehns and I just stood there. She maintained her hold on me and followed the line up to the bus door. I peeked at Kohkwehns and I noticed there were tears in her eyes. I had never imagined her to break down in tears but she kept holding on to me tightly as she walked with me to the bus door to say her final bye-bye. I looked at her again. Our eyes met quickly for our "Good-bye." Mama was now with us. She, too, looked weepy, but said nothing. Kohkwehns led me up to the door of the bus. I boarded and that was my departure. I noticed Kohkwehns as I took my seat on the bus. She came to the road and waved; somehow, I felt that maybe I wouldn't see her again. And that's what happened. I never saw Kohkwehns again.

I boarded the bus, it took off, and I was on my way, first to Wikwemikong and then to Spanish. As I remember, we picked up children all along the way. There were parents standing with their children who were ready to board the bus. A belief in Jesuit education had come to our community and the parents were anxious for their children to be part of it.

The bus ride was something else. Since we were crowded into the bus, it was not long before a lot of the children started getting sick—which amounted to the entire busload getting sick. I guess it was too much to expect some sort of relief to our misery. We arrived in Spanish as night descended. I found out then and there that you had to fend for yourself. We got off the buses and then we couldn't figure out where to go. Finally, a priest materialized to lead us indoors and up the stairs. What a strange experience it seemed. We were all shooed into a huge dormitory, there to find a bed with bedding. We all tried to beat each other to the best location. I found a bed that fit me; being in grade nine and tall for my age, this was not easy. The bed had bedding; the only thing was, I now had to make it.

It was at this point that a priest, so we thought, appeared. He was not a priest yet, but he was there to aid us. We eventually learned that he was called a "prefect" and the prefects were to look after your every need. They were just like young priests and you had to respect them just like an older priest.

Succeeding in the entrance exams, I was attending high school at Garnier Residential School in Spanish, Ontario. There were no First Nations teachers there. Our teachers were all men of the cloth, Jesuits to be precise, of diverse European backgrounds—German, French, and Irish. They were Old World classical scholars and their goal was to make us achieve intellectual excellence. I had never before known that people spent their lives reading books and studying as academics. The Jesuits taught the Ontario curriculum, with a strong emphasis on Roman Catholicism.

I was among some of the first high-school students at Garnier Residential School; high school was a new venture for the school. The time had come when, by law, students had to be kept until they were sixteen years of age. Previously, students had been sent home with whatever they had learned by their sixteenth birthday but it was clear that many did not have enough. Since students could not be sent home until they were sixteen, if they had completed grade eight when they were twelve or thirteen, they might as well be given more education. So, that's how the idea came about. Let's go on to grade nine, then ten—and the whole idea of a high school emerged. We were among the first groups—the guinea pigs, so to speak!

Father Rushman told us that this was where we would spend our days. He knew me from his days at Wikwemikong. He became very direct and said, "You have a life here. You will succeed if you give us your highest cooperation," and with that he sent me on my way, saying, "You will be awakened early tomorrow morning." And that's what happened. As was expected, the next morning, a loud bell rang to rouse us all from our sleep. It was then I noticed an entire dormitory of boys, ready to get up. We all washed, dressed, did our own beds, and then headed downstairs for breakfast. It was as I expected—porridge, a meal that would continue as long as I stayed in Spanish.

After breakfast, a prefect informed us all of the clothing issue in a room down the hall. We went to the designated room and began our search for outfits, old military uniforms, that would fit. The prefect kept admonishing us to hurry up and find something to wear.

Over the last number of years, the prevailing view of residential schools has been that they were places of abuse and deculturalization. This view, espoused by academics who were not students themselves, has marginalized me and my classmates. Our stories have been requested, and when they didn't fit the abuse theory, they were discarded.

My first such experience was with a professor who has become very well known for his work on residential schools. He and I were colleagues and he asked me to spend some time with him talking about residential school. I remember visiting with him for many years. Yet, when I looked at his book, it was as if I had never been involved. I could not see my perspective in his work at all. It made me feel that, to him, my views and knowledge were unimportant and had been disregarded.

Then another researcher approached me and asked me if I had been sexually abused while at Garnier Residential School. When I said I had not been, her response was that I must be in denial and my healing would only take place when I admitted that I had been abused. She plied me with a book designed to help me come to terms with my sexual abuse.

So, you can see how this era of healing the wounds of residential schooling has taken over the story to the point that those of us who saw some value and, to some degree, enjoyed the experience are no longer asked for our knowledge. This was very clearly pointed out to me when I learned that one university was no longer teaching *Indian School Days* by Basil Johnston because it was not true. Now, I went to Spanish with Basil Johnston. I know it is true. To my knowledge, it is completely authentic and describes in accurate detail our lives in Spanish. However, apparently, for the academics who want to perpetuate solely the idea of residential school abuse, the book is not true. Ironically, an official Jesuit history of the school also attacks *Indian School Days*. To those of us who know that Johnston's

Cecil in a Mountie jacket taken from rummage provided by Garnier Residential School.

book is a true reflection of the way it was, it is again a devaluing of our experience to have this book attacked by those who do not know!

To me, academics created a new theory of making our people victims. We are the red objects of white subjects. We had things done to us. This serves the mainstream institutions, because they can maintain that we are not capable of looking after ourselves. But for those of us who do not want to be considered victims, for those of us who survived and thrived, this interpretation is insulting and demeaning.

Let's think about the context of my Garnier Residential School experience.

First, residential school merely means schooling where you also live. There are many historical tales explaining why this was necessary in those days. I will not bore you with them. However, for me and other grade eight graduates from Buzwah Indian Day School, Garnier Residential School was the option available for us to get further education. Garnier, or Spanish as it was more commonly called, was the next step in our education. We certainly knew of residential school and other students who were there and we kind of looked up to them.

Garnier Residential School (named after Charles Garnier, a Jesuit missionary killed by Iroquois in 1649 and canonized in 1930) was run by the Roman Catholic Church. To my community and people, this was not a problem. Roman Catholic priests had been part of the lives of the Odawak of Wikwemikong or the Pottawatomies or Ojibwes since the 1600s. It has been said that we have been Christianized since the first boatload of Catholic clergymen hit North America. The first mission in the mid-seventeenth century is commemorated on a plaque at Ten Mile Point, Manitoulin. Since then, we have been under the influence, so to speak, of the Roman Catholic Church. By the time I went to Spanish, some Christianity had rubbed off the priests and on to my family during the 300-or-so years of evangelizing. So, the concept of residential schools pounding Christianity into our little heads doesn't really fit in our situation. We were as devout as the average little Catholic boys anywhere!

Along with Christianizing, the residential schools are said to have been developed to *civilize* us. Now, here we get into some very murky waters because one person's *civilized* is another person's *savage*. We boys and girls from Buzwah certainly thought we were civilized. However, looking back at what the priests set out to teach us, we had some gaps in our knowledge. We did not come knowing how to do ballroom dancing, for instance, and the priests took it upon themselves to teach us. We did not know the operettas of Gilbert and Sullivan. The priests saw it as their duty to introduce us to the English cultural phenomenon. So with great abandon, I can now lustily sing songs about major generals, pirates, and mikados. I have yet to use this civilized behaviour to get a job or further my education.

I have found that very few of the *civilized* people I have met since were schooled in Gilbert and Sullivan.

Did I mention our cultural education included silent movies, particularly those starring Tom Mix? It appeared as if the Jesuits were trying to turn Indians into cowboys. At least that could be one explanation. Cowboys must have been more *civilized*.

The residential school was a very big place run by priests and prefects and what they called brothers. They were all hard-working men who kept the school going. I had a number of old brothers and several Jesuits who taught me.

There were very strict schedules; everything in our life was dictated by time. We learned Latin, Shakespearean plays, and, as mentioned, operettas. On top of that, I learned how to take a motor apart and the intricacies of electrical wiring. I learned the mucking related to doing plumbing and the drudgery of farming. I found out that academics, especially Jesuits, do not work with their hands as a rule. They realized early that my grandfather had taught me skills that were sorely needed to keep the large rambling building that housed us from falling apart and the importance of the trades that the Jesuits had not learned in their scholarly pursuits. The priests might have been able to hit a nail with a hammer, but they never did. Any of the physical work done around the place was done by the brothers or by those of us who came to Garnier already trained by our families.

When the Jesuits put on the Gilbert and Sullivan operettas, the carpentry and engineering skills I had learned from Pa were called into action. I was the set builder and my greatest achievement was building the ship used in *H.M.S. Pinafore*. I constructed it so that it propelled itself onto the stage. Oh, the thrill of seeing my creation, filled with my

At home from summer vacation during the last years of residential school in Spanish.

classmates singing lustily, cruising onto the stage on opening night!

Our days were broken into little segments and we were expected to adhere totally and completely to the preordained pattern. When we sat down for supper and someone was missing, everything stopped and everyone looked for that person. I never dared to be missing, although once in a while one of my friends would fail to show up.

The Jesuits had high expectations. Excellence was expected in all things; nothing less was acceptable. Their role modelling of being scholars inspired those of us with academic minds to work to our potential. There was no stigma attached to being First Nations kids. We were expected to learn. Hard work and studying was all that was required for each of us to acquire the content. Not all of us did, but the priests assumed we were all intelligent enough to do it. From the priests in residential school, I learned that studying can be a life's work. It can be satisfying. It can be a vocation and an awakening to worlds and experiences not even dreamed of.

However, even though we were being taught by the Jesuits, the academic clerics, it was impressed upon us that

Cecil (back row, centre) in front of his Uncle Adam Corbiere's grocery store in Wikwemikong, circa 1949. Adam Corbiere (back right) was Cecil's mother's brother. In the front row, left to right, are his children and Cecil's first cousins, Jeannette, Elaine, and Robert. To Cecil's left is his Uncle Adam's wife Rita's younger brother, Orville Trudeau.

we could never aspire to be one of them. I remember one day when Father Oliver was explaining what it would take to be a priest. Piety was the first and foremost characteristic he said. He continued, "*None of you here will ever measure up.*"

The Jesuits tried to make sportsmen out of us. We had a hockey team, but the catch was that we had to construct a skating rink. As chief maintenance helper, I was part of the crew that had to put up the rink, the boards, and electric lights. There always seemed to be one light burned out and, consequently, the whole string was in darkness as it was wired with a single wire. Julius and I spent hours before a game trying to find the short. Finding that one bulb was a nightmare—or a challenge.

I progressed from maintaining the rink to managing the hockey team in my last year at Spanish. The *Sudbury Star,* on February 5, 1953, had a picture of our team and the headline, "Garnier School Team Leads League." That day we trounced Sudbury High School, remaining in first place in the North Shore Juvenile Hockey League. Our team

In addition to hockey and football, Cecil (left) was also involved in baseball at Spanish, along with his friend Bobby Sunday (from Akwesasne).

included: Agillius Ominika, Billy Kenoshameg (goalie), Ray Kenoshameg (goalie), Emette Chiblow, David Fox, Alex David (backup goalie), Lloyd Commanda (assistant manager), Harvey Ermatinger, Tim Dayliuth, Dominic Contin (captain), Terry Jacobs, Gilbert Whiteduck, Gordon Manitowabi, Peter Armstrong, Alan McGregor, Bob Sunday, Tim McGrath, Boniface Abel, and Rev. H. Barry.

The Garnier Residential School was a farm, so you'd be in the classrooms all day and then the rest of the time you worked on the farm. There were all sorts of other jobs that one could do and I was in what might be called today the maintenance shop. I knew I had to repair things and had the run of the whole building, which, upon reflection, was a tremendous advantage in the long run. You get very good at what you do, as well. In fact, I got so good that I could pick every door lock in the place. Every door seemed to be locked to begin with, but sometimes you were asked to figure out how to open one when the priests lost their keys. So, that gave me another skill—picking locks!

One of the first tasks I was given upon arriving at residential school was replacing all the broken windowpanes in the whole four-storey building. Those that weren't

The Garnier baseball team with Cecil (far right, back row) as manager.

broken needed to be washed. Either way, it meant climbing
on an extension ladder to the top windows. I think my
reputation for being able to climb and fix things preceded
me to the school. Father Rushman was the former head at
the Wikwemikong Residential School and knew the kind
of work that my Pa did and that I was Pa's able helper. He
approached me and said, "We need to repair the windows.
They are damaged and, in repairing them, we have to put
in new panes. Can you do that?" He wanted to repair
every window in the school. Not really knowing what I
was getting into, I agreed to do it.

I had limited equipment, which I carried in a kind of
toolbox. At the far end of the basement was a table of
glass, but I had to learn how to cut it to fit and make the
tacks to hold the panes in place. Pa had impressed upon

me the importance of these little nails. He was a tinsmith and would cut these triangular nails to put in windows. At the residential school, I had to make these myself. There was a tin shop in the basement of the school and Brother McLaren, who we called Muggy, watched as I fashioned the necessary hardware.

The only tricky part was carrying the pane of glass up the ladder for each window. I had a tray, a toolbox thing, with my pliers and a coal chisel to hammer down my nails. I carried the toolbox with the tacks and the panes of glass I had cut up the stairs to the ladder. When I got to the top floor where the window hole was, I cleaned up the window sashes, put in new panes, and puttied around them. This was difficult from the extension ladder, but we found another way.

Someone (the brothers, I suppose) had built a contraption that you stuck out the window. It was anchored on the inside and stuck out the window and attached to the inside wall. George Kanasawe told me about this climber and we found it in the attic. At first, we couldn't figure it out, but when we got it together it worked beautifully. It had hands on the inside of the wall and hands on the outside and attached to the wall. It picked into the wall. It worked pretty well and when I got the hang of it (no pun intended), it revolutionized my jobs of washing windows and replacing panes. I got on it from the inside and climbed out the window on it. It was much safer than being perched on the extension ladder. It probably saved my life!

Herman Kanasawe was the person who got the water for the squeegee. There were times when he wanted to get on the platform, too. We quarrelled about who should climb out, but I maintained that as long as I was the first one to climb out on it and it had stayed good, I had rights to the contraption.

This job was a Saturday afternoon preoccupation. I started the job when I got to Spanish in the fall and I was still replacing windows when the snow began to fall. I remember Father Rushman telling us to keep on with the work, even though it was already winter.

One day Father Hannin collared me and told me that I was to build a tabernacle for him. I had no idea of what a tabernacle was or how to make one. He was not the sort of person who was prepared to tell you how to do anything. He just ordered you to do it by whatever means you could manage. Father Hannin made it clear that it had to be circular with a dome, it had to have a door that locked, and you had to be able to turn it. So I made the door and then had to figure out how to make a lock that locked when you closed it. This tabernacle fit the liturgical concept of not only the Blessed Sacrament but also all the Liturgy of the Mass.

The domed creation could open as a server pushed the door curtain back. Father Hannin had seen one of these tabernacles on his travels, but I had never seen one; I hadn't a clue what it should look like. So I was at the mercy of Father Hannin (the school disciplinarian) when I didn't understand what he really wanted. I just kept putting together a very crude structure using very heavy material (whatever I could find). Since Father Hannin wouldn't give me any material, I had to scrounge around in the basement for anything I could transform. For the base, the materials were very unsuitable, but he wouldn't let me heat the wood to make it more pliable, perhaps because he didn't trust me to use the fire. Maybe he thought I'd burn the school down.

For the dome, I found a can of very heavy caulking material to use. I found that by heating this material, it became soft, so I could mould it into a dome shape for the roof of the tabernacle.

It was amazing how it turned out—a round thing that sat on the altar. The church people put a curtain on it and everyone was impressed. It stayed on the altar for a long time before it disappeared. I went back after being away for a year and it was gone!

Another time, Father Hannin told me to construct a greenhouse for him. Constructing a greenhouse relied on some principles that I felt had to be taken into consideration before I could begin—like digging a hole in the ground and making a bedding of some kind where the greenhouse would sit. This did not seem like an awesome task to start with. A hole was dug—large enough for a variety of plants. Keeping Father Hannin's temperament in mind, we were obliged to build a greenhouse, no matter how it turned out.

Alla-butt and I surveyed the back yard of the Jesuit institution and selected a spot with a big enough piece of level ground. Oh, we messed around. A couple of the other boys, Herman and Tommy, helped and we began to dig, as we all felt that any building needed a basic foundation. We dug a shallow trench together, which turned into the foundation for our greenhouse. We soon managed this aspect of the task.

The building was glass-walled with glass salvaged from another building. We were very scared of Father Hannin since we just went ahead using scrap building materials that we found lying around. Our main concern was to finish our greenhouse in some logical manner with its own doors and windows.

Father Hannin did not want a big garden affair; all he wanted was about a dozen plants in cans that would grow into sizeable vegetables, I suppose, to feed the whole school. We managed and soon had a crop in our own greenhouse.

The students shared a subculture that subverted some of the best plans of the school administration. We developed a barter system; there were jobs that we had to do that gave each of us something to bargain with. The ones who worked in the bakery had scraps of bread; others had butter. No matter how onerous our tasks, we found opportunities to support our underground economy.

Many people of the village of Spanish treated us kindly. The bakery in Spanish had gingersnaps that we could get if we went to the store. Another store was operated by a Mr. St. Denis, whom I remember fondly. He never failed to treat us with respect. We developed a relationship with the town of Spanish—walks on Thursdays, gingersnaps in the bakery, a stop at Mr. and Mrs. St. Denis's store became our routine.

Often it is emphasized that, in residential schools, speaking Indian languages was forbidden. This is true; however, we all spoke Ojibwe and all you had to do (well, the way we used to do it in Spanish) was to go underground. What that really meant was that we spoke Ojibwe to each other when we were in the basement. I brushed up on my Ojibwe, which I had learned on the playground at Buzwah Indian Day School. Garnier Residential School provided me with a chance to learn Ojibwe from young men who came from other Ojibwe-speaking communities in northern Ontario and to broaden and expand the vocabulary with which I came to Garnier.

The priests were always concerned about our raging hormones, and since the girls were across the road under

On the front steps of the South Bay Church. Clockwise from back left: Cecil, brother Don, sisters Elizabeth (Liz) and Loretta, and Cecil's grandmother, Harriet King (Mama).

heavy guard by Anne Berrigan, the head of the girls' school, the prevailing situation was one of sanctity and chastity. However, in our school, one winter, probably at the height of our hormonal development, the rumour surfaced that our food was being laced with saltpetre. I will just assume that most of you know what that is, but we knew it was to subdue our basic urges. I do not know precisely whether it really worked, but I did get a call from another male graduate about five years ago who claimed that he thought the saltpetre was finally taking effect.

At residential school we were never bored because there were always lots of things to do. We worked in the barns, bakery, shoe shop, sewing room, chicken coop, and cannery. We tilled the fields for potatoes, turnips, cucumbers, and tomatoes. I worked primarily in the maintenance of the buildings, fixing what seemed like endless leaks in the plumbing as well as the roof. It was such a good thing Pa had taught me how to fix things. As a qualified tinsmith, painter, and sheet-metal worker, he could fix anything! The Jesuits could explain anything relating to the theory of how the generating system worked to give us an idea how to find and solve the problem. But they could not put the theory into practice. We had to figure it out.

Brother Bejmoss was the boss in the cannery. He was one of those wild, passionate creatures who went through life swearing in French. His hair stuck out and he would be angry at the stoves and literally tried to beat them up. Canning was a hot, steamy job and he tended to sweat a lot. So, he worked stripped to the waist. The sweat from his upper torso ran down, soaking his pants. He always looked like he had wet pants. Ten of us boys worked there with him each canning season. As a treat, he made a drink for us out of brown sugar and cinnamon.

Then there was Muggy, another brother, who used to talk to the three furnaces that heated the school as he stoked each one up for the night. Muggy was also in charge of making shoes and baking bread. He had a squad of boys who followed him around.

There was Brother Voisin, commonly called *Choiman*, in the cow barn. The boys there learned the dairy trades— milking cows, making butter, and supplying the entire building with milk and butter. Dairy duty was one of the favoured jobs because when the butter was taken from the churn to be moulded into blocks, pieces would "accidentally" fall off, and an enterprising boy would grab it and store it in a secret place to be traded later in the boys' underground barter society.

Then there was the horse barn with Brother Vandermoor. From him we learned the agricultural skills needed to run a farm. Despite the fact that many of us came from farms ourselves, one goal of residential schooling was to make farmers out of us. My people, the Odawak, had been involved in farming since the eighteenth century, growing corn for the fur trade and providing maple sugar in such quantities that it required ships to transport it to Chicago for sale. My grandparents had a large garden and kept sheep, turkeys, cows, horses, and pigs. I never liked farm work and by the time I arrived at Garnier, I was totally convinced that farming was not going to be my life's work, but at the same time, I did not find the fact that we had to work on the farm at Spanish a great hardship. If I were at home, I would be shovelling "it" there, too.

There were other brothers who were responsible for teaching other skills. However, in the school, as we ran it, each of the jobs we had as students had a payoff. We were not victims of the brothers; we put the skills learned from them to good use. Those working in the cannery somehow acquired sugar and used that as a trade good to get other merchandise. The barter system was in full swing in the dormitories and refectory. The boys from the bakery, of course, had fresh bread to trade. Mind you, just crusts, but nevertheless they were excellent with the butter the boys in the dairy smuggled out of the cow barn. The boys who worked in the kitchen tended to get jam and cookies or baking of all kinds. If you could get two crusts and a piece of cake, you could make the best sandwich!!!

Now, working in the laundry had its perks as well. Since the laundry was in the girls' school, a mountain of messages accompanied the laundry from one side of the road to the other. Our raging hormones were somewhat assuaged to find a handwritten girlish note in one of our pockets. All the girls seemed to know whose pants they were cleaning.

Recalling these things, I realize that this was our world. We created a culture within the institution's culture. We found a way to circumvent the forces that dominated.

One example shows how this worked. One of the prized trade goods in our adolescent boy subculture was tobacco. However, only the priests had tobacco, and our challenge was to get that tobacco into our hands. Our plan was put into operation at mealtime. Since there were two dining rooms, one for the priests and one for us, the boys were called to meals at a slightly different time than the priests. In the five-minute time period between when the priests left their rooms and we were expected in the refectory, some of us would use our numerous skills in opening locked doors to get access to the tobacco locked in the priests' private rooms and get back to our appointed places in the dining room without being missed. The margin of time was very tight. Sometimes, creative explanations had to be given when the miscreant's disappearance was noted.

Our worlds of work and trade and developing our own culture in the school were full. We had no time to think, or be lonesome, or pine. As I said, our underground culture functioned in Ojibwe. Contrary to common wisdom that all Indian children lost our languages in residential school, as a matter of fact, I improved my Ojibwe at residential school to be part of that culture with its own language and codes. We were told that we were to speak English, which we did within earshot of the priests. I certainly cannot say that we were punished for speaking our own language because it was hidden from them.

Academic life was the heart of the school. Jesuits are academics who believe in scholarship. We were trained to love learning and to seek knowledge. The Jesuits taught us a resolve where failure was not an option. When you undertook anything, you completed it and displayed your best craftsmanship and imagination. Never would anything be half done. Nothing was attempted unless you could achieve it. The Jesuits demanded that you carry through on any commitment to a job, no matter how trivial or difficult. The same applied to sports. When matched with insurmountable odds, we were still obliged to win the game. For the most part, we showed we were capable of meeting the Jesuits' high expectations. So, just think if we had stayed at home instead of going to residential school. What would the expectations have been in that situation? My grandfather never allowed me to do anything by halves, but both he and my grandmother knew that I had to go to residential school to hone my academic skills.

We did not think of ourselves as pioneers, but the *Sudbury Star* reported the graduation of the first class of eight high-school students from the Garnier Residential School for Indian Boys, believing it constituted the first full graduating class of its kind from any Indian school in Canada.

The priests decided to make graduation a very grand affair. They wanted the place and all of us ready to celebrate properly. I remember the priests gave us lessons on how to use a fork and a knife because, up until that time, in the residential school we had only ever eaten our meals with a tin plate, a tin cup, and a spoon. We managed with that for our years at the school, but for the graduation we had to appear civilized, I suppose, and demonstrate that we knew how to sit at a table properly. That happened.

Then the priests decided that we would have a graduation ball. It was to be a big event. Again, we were total clods in this regard, so they decided to teach us ballroom dancing—in particular, waltzing. I guess the priest was good at it, because he attempted to teach us. Basil Johnston was my dancing partner all that year. I remember him fondly for that, though he was very *aukodehgizig* (prickly) about it.

Basil was a bookworm and he excelled in academic things. He read and wrote; physicality was not normally his strong suit.

The ceremonies were held on a Wednesday evening, June 7, 1950, in the large auditorium crammed with parents, chiefs from a number of surrounding reserves, members of the Department of Indian Affairs, residents of the nearby community, and clergy. Basil Johnston delivered the valedictory address, in the words of the reporter, "speaking with emotional sincerity." He "made an impassioned plea to all Indian parents to realize the urgent need for greater education among Indian children in order that they can take their true place in Canadian life." He went on to say, "Indians need education: they need their own teachers, lawyers, doctors and politicians." He said that "only through having the courage to continue our studies and determination to use our talents for advancement can we become true citizens of Canada. We have talked of our rights as the first citizens of the country but few of us are prepared to safeguard those rights. We must be alert to take advantage of our opportunities." He received thunderous applause from the large audience.

Rev. R. Oliver, principal of the school, told of the struggles to get a high-school course at Garnier. He said that there were many years of "discouraging rebuffs when they had proposed the introduction of a full course of training for the Indian boys and girls at Garnier and St. Joseph's Schools." He explained that the school authorities held the "firm conviction" that only through raising the educational level of the Indian children could they ever hope to better themselves and improve their standard of living and status in Canadian society. He said that the first grade nine classes had started four years before and these were

4. RESIDENTIAL SCHOOL **135**

the ones who were graduating with their high-school diplomas. The numbers of students in high school at the schools continued to increase. In 1950 there were forty-five boys and thirty-eight girls in the high-school program. The graduates represented many communities: Basil Johnston, Cape Croker; Dominic McComber, Montreal; Arponse Trudeau, Wikwemikong; Francis Commanda, North Bay; David Jocko, Golden Lake; Julius Neganigijig, Sheguiandah; Alfred Cooper, Wikwemikong; and Ernest Nadjiwan, Cape Croker. The students were not ending their education there; two of these were enrolled in university for the fall semester.

Four more boys graduated from grade eleven and had already arranged to attend four-year trade training courses at Toronto technical colleges. They were Maurice Pelletier, Cutler; Adam Roy, West Bay; Russell Jocko, Golden Lake; and Clement Trudeau, Wikwemikong.

Girls in grade eleven who received the special awards were Mary Evelyn Atchitawens, Mildred Cameron, Dora Contin, Annie Gakasheyongai, Lillian Kitchikake, Marion McGregor, Lucy Neshkewe, Elizabeth Pitawanakwat, Violet Shawanda, Honorine Trudeau, Rosemary Wakegejig, and Matilda Wemigwans.

Representing Indian Affairs at the graduation was R.P.G. Laurence, Indian agent for The Soo district. He said that the department was putting more stress on education in order that the Indians might become more self-reliant. He encouraged the wholehearted cooperation and support from the parents.

When the formal part of the evening was over, we all went to the centre of the room and the dancing began. All the students had to dance because this was the moment for which Father Oliver had prepared us. Of course we had to dance with the partners we had trained with. So Basil and I showed off our stuff to our family, friends, and complete strangers! The music was supplied by the Cutler Orchestra comprised of Howard Pelletier, director; Lawrence Lewis, piano; Henry Lewis and Howard Pelletier, saxophones; Peter Day, Maurice Pelletier and Emile Hughes, violins; Victor Pelletier and Alec Day, drums; and Wilfred Commanda, trombone.

I have only recently realized what an opportunity I had in going to residential school and being trained to do academic work in such a way that I was able to go on to teachers' college. I have lived in a small prairie community, a Doukhobor and German settlement. I was active in the local church and have made friends with a number of men my own age. I was surprised when one of them said that he wished he could read like I did. When I said, "You read," he said, "I know the words, but I would not be able to read like you." It was only then that I realized that many farm kids of my age did not get the opportunity for the schooling that I had been given. Think about the other rural children on Manitoulin in the 1930s and 1940s. What schooling opportunities did they have? I do not claim that these were the experiences of everyone who went to Spanish. As one Ojibwe person asked to tell whether he would tell the truth when testifying in court said, "I don't know if I tell the truth, I can only tell what I know."

I was chosen to deliver the valedictory address at the graduation of boys and girls from St. Charles Garnier and St. Joseph's in June 1953. When I learned that I would have to write a speech, I asked Father Rushmore for his help. He looked at me with dismay and said, "You have been here for four years; surely you have something to say." Recently, among some papers of my daughter Shoo-Shoo,

Delivering the valedictory address for the graduating classes of St. Charles Garnier and St. Joseph's in 1953.

I found the text of that speech. I offer it here as a sample of what I had learned during my time at St. Charles Garnier Residential School:

> The Principal, Reverend Fathers, Brothers, Ladies and Gentlemen;
>
> Tonight it is my difficult but privileged task to bid farewell, on behalf of this year's graduating class, to the home of our endeavours of the past years. It seems but a short time since we entered these familiar surroundings. At that time, graduation was in the dim, distant future, as it now appears to many of you.

Many are the cherished memories dating back to that first awesome day when we entered these schools. We were very immature then and we had to learn a great deal, but time passed quickly and gradually we began to feel that we were a part of Garnier and St. Joseph's—and weren't we really glad of it!

We followed, to the best of our abilities, in the footsteps of the former graduates of these two schools. Their standards, their principles, their fine traditions were our inspiration, our guide, and now we, in turn, hope to be an inspiration and a guide to you who are yet to follow. We hope, through our accomplishments, to be an example of the bright future that a graduate is entitled to, and in so doing, to encourage more of our race to take advantage now of the great value of education. Then you, also, shall be the proud graduates of a proud Garnier and a proud St. Joseph's.

We all realize how advantageous it would be to have our own teachers, lawyers, doctors and politicians, men and women who will work hand in hand with those who now are working for our rights and prosperity. We need men and women who will be exemplary leaders in our own communities. Our reservations need modern improvements. And this demands leaders—men and women of vision, initiative, and energy.

Our graduation this evening, ladies and gentlemen, is an introduction towards this leadership. It is a beginning and yet an end. It is the beginning of our years to take on the responsibilities of leadership. It is also the closing or end of our years called "Growing-up."

We have gathered here tonight in our last formal get-together to say farewell. To express fully the mingled feelings that are in each one of our hearts tonight would be impossible. We regret very much leaving Garnier and St. Joseph's, but yet we are exceedingly proud that we have accomplished something for our school—a reward which will remain a cherished gem all through our lives! Yes! Ladies and gentlemen, we have reached the goal of our endeavours, and so we are here to bid our fond farewell. We say farewell to our teachers, to our fellow students—to our familiar surroundings. No more will we be entitled to the youthful hilarity which once echoed through the halls of our schools. No more are the gags and the pranks of childhood attributed to us, for now we have passed that age; it is in the past and our future lies ahead of us.

Yes! We have now a responsibility. We have now to put into practice the principles we learned in our study. We now have to venture out on our own. But we've no fear, for with the ideals of Garnier and St. Joseph's to guide us and with the Grace of God, we are quite prepared for the future that faces us.

We owe it to Garnier and St. Joseph's, to the priests, brothers, sisters, and the teachers who have been our cherished friends—kind, understanding friends—who never laughed at our foolish schemes or weighty problems, but gave us wise direction and courage enough to see us through. They taught us well, but educated us better, with the true Christian education that leads us to God. We found Him in the tabernacles of our chapels, ever accessible, and to Him we say "Thank You" for the privilege of our years of happiness with the priests, brothers, sisters, and teachers of Garnier and St. Joseph's.

We thank Him also for our dear parents, whose clear-sighted faith has strengthened them in a programme of sacrifices on our behalf, sacrifices of time and money and self in order to give us the advantages of a Catholic education and the many "trimmings" so necessary for the "whims" of a high-school boy or girl. A heart full of gratitude is yours, dear parents.

Soon, Canada will have many Indians who will follow various vocations. Even now, the day is not too far off when some of the students of Garnier and St. Joseph's will follow the call of Christ. This, my friends, we will always owe to the perseverance and direction of the members of the Society of Jesus and the Daughters of Mary.

And so, we have written our pages in the annals of Garnier's story and that of St. Joseph's. May they ever remain there!—a glory to our school!—and a credit to ourselves!

May God bless you all!

I thank you,

CECIL KING

(Graduation Exercises, Tuesday, June 15, 1953, Garnier Arena, Spanish, Ontario. Published in Graduation Programme, 1953)

St. Charles Garnier Graduates of 1953:

Boniface Abel

Dominic Contin

Arthur Coco

Harvey Ermatinger

Terence Jacobs

Cecil King (This tall, handsome "Gable from Buzwah" has been with us since 1948, excluding one year. Cecil is noted for his willing and extremely effective leadership, courage, kind-heartedness and care of little boys. A master of all trades, he has a true blend of capability and affability. To our Valedictorian, God speed you to success in the teaching profession, Cecil)

Timothy McGrath

Alan McGregor

John Pelletier

Joseph Schnurr

Gilbert Whiteduck

(*The Club Star*, "The Graduation Issue," vol. VII, no. 3, June, 1953)

5. LIFE AFTER RESIDENTIAL SCHOOL

The summer after I graduated from Garnier was hot, so much so that we had threatening forest fires and men and volunteers were needed to extinguish the fires and safeguard our homes and village. I was finally apprehended by the fire ranger and, under his authority, taken with a number of other men and boys to the fire front. I remember being ordered to shoulder a water tank and pump and follow the fire chief. This was a miserable job, to say the least, because each time I went for more water for my tank, appointed people simply dumped the water from their containers from atop the water tank truck. I worked almost the whole summer and this was my first job, so to speak. We managed to keep the fire under control. So this was my experience as a firefighter, which may have taught me some other skills, such as the science that was involved. The fire chief had trained at a tech school somewhere in Ontario and knew some skills of fighting forest fires, which he employed to extinguish a fast-burning fire front. I discovered there is a science to this and I was learning something entirely new—along with the true meaning of "employment." Finally, the rains came and the fire went out.

Things had changed when I went home to Two Clock. Kohkwehns was gone. Mama was sickly and I feared that she, too, was going to leave us. There was sadness in our formerly happy home. There was emptiness for me without my protector, companion, and teacher in my life. Pa was forlorn. Our household was not a home anymore. Pa didn't seem to talk to us or anyone now. This was a new era and I could not handle it very well.

Kohkwehns had passed away in the winter after we had said what was to be our last good-bye at the black bus. She had been getting sicker through the year when I left. We did not know what her problem was. Kohkwehns was treating herself with all her knowledge of medicines, but I could tell she was worried. The doctor kept coming to the house and I would be allowed to sit in on these visits. Over the winter after I had gone to Spanish, Kohkwehns got sicker until she left us. I was not able to leave residential school to be there for her funeral, but I was told that her coffin was made by Pa in his workshop and the interior was prepared by women in the community.

● ● ●

Herman Kanasawe and I decided to go to Toronto and look for employment. Herman was my buddy from Buzwah Indian Day School and it stood to reason we had talked about many things, including the prospect of leaving Buzwah. Herman claimed that he would like to go to Toronto and seek his fortune. Because his brother George worked on boats in Toronto, Herman's initial plan was to look for work on a boat that would take him to the city.

I didn't know if it would be possible from Buzwah, but it was a thought. Herman had numerous ideas—some were tempting and others were just thoughts or jokes!

In the end, we decided the best idea would be to get to Toronto another way. Herman would try to get work on the boats there, hoping his brother could get him a job. Toronto was—and still is—far from Buzwah, with no direct highway. So hitchhiking was the normal way to travel. I could hear Napo admonish us, as the only one serious enough not to leave Buzwah. He always said we should be ashamed of ourselves. However, we had no reason to stay in Buzwah, and since we now had to go for higher education or employment, it seemed our fate was sealed. We had discussed our choices, either getting employment, or going to "university," which sounded good. Herman didn't care because he knew he could always sail the Great Lakes on the *Caribou* as his brother did.

We had not even determined the direction we would head, but we had decided we were going. Herman was all set for Toronto. For me, I didn't know. However, after some debate with Herman, I agreed to head to Toronto. We really had no idea where it was. Herman had some Ontario maps and had located Toronto, but we had no concept of how far it was or how we were going to get there. This did not change our determination to start out on our journey.

We really had no money for such a venture, but I had assumed that Pa would give me some. I now realize that Pa must have been very disappointed in me. Every summer since I was a little boy, I had spent my summers working with him. I would do the climbing and jobs that I under-stand now must have been too dangerous for him to do at his age and health. He must have decided that if I was

Cecil hugging his cousin
Rose Corbiere outside of the
Wikwemikong arena.

insisting on setting out in the world on my own, that he would make sure that I did it on my own without a financial support system. I had convinced Herman that I would have the resources to support our travel. When we set out, I had to tell him that I didn't have any money. We left Buzwah anyway.

Leaving Buzwah, you had to start off by boat from Two Clock and paddle across the bay to Manitowaning, and this is what Herman and I did. Herman and I started out late Sunday evening from Manitowaning to South Baymouth, where we intended to get on the ferry (the SS *Norisle*). We got a ride right away, but when we got to the ferry we had to beg a bit to get on, but we succeeded and were on our way to southern Ontario. On the Bruce Peninsula, where the boat landed, on the first leg of our vagabond journey, we were not lucky at all. Nobody wanted to give us a ride, so Herman and I started walking towards Toronto.

Night was falling, but we were not deterred. We became conscious of darkness and, since we were not getting any rides, we decided to bed down. We were in the bush somewhat near the road to Toronto. We had studied a map before leaving Buzwah and so had a general idea of the road to Toronto (on the Bruce this is not too hard to find as there is only one road heading south). We were not too brainy on Toronto itself as a city. Herman talked about Toronto and his experience there. I had nothing to say. Herman vaguely remembered Toronto from having been there to sell blueberries a summer ago.

We were lucky. We made it to Toronto in one day. We got a job with King Construction, which was building Highway 401 west of Toronto. Neither Herman nor I was fit or equipped to do construction work on a highway in the blazing southern Ontario sun. We didn't last long. Herman had found his brother and got a job on the boats. I didn't want to work on the boats. I was afraid of getting seasick!

So I was alone and had to find a job. I went to Buffalo, where my brother, Don, was working in the Ford plant. I got a job putting the left front fender on the new cars. I stayed long enough to get promoted to putting the right front fender on, but this work wasn't for me, either. I did find it fascinating how the assembly line worked—taking pieces of cars, having different people putting individual pieces on, and ending up with a complete working model!

I soon found that Toronto wasn't such an alien place. There was a network of Wikwemikong connections that supported each other in getting work and housing in the city. My mom and dad had been in Oakville since 1948. Mom had a job at a cosmetics plant and Dad worked in construction, which was his line of work. Joe Trudeau from Wikwemikong was familiar with the seasonal fruit-picking jobs and helped me get a job in the strawberry patch of McAdams. There were huts for the workers to live in and for about two weeks this is where I lived and worked. After that, it was on to the peach orchards in the wine-growing area of the Niagara Peninsula.

Did I mention that I worked in a Heinz plant where ketchup was made, and I had to clean out the ketchup vats? I thought I would never eat ketchup again because the rotten tomatoes were so putrid. Then, I moved on to tobacco picking and made a lot of money. It really was not a hard job because an old horse set the pace. As long as you picked the leaves as fast as the horse walked, you stayed out of trouble.

I learned a lot about work that summer. I learned that most jobs I was qualified for were seasonal. When one ended, I had to look for another. Each of my jobs lasted about two weeks. I learned that such jobs were low paying and prone to lay-offs, and a person had to move around to stay continuously employed. I found that getting a job in the city was easier if you had a contact with the employer. In other words, you would be hired if someone who knew you was a good worker and had gotten a job there before. I learned that the jobs that many people did were no cleaner or more interesting than the farming that I was leaving the island to escape. Earning a living in the south often meant doing demeaning, disgusting things under the watchful eye of someone who could tell you to leave in the blink of an eye. This made me take a second look at my options.

In 1953, when I had graduated from Garnier, I had intended to take an engineering course. My experiences with Pa King and the skills that I had already acquired convinced me that I should pursue a career in the practical sciences. However, H.G. Mingay, regional inspector for Indian schools in southern Ontario, had other ideas for me. He suggested that I should go to Toronto to take a summer course in school teaching. Mr. Mingay said if I still wanted to be an engineer after the course, fine, but if I liked teaching, I could study to be a teacher instead.

I decided I should give this a try; teachers were part of my family's experience. Mama had taught at Henvey Inlet. My aunt, Elizabeth King, was the teacher both in Buzwah and in South Bay settlements on the reserve. Her sister Stella taught both on- and off-reserve. Her daughter Rose became a teacher. She took on the profession of teaching on- and off-reserve. Furthermore, I had had exceptional First Nations teachers in my own education at Buzwah School.

This was the era of the "Six Week Wonders." We were the province of Ontario's response to the post-war baby boom. Teachers were needed to meet the demands of the burgeoning school populations born after the war. Prospective teachers were given six weeks of training in the summer and then sent out to take over classrooms in the fall. I went to Toronto for my first pre-teachers–college course. This was a Department of Education course. One advantage of these summer courses was that a number of "green" teacher trainees from all over the province came together in Toronto for an intense introduction to school teaching. Each of us knew that we would be placed in front of a group of children in a couple of months and we would be on our own.

Getting to Toronto was the first challenge in taking the course. Buzwah was part of Wikwemikong First Nation, which was situated on the northeastern corner of Manitoulin Island, and there were two possible ways to get to Toronto from there: catch a ride south to the ferry at South Baymouth, then hope to get a ride from Tobermory to Toronto, or go north to Highway 1 and hope to get a ride east. I chose the second way. I first had to get to Little Current, 27 kilometres from the reserve, to cross the bridge to reach the mainland. From there it was 66 kilometres through the

Killarney Mountains to Espanola and the Trans-Canada Highway. From there, to get the bus to Toronto I had to get a ride the 200 kilometres to North Bay. The most significant thing was that on my other trips to Toronto I had been in the company of people who knew the town. Now, I was on my own. Neither of the previous trips had prepared me to make my way to Toronto by myself. I was just a young man from the bush making my own way to the "Big Smoke," as we called Toronto. I was very nervous about what would happen next!

I think Pa must have had a hand in preparing that part of the journey for me. On the bus to Toronto, there were six of us from the Indian reserves. One of the boys travelling with me was Alan McGregor from Birch Island. He had a sister living in the big city. It turned out that his mother had arranged with her daughter to provide a residence for her brother and me. What a relief! I was familiar with the bus depot in Toronto, one of the places that Herman had taught me about. He would come down from the north on the bus to sell blueberries. He had shown me how to get to Yonge Street from the bus depot. As everyone knew at that time, you can get anywhere in Toronto from Yonge Street. Pa had given me enough money to get a cab from the bus depot to our residence.

By the end of the course we were informed of the jobs that we would have where we could practise our teaching skills for the next school year. My cousin Mary Lou Fox was lucky. She got a job teaching grade two in the school where her mother and aunt taught. This was in Espanola, where her mother had taught for many years and the town where Mary Lou had spent her high-school years.

I was not so lucky. My very first introduction to an actual classroom after the Toronto summer course was an offer by Mr. Mingay, head inspector of Ontario Indian Schools. One of his responsibilities was to staff Indian schools with Indian teachers if he could find them, and I guess I was one of his conquests. My six weeks at summer school led immediately to a job at Excelsior, or West Bay, Manitoulin Island, Ontario. I accepted his offer and prepared for West Bay, better known as the Excelsior Region in those days. Although I was hired by Indian Affairs to teach in West Bay School on the reserve on Manitoulin Island, it was not my community. Even though I had some relatives there, it was not familiar territory to me. I soon got to know the members of the community, who were very supportive of me. It helped that I could speak Ojibwe.

Pa offered to take me to West Bay since I did not know the community, and Pa perhaps understood the dilemma, had some understanding of my predicament, and wanted to help me. That is what happened. We left home at Two Clock heading to West Bay on a bright Sunday afternoon. He reminded me that he knew an old shortcut road across certain farm lands, and this is the road to West Bay that I became familiar with in my introduction to the community.

The first vision of a building that looked like a school came soon enough. We stopped at a small gas station to inquire who was in charge of the school, and the lady of the gas station seemed to know who we were. She gave us directions and the key to get into the school. This was the beginning of a new journey into employment. Pa went with me to the school, and as I recall, he even carried in my suitcase. He seemed so happy I had a job. My future was indeed shaping up.

Pa then said, "I will leave you here. Be careful and respect these children. If you show help to any child, they will side in with you." I saw this happen many times. Pa left me to my own devices. I prepared a meal, cleaned the kitchen, and put some thought into what I would do the next day. I wondered about my class and how I would react to them. At this point I made a bed to lie down. This ended my day, and I fell asleep wondering what my first day in my own classroom would be like! This was a daunting exercise.

Well, Monday came soon enough. I prepared a breakfast of some sort, ate, and went to my classroom—or to what I thought would be my classroom, and it was. I sorted out some textbooks and considered what would be appropriate for my new students. It was nine o'clock and a tiny little girl came in to ask if she could ring the bell. I gratefully gave her permission—and this was the start of it. She was faithful and absolutely dependable. She was a part of my school and she seemed to grow with it.

My students started arriving. They were a mixed and joyful lot ranging in ages from six to perhaps ten. By then I had figured out the subjects and how they fit the Ontario curriculum; I was ready to go. I separated the students according to the information that existed at my desk. It was easy to peg the individual students to their proper age–grade designations. The first day was indeed exciting and the students were content where they happened to end up. My classroom was going without a hitch. West Bay Indian Day School had succeeded in measuring up and the students were happy.

I developed some sports programs and had intramural sports, pitting one group against another. I started with softball in the fall months, which both the girls and boys seemed to enjoy equally. There were some stars at this early time. We played until freeze-up. Winter came as it was supposed to; the lake froze up as it did every year. Skates came out and there were some star skaters. The year carried on until the Christmas break. I had made it through the first term in teaching and, basically, I was still in pretty good shape.

We did get in sliding as a favourite pastime. Sliding went on anywhere and all the students enjoyed their homemade sleighs. The boys and girls all had their own hills for sliding. I hardly knew where everyone disappeared to at recess time, but I figured it out. They wanted to get one slide in on their hill. The winter went on and the school subjects were mastered as the curriculum stipulated. School continued into the warm months and then closed down for summer. Everyone was excited about that as all went on holidays. It had been a good year and the students joyfully looked forward to the next year and their teacher was of the same frame of mind.

I returned to Toronto for the summer to take the second pre-teachers-college course. The new school year arrived with the same students; they all seemed positive and I was more than ready. I now had a year as a teacher under my belt. School work was indeed enlightening, and there were no unforeseen hitches. Another year passed and the time came to investigate the possibility of a move. The urge to be a principal was in my blood. With this in mind, I approached Mr. Matters, superintendent, Indian Affairs. He welcomed my approach and provided me with a list of schools that were destined for closure and those schools that had vacancies either for staff positions or principalships. Mr. Matters was impressed with my time at Excelsior and felt he could oblige me in my wish to move. I chose Northwest Bay First Nation (now Naicatchewenin First Nation) in the Fort Frances District of Indian Affairs.

With the two pre-teacher-college courses and an initial teaching stint at West Bay completed, my new wife,

Virginia Pitawanakwat, and I headed for Northwest Bay to begin the school year. Virginia and I had known each other in Spanish, and my brother, Don, actually studied math at the girl's school with Virginia. But when she was fourteen she wound up at the TB sanatorium in Hamilton. My brother and I visited her there. Her grandfather ChinDan Wemigwans from South Bay, a satellite community of Wikwemikong, was friends with Pa. We married at the Kaboni Church in Wikwemikong in the summer of 1954.

Our adventure to Northwest Bay began in Sault Ste. Marie. From there we had to catch a boat to Fort William, where we took a bus to Fort Frances. We looked up the Indian agent and he gave me the keys to the log house that served as the teacherage in Northwest Bay. His instructions on how to get from Fort Frances to Northwest Bay were a little unusual. He told us to stand out by the side of the main street and stop the first logging truck we saw. He said we could get a ride in the truck all the way to our new home. He did caution us that the house was rather unusual and looked like it wasn't finished but we would have no trouble finding it.

It really was a very tasteful cedar log house. While it was made entirely of prepared cedar logs, the logs were axed flat on one side and rather than lying oblong were situated in an upright or vertical arrangement. Our house was unique in comparison to the regular log house. The teachers' residence and the school were located beside a fast-flowing river to complete this sylvan picture. It was indeed most scenic. The living room was located so near the riverbank that I could fish from the living room window. As part of the scenery, there was a lagoon up the hill from the house and another on the other side of the building.

We moved into the house, which was very rugged inside but quite cosy. We made a fire in the kitchen stove with the little bit of wood that was there. Virginia made supper and some young men arrived later with playing cards and we had a very nice first evening in our new home. The band brought a little bunch of wood at a time. There was no running water and we had to carry the water for cooking and bathing from the river and use the facilities outside. We walked to the store for our groceries and it seemed like miles.

I walked down to the school building and investigated what there was to teach with. There wasn't much, but there was some scrap paper and a bundle of scribblers. There was a classroom and there was a desk and there were different accounts of what the individuals who had been there had experienced. When I arrived, the band believed that I was a qualified teacher and I was there to stay. I figured out how many children there were and got ready for the first day.

It was only the fifth term of school at the reserve school and few of the children spoke English. Teaching the children English became my priority because, before the general schoolwork could start, the children had to understand English. I found that the "little ones" picked up the new language quickly, but the bigger children were more self-conscious and too shy to speak. I found it hard to know whether they understood or not because they just didn't say anything. There were not many students—twenty maybe. They loved to hang around the school and they seemed to respect this image of an educator who looked like them, only older. But they were not really "schoolified" yet, and their parents had not yet been evangelized by the Roman Catholic Church. Basically there was no

Church interference unless you wished to affiliate with Fort Frances Diocese.

So the routine of running a school began!

I see now why I was chosen for this assignment. Mr. Mingay must have known that a teacher with Ojibwe as well as English would be able to bridge the gap between the children's existing knowledge and the school. I don't know how a unilingual English-speaker could do this. I guess that is why punishment had become the accepted teaching methodology for teaching English in residential schools.

I liked the Northwest Bay assignment because the country was very wild and there was plenty of hunting. There were few modern conveniences, but the view from the house was beautiful. My year in Northwest Bay and the woodland scenery and the roar of the rapids in the river made this place truly a godsend. I liked it, but Virginia did not like the remoteness and the wilderness, and we left when the school year was over.

I had had a chance to see different types of educational experiences for Indian children. Although I thought that the Church residential schools did a good job of educating children, they could not prepare students to live with other Canadians. By this time, I had decided that I would like to work in a city or consolidated school to get the experience of urban and integrated education for Indian children. I believed that by attending secondary day schools with other Canadians, Indian children would get a broader outlook and learn to get along with others. I realized that when they attended an all-Indian school until their late teens, young Indians had to adjust to living in a white community afterwards, whereas if they grew up with all types of youngsters in a day school there was no adjustment needed.

After teaching at West Bay and Northwest Bay and having taken two summer courses in Toronto, I had to enrol for one year at North Bay Teachers' College. My wife took a job working at the Indian Affairs department in North Bay. I was one of six Indian students at North Bay Teachers' College and my favourite cousin, Mary Lou Fox, was one of the other students. Her grandmother, Elizabeth King, had taught at Buzwah and South Bay. Mary Lou and her mother had left the reserve when her father was in the army, and Mary Lou's mother, Rosie (King) Fox, Uncle Charlie's daughter, had moved to Espanola, where Rose began teaching in the separate school. Mary Lou had found that the move to the Espanola High School took a little getting used to, but she found it really easy to get along with all kinds of people. She was vivacious and had a great sense of humour. She did not plan to teach on a reserve; however, she was very committed to helping maintain the distinctiveness of the Indian people and the traditional language. Mary Lou often called my sisters, Elizabeth and Loretta, who were in training to be nurses at St. Joseph's Hospital. This allowed her to speak and maintain her Ojibwe.

A newspaper reporter from the North Bay newspaper interviewed the Indian teacher trainees to see what made us tick. In his article he commented that, "all the Indian students also express themselves with a clarity and precision in English which makes a great impression on those with whom they come in contact." Anita Wakegejig, who had graduated from the convent of Mary Immaculate in Pembroke, was the daughter of a teacher and had wanted to be a teacher from the time she was a little girl. She was determined to return to the reserve to teach because she said she wanted to "help her people." Lillian Pelletier, another

Manitoulin Indian girl who had attended St. Joseph College in North Bay, had received her elementary education from her mother, who was the teacher on her reserve. She said it didn't affect her education because her mother treated her like every other student. Eunice McGraw, though born in Wikwemikong, had lived in Blind River with her father after the death of her mother. She was educated at Shingwauk Anglican Residential School and Sault Ste. Marie Collegiate. Eunice wanted to teach in a white school or up north for a while to get experience. She believed that young people were going to leave reserves, and although she would be willing to teach on the reserve, she would do it only after all the students she had gone to school with were gone.

Part of my time at North Bay Teachers' College was spent in student government. I was surprised when I was elected vice-president of the first-term students' council by a landslide. The job description of the students' council was to plan the extracurricular activities of the school, and we managed to provide a very busy social calendar for the students. During the term we organized a Hallowe'en masquerade, hard times party, open house, Sadie Hawkins night, and a sleigh ride. This was in addition to the Friday-night socials. The council presented the first Friday assembly of the term and a literary program for the rest of the year.

The climax of the first term program was a Christmas formal dance, scheduled for Scollard Hall because the auditorium at the college was too small for the anticipated crowd. Two giant Christmas trees and the wishes of *Good Cheer* written out and attached to the wall were the major features of the decorating. I think my experience with the Buzwah Indian Day School Christmas concert must have prepared me for this.

The council's activities were under the guidance of Miss Agnes Johnson, staff advisor, and as I recall, the president and I rarely saw eye to eye.

I was a member of the North Bay Teachers' College choir, a large choir of about ninety voices. I was part of the strong section of male voices. The highlight of the year was our trip to Sudbury for the music festival. We sang all the way in the buses and in our respective classes at the festival. The women received a mark of 82 and we received a mark of 84 for the men's rendition. I remember that we won first prize in our classes. However, the account in the yearbook was a little sobering because it points out that we had no competitors in either of our classes! First place was assured!

It was at North Bay Teachers' College that I learned that kids were not all created the same; I was introduced to the IQ test. As teacher trainees, we had to learn to measure students' capabilities and aptitudes. To learn the complexities of the IQ test, we each had to have our own IQs tested. To everyone's dismay, I scored 60.

As you all know, an IQ of 100 is considered normal and anything under 100 is subnormal. An IQ of 60 was enough to deem a student uneducable. It was embarrassing to say the least. Now, remember, I had passed my entrance exams, studied under the Jesuits, and had graduated high school in Ontario at a time when final exams were set for all students in the province by the Department of Education.

My IQ score spoiled my professor's lesson. He tried the most ingenious theories to explain how someone with an IQ of 60 could be enrolled in his measurement class, let alone be training to be a teacher. If that standard of measurement had been applied to me in Buzwah, I would have been majoring in "sandbox," and if it had been applied to me at Spanish, I would now be working as an assistant on a pig farm. Happily for me, I was not tested and judged at an early age. I was not a scared little First Nations kid who was tested and found wanting. When I learned of my subnormal IQ, I was a confident young man with a history of success and academic achievement, so my belief in myself was not shattered, as a young child's can be when we tell him or her that he or she cannot learn with the other children.

In teachers' college, I learned that standardized tests can label you, humiliate you, and be used to say that you are intellectually inferior to your peers. I felt what so many young First Nations kids feel when they are singled out from their classmates for not measuring up to the norm. I learned through personal experience that tests can be used to judge you and may have no reality in fact. Today, I am a professor emeritus at Queen's University, a person who has earned a bachelor's degree and master's degree from the University of Saskatchewan and a PhD from the University of Calgary, with an IQ of 60. What if I had accepted the limitations that such a label puts on one?

Since I went on and got a few more educational credits, I must be one of what they used to call "overachievers." I have been a lot more educationally successful than the tests predicted and the experts would have believed. But how many of our First Nations children are judged by tests and experts and never have the chance to show that they are overachievers because the course of their future schooling and their educational opportunities is sealed by the scores they got on a test in grade four or even kindergarten. Given the chance, I bet we could have schools filled with overachievers.

I learned a lot of useful things at teachers' college. I learned the power of oratory. I learned that I had the power to sway an audience, to have them eating out of my hand. I gave a speech on Cyprus to an assembly. Mrs. Irwin, the social studies methods instructor admitted that she was nervous when I went up to speak because I had not cleared my topic with her in advance. However, the speech was a hit. The principal, Mr. Beecom, berated the student body and said that my speech was an example for the whole class on how you could speak with passion. That I could move an audience was an awakening for me.

We learned other lessons. One of the most significant for us was when Mr. Husband, our physical education instructor, was humiliated by Mr. Beecom in front of us. Mr. Husband was teaching us how to teach folk dancing. When the principal arrived in the classroom, we were in full flight of some exotic dance from afar. When Mr. Beecom saw what was going on in the class, he told Mr. Husband that he wasn't paid to dance. He said that classes were supposed to be serious, not frivolous. We realized that teachers could be misunderstood, too, and we all felt sorry for our poor teacher.

I went to North Bay Teachers' College when the emphasis was on building replicas and having a visual to teach from. I remember constructing a replica of Stonehenge for one of the classes I was teaching in my practicum. The only problem was that I had to carry it with me on the bus back and forth from my rooming house to the school every day. I must say that Stonehenge took a beating during its travels those days.

My experience up to this point had been with the federal system of education for Indian children. At North Bay Teachers' College, I was not only in a provincial institution for the first time, but the tone for my teacher education was set by the Ontario Department of Education under the direction of the Minister of Education. During my time at teachers college, the minister was W.J. Dunlop. He addressed the graduates in our yearbook:

> Those who join our profession know that they are becoming members of the public service organization in which there is almost boundless scope for assisting in developing citizenship of the highest order, in which there is plenty of opportunity for good, hard work and for achievement that is thoroughly worthwhile.

Minister Dunlop did not stop there and it was his next description of teaching that was new to me. He went on,

> But there is fun in teaching—plenty of it. The classroom should be, the brightest, happiest, most cheerful place in the community if the teacher begins with the right idea and adheres to that idea. When you have learned to be cheerful under all circumstances; never to scold or nag; never to be really angry, although at times you may pretend to be so; always to be calm and dignified—then you are master or mistress of all situations and discipline is easy. By the way, don't forget that the three R's have not gone out of fashion.

The minister's words reminded me of Kohkwehns. She had taught me to encounter the world with joy and wonder. She taught me so many things by letting me experience that world, in contrast to the way Mama taught. Mama had the stern autocratic approach of the Victorian schoolmarm; discipline and rules dominated her teaching technique. The Jesuits stressed that teaching and learning were serious matters. No one, in many years, had suggested that *fun* should be part of the educational experience. This was one of the wisest teachings I received at North Bay Teachers' College and it freed me to teach in Kohkwehns's style.

My year at North Bay Teachers' College strengthened my relationship with my cousin Mary Lou Fox. Now we were professionals, both dedicated to bringing the best education to Indian students. We discussed the methods of teaching that we were being taught and how these methods worked with Indian students. A cultural gap became apparent to us. This was the beginning of a long conversation about Indian education, language, and culture that continued until Mary Lou's death in 1998 when she was sixty-three. I found strength in her support and I knew that, at times, my knowledge and understanding of her struggles were valued.

After completing teachers college, I was hired to teach at Dokis Bay Reserve, an Ojibwe community on the north end of the French River. It was very isolated, with no road to speak of, although a roadway was in the process of construction. I was a little early to have the pleasure of driving on a new road surface. There was a Roman Catholic church, a sawmill, a post office, and, of course, the school. The marine boat that plied the French River up and down every day was the only excitement in Dokis Bay.

I was hired to be head teacher and any other roles that Indian Affairs could think up. But, in fact, I was a principal—in my first year as a qualified teacher. I saw this as a daunting experience. The school, being isolated, had a group of students to challenge my teaching skills, and I enjoyed settling in as head teacher. Dokis Bay Indian Day School was a brand new building that I had the experience of breaking in. It was a nice school and Virginia and I settled in to start our new family.

There was a huge community celebration when the new school was opened. Guests arrived in Dokis Bay for the event. The visitors—Mr. Matters; Rev. Leopold Porcheron, S.J.; separate school inspector R.M. Surtees, North Bay; civil servant W.E. Sinclair; and the *North Bay Nugget* reporter—were driven in by Henry Gauthier, the Indian agent from Sturgeon Falls. The reporter described the torturous two-hour, twenty-mile trip made by the guests from the outside through muddy roads from Highway 64 to the island village. The reporter told how Gauthier steered the vehicle through bottom-scraping holes and slippery hills. He stopped frequently and stood out in the downpour, wiping his mud-splattered windshield. According to the reporter, the monotony of the trip was broken by the jovial storytelling of Rev. Porcheron.

Fred Matters, superintendent of Indian agents for the Northern Ontario region, turned over the keys to the new one-room school. The members of the community celebrated the event proudly, despite having to trudge through the mud and rain to be there. Elders Frank Dokis, a seventy-eight-year-old trapper and hunter, and Emile Restoule added stories of the past. A turkey dinner prepared by the homemakers' club was served at the home of Mr. and Mrs. Emile Restoule.

I was involved in teaching adults as well as children. In 1957–58, I taught adult education academic upgrading in Dokis Reserve. We also became parents with the arrival our first born, Denise, in July of 1957. My teaching incorporated Ojibwe as a way to explain concepts. I found this ability to be invaluable when working with adults. We had a lot of fun. Emile Restoule was often in the school and would add translations into Ojibwe, which would create total chaos in the class as he stretched the language to outrageous lengths. It convinced me that learning English could be enhanced by working with people in our language.

I stayed at Dokis Bay for three years, worked in their sawmill, and generally fit into the life of the community very smoothly. The chief of the Dokis Bay Reserve was a very impressive individual who was very interested in his new school and, I suppose, the teacher. First Nations chiefs do take their roles seriously and generally are proud of their operations. After three years, it was time to move. I got an offer from St. Joseph Elementary School in Hamilton.

Teaching grade three in Hamilton was a very different experience from the close-knit First Nations communities that I had taught in since becoming a teacher. The parents were very concerned that their children do well in school. It was my first time working in a cultural community that was not French, English, or Ojibwe. The Italian Catholics who were the foundation of this Catholic school and church were incredibly hospitable to me. I don't know if all the teachers got the same treatment, but I remember many dinners with my students' families. The father of the house would stand at the head of the table and the wine would flow. There were platters of spaghetti and forms of pasta which I had never eaten before. I remember one of these feasts laid on by the family of one of my weaker students. His father raised his glass and addressed me, saying that his son had to pass. To this day, I regret that I did not find a way to pass him.

Virginia and I decided it was time for our family to move back home. In 1960, I received an offer from Pontiac School in Wikwemikong. Since we had collected quite a lot of furniture through our various moves, I had to hire

Cecil and Virginia King
(née Pitawanakwat)
in Hamilton, circa
late 1950s.

a flatbed truck to transport our personal effects to our new home on my grandfather's land, where we would stay until we could find somewhere in the village near the school. By the time I returned to the reserve, I had a wealth of experience teaching in different locations and school systems. While most was in small, federal Indian schools, my teaching in Hamilton was in an urban provincial school. I thought that I was very well prepared to teach back home.

6. MY CAREER UNFOLDS

My return to my home reserve was traumatic, to say the least, after having been totally in charge of the schooling of the children and adults in three different First Nations communities. I had come full circle in Ontario to end up at home on my own reserve. I felt fortunate. However, moving back to Wikwemikong in 1960 was also a bit of a disappointment; in my absence since 1954 it had indeed changed. From where the First Nation was when I first left to the picture I now saw, it was as if it had gone backwards. Gone were the Wiky (as we called Wikwemikong) band and the church choir. The clergy were not interested in change and, basically, the nuns had taken over the church tasks, which used to be community responsibilities.

Wikwemikong had become modern, but the change was not to the advantage of the people who had lived there for several generations. There was local farming, and generally those with farm implements and farm animals, like my grandparents, had settled to tilling the soil. Gone was the labourer of the woodlands, and with them, all the traditional ways to support one's family—logging, crafting, medicine picking, fishing, and maple syrup making—since these were determined to be an unprofitable operation. Employment was no longer easy to find. However, families had grown and individuals had freshly constructed dwellings, and the number of these was increasing, as was the number of children, so that the schools had to be enlarged to meet the increased enrolment. This was the situation of the village as it existed on my return.

The school was now run by nuns. Schooling had been reorganized to meet a new era, and all of Ontario was gearing up for an expansion of educational offerings. Ontario was growing and so were the education programs of the school. I was told by Mr. Matters that Pontiac School in Wikwemikong would now be operated by the Sisters of St. Joseph. Furthermore, I would teach English literature to start with and be under the authority of a nun principal. I was agreeable to this arrangement at the start. I had thought that I might be principal since I knew the community, was a qualified teacher, and had teaching and administrative experience. This didn't seem to be beyond possibility because ten years earlier local First Nations teachers had been in charge of Buzwah School. However, I was advised that the nuns were in charge and that we were lay people and therefore inexperienced in running a school. I was particularly upset with this arrangement when I found out that the nun who was going to be principal was someone who had been a classmate at North Bay Teachers' College.

While this upset me initially, I saw there was nothing I could do about it. My teaching year at Wikwemikong had begun and I was relegated to the bottom of the heap with no regard for my previous experience. The control of education in the community was firmly in the hands of the nuns. This further indicated to me that the Wikwemikong Band was slipping backwards from where their education had reached and, at this point in my thinking, having nuns in charge of education was not advancing the interests of the community when the band authorities had had no involvement in any of this process. The Church was taking over education, as it had in years gone by. While I was educated at Buzwah under the direction of First Nations teachers, my cousins who were brought up in the village of Wikwemikong had been schooled under the watchful eyes of the nuns. Or, as Mary Lou put it, "the school was run by Catholic sisters who wore black robes." The First Nations teachers who taught there and the students who attended were not allowed to use Ojibwe.

Instead, the nuns set a plan in place to bring French into the school. It seemed as if our Ojibwe was intended to be shelved, as it didn't fit the philosophy of the regular school program. This was not supported by me, the other Ojibwe teachers, or the community. We believed that it was time that the schools in First Nations communities supported the preservation of our own language—Ojibwe.

Perhaps it was this effort to place French on the curriculum in First Nations schools that ignited many of us to lobby for the teaching of Ojibwe in the schools within our territory. Mary Lou Fox and I and a number of others became very engaged in promoting the Ojibwe language and, independently, Estelle Shawana, from Cutler, was preparing lessons and developing workbooks for teaching the language. As trained teachers, we realized that teaching had to have a structure, and to this point there were no plans for teaching Ojibwe to children in Ontario. As we started to work on it, we saw how complicated the issue was. We needed to agree on how we would write the language. There were books around our communities that had been written by missionaries when they came to our communities, to help them learn the language themselves. However, as the Church became more intent on teaching us English or French, these dictionaries and vocabularies had been abandoned. Instead of them learning our language, we had to learn theirs!

We began to talk among ourselves about what we needed to do to get Ojibwe taught in the schools. We were the people whose parents and grandparents had been convinced that, for us to succeed at school and in Canadian society, we had to learn English at home and not Ojibwe. We were the people who had experienced the effect of this. We saw the devaluation of our elders, our traditional cultural ways, our ceremonies, and all the ways of knowing that were spoken in Ojibwe. As I previously stated, I myself had the opportunity to learn the traditional songs from my uncle, Waabiginees, but could not because my grandmother did not want me to learn Ojibwe. For me, it was my classmates who tutored me in the Ojibwe language and worldview.

As teachers, my colleagues and I could see the result of schooling as it was. We believed that students were turning off because the school had very little of value to them in their lives in Wikwemikong. We were not teaching the students to be good Ojibwes but trying to change them into something that others wanted them to become. We believed that success in school had something to do with being proud of who we were.

In 1950, the Department of Indian Affairs's goal of assimilation provided a rationalization for an attack on Indian culture and language. The goals of the Roman Catholic Church and its teachers were similar to those of the Department of Indian Affairs. Now I understand.

Then I didn't know why my whole being felt that we were moving in the wrong direction.

Early in his time as prime minister, Pierre Elliott Trudeau summarized the place of our people in the country as he saw it. This was the background thinking on integration.

> We have set the Indians apart as a race. We've set them apart in our laws. We've set them apart in the ways governments deal with them. They are not citizens of the province as the rest of us are. They are wards of the federal government rather than of the provincial or municipal governments. They have been set apart in law. They have been set apart in the relations with government and they have been set apart socially too. (Part of speech delivered in Vancouver, August 1969. In R.P. Bowles, J.L. Hanley, B.W. Hodgins, G.A. Rawlyk, *The Indian: Assimilation, Integration or Separation*, Scarborough, Ontario: Prentice-Hall of Canada, Ltd., 1972, p. 71)

It was ironic that, just at the time when Indian people across Canada were coming to realize that the various provincial education systems—with their emphasis on the two official languages—were threatening the survival of Native languages and that elements in a standard curriculum might be irrelevant to the situations in which Indians lived, that the Wikwemikong school, with Ojibwe teachers and elders well-equipped to support the language, was not allowed to do so in the school.

Despite my reservations about the school, it was time to settle down and raise our family. When the time came for me to build my own dwelling, and after having researched house designs, a mental plan, at least, came to fruition. Of course, I needed some start-up money, as neither my wife nor I had set aside funds to build a family home. Since our family was growing, a dwelling was needed, as my son Daryl was born in 1961. We lived in the second house on Pa's land for the first year that I worked as a teacher in Wikwemikong.

This is how we got started. I knew borrowing was the route to consider—and I did. Since I had land, a village plot in Wikwemikong, I approached the chief and council in a meeting to apply to them for some help to build a home. Fortunately, I had allies on the band council who supported my request. I very easily qualified for a loan of $5,000. I suppose the band council viewed our situation with two incomes as being a favourable risk for a loan. Anyway, now I could start.

My in-laws, Mr. and Mrs. Dan "Pete" told me about a stand of Norway pine that had survived all the other cutting that had been going on for at least two generations. This stand of Norway pine was pristine, so it seemed—verdant, straight, all of a particular size, and very ready for selling by the lumber cutters. It was only a matter of time before they would disappear.

My father-in-law then urged me to find someone who knew the art of making logs for sawmill readiness. He said he would walk us over and show us exactly where his pines were growing. They would have been well hidden, even from us, were it not for my father-in-law's surreptitious knowledge, which he was willing to share with me. I also think he saw the opportunity of capitalizing on the $5,000 that he knew I had at my fingertips. It certainly was an enticement.

My father-in-law's name was Daniel Pitawanakwat. This name, for economic reasons or just for plain efficiency, over time became "Dan Pete." His wife was Margaret, and between the two of them, if there was any scheming to be done, they were notorious, at least to me. I had no doubt that Margaret, too, saw the possibility and opportunity to channelling some of my loan into their hands.

At Dan's request or advice, I approached Ambrose Kitchikake, who very readily agreed when he knew he would be in cahoots with Dan Pete. Ambrose suspected where the pine stood and was totally ready to attack the forest. Ambrose had an old tractor that basically worked, and hitched to it a reasonable rubber-tired wagon. Ambrose lived alone and liked having a trickle of money coming in to supplement his veteran's pension. He was a very seasoned woodsman and he had the equipment—a sharp axe and an old chain saw that worked. Ambrose was ready to roll.

Dan's sawmill was ready. It was not new, having been used considerably in sawing pine logs for other house builders, but basically it worked all right. Therefore, Dan saw its possibilities in my case. He would saw the logs into the precise amount of lumber that I needed to build my house. Dan had long before figured out, in his own way, the amount of lumber I would need based on the outline of what the house was to look like. He could read a blueprint sufficiently to figure out the amount of material that would be needed. This included the number of pine trees Ambrose would have to cut and deliver to his sawmill. Dan informed Ambrose of his limit to result in the exact amount of lumber, and no doubt Ambrose appreciated this knowledge. Of course, Ambrose now became the key element for Dan's sawmill production.

Ambrose began immediately and, for precisely six days, sawed down every pine tree within the designated area. Ambrose, with his tractor, would skid each log to a central location where the logs were rolled up into sizeable piles, ready to be transported to a sawmill—yes, Dan Pete's saw-mill. The transporting of the logs was not an insurmount-able task, for Ambrose had devised a practical rack on his rubber-tired wagon in readiness to load logs for transport to the sawmill. Since Ambrose lived alone in a cabin he had built in the bush and worked alone, I tried to help him by reporting to work on the days Ambrose proclaimed he would go to his cutting area. While Ambrose seemed to appreciate my offered assistance, he indicated to me in every way that this was his job and that I would be paying him.

Dan, in the meantime, had fine-tuned his sawmill into absolute readiness, an enterprise that consisted mainly of rubbing grease on everything. Nevertheless, the mill was more than ready and it ran very smoothly. My lumber rolled out ready to become my new house! The lumber had to be seasoned—piled to dry out. After it was suffi-ciently dry, I transported the lumber to the planing mill in Manitowaning in Dan Pete's truck. Mr. Harry McMullen dressed the lumber and then I hauled it back to the chosen location for the house.

My Uncle John, an experienced house builder, was joined by Pa and my dad to build the house's foundation, which was completed in July. By the end of summer, Uncle John had completed the whole house except for the roof. In September, with a crew of available men in Wiky, the house was made liveable. As I entered my second year of teaching, we moved into our new home. The school was close to our house and I walked to class.

My students were quite vibrant. In March that year, we teachers decided to have a field day to honour our teaching and draw attention to the success of the school programs. We held a meeting of the staff and all decided on a theme for a school parade. All classrooms took part, some doing very little while others pitched in to make our parade a spectacular event. I taught grade eight and I wanted to do something totally different. I decided to create a replica of Paul Bunyan and Babe the Blue Ox.

I rounded up my class and explained to them what I had in mind, and generally the students thought it was a grand idea. The first undertaking was to get a rubber-wheeled wagon from somewhere. One was found. My boys were quite adept at art and very soon a sizeable ox took shape on the wagon. There was a group shaping the man, Paul Bunyan. The figure was a challenge, but our float was a grand success, as was the parade.

I held a number of positions at Pontiac School, moving from teaching the regular academic program in grades six, seven, and eight to teaching the physical education program in grades eight, nine, ten, and eleven from 1960 to 1963. Also, in 1963 our daughter Anna-Leah was born. Since receiving my teacher training in North Bay in 1956, I had continually worked to upgrade my qualifications. The summer after receiving my initial training, I was back in southern Ontario at McMaster University, where I completed the Elementary Physical Education, Unit 1. The next summer, I returned to Hamilton to complete Intermediate Physical Education, Unit 2. During the summer of 1964, I completed the Ontario Department of Education Intermediate Physical Education and Health course in Toronto. With my phys. ed. training and my experience managing the teams in Spanish, I was soon organizing local sports programs, which seemed very opportune since we had a group of athletes available.

In the meantime, word came that the friendship centre in Toronto had started classes in cultural expression. We felt that we had to develop our own cultural expressions—language, singing and craftwork—for cultural advancement in our own home life.

In 1959, I had received credit for the Junior Education Elementary Program and I spent 1963–64 as principal's supply for the Sudbury Separate Schools in the provincial school system, which meant I would fill in for principals at different schools should they need to be absent for any reason. This provided a chance to compare and contrast the education offered in an urban Catholic system to the Catholic education offered our students on the reserve under the direction of the Sisters of St. Joseph and the Department of Indian Affairs.

It was an exciting time to be an Indian teacher in Ontario. Even on the reserve and in the family, we discussed education. Within the community, others were empowered by the opportunities that were available. Our friends were scattered throughout the province and would come back to the reserve full of new ideas. Cousin Mary Lou had become friends with Rosemary Pelletier, who lived in The Soo with her husband, Don Fisher, when Mary Lou was teaching there. Rosemary's brothers were involved in the awakening of political consciousness among Canadian Indians, and Rosemary became absorbed in the ideas her brothers spoke of. She passed the ideas on to Mary Lou, and before long we were all enthusiastic about seeing change come to our communities.

The year 1960 was the beginning of a new era for us as Indian people in Canada. That was the year that we received the right to vote in federal and provincial elections. It was the year that we were allowed to go to bars and to drink alcohol. I and the young educated employed Indians on the reserve felt very empowered. As the Indians of the

United States and Indians across Canada were returning to their traditions, we began to talk about reviving the celebration of our culture on the reserve. We were aware of powwows in various places and began to question why we couldn't host one at Wikwemikong.

Powwow dancing had been part of the development of cultural expression and had become a regular activity in the village. Rosemary Pelletier was instrumental because she purported to be an expert on powwow dancing. By this time, Wilfred Pelletier, Rosemary's brother, had associated himself with singers who lived in Toronto and invited them up to Wikwemikong to participate in our powwow. This was done when Rosemary and Don Fisher were home for a summer holiday.

We decided that we needed to take our idea of hosting a powwow to the band council. I'll always remember the remark of one councillor, who said that "we were just making a lot of noise which would ultimately pass." Perhaps it was that comment that motivated us to make the powwow a reality, with or without the help of the council. Eventually they did chip in $200 and, after much discussion, the Wiky hockey rink was turned over to us to hold our powwow. This was by no means a gift and skepticism prevailed.

Once we had the use of the rink, the reality of what we were doing set in. We had to build a stage; we needed lumber and lots of it. The stage had to be big enough to hold 100 dancers (we were thinking big). The stage had to be rigid to withstand the pressures of 100 dancers in motion—a fact that almost killed us all, but we soldiered on. I was able to borrow a pile of two-by-ten timbers from the schools and logs to serve as sleepers under the stage—with much scrounging! Of course, Dan Pete was involved in the planning because we needed lumber treated at his sawmill. A bunch of allies came forward and we set to work and built the stage that would be about three feet from the ground. Somehow the stage materialized in record time. Furthermore, it was a strong stage that could withstand teams of horses on it!

Up to this point, being busy with the practical things necessary to hold a powwow, it just did not occur to any of us that we needed to formulate a committee of some sort, but it was becoming evident that someone had to claim ownership. Nobody wanted it at the time except us few renegades who wanted to prove a point: that if our ancestors could do this, then so could we. We believed that a powwow was a community project and therefore it should belong to the Wiky band council. This thought terrified them all; the chief and council really didn't want the powwow, not only because they had never held a big cultural event and feared opening up the community to strangers visiting, perhaps eventually increasing liability to reserve policy, but also because the Roman Catholic Church, who had deemed the drum and dance evil, still had a stronghold over band members, making them wary of such practices. So, we formed the powwow committee.

Many of the Old Ones were intrigued by what we were doing. I remember Pa saying, "Do you know how to dance?" "Who is going to sing?" He knew I had no skills in this department, and now that I think of it, he may have wanted to be asked. We never thought of asking the Old Ones.

There was a lot of preparation needed and Rosemary was a very good organizer with lots of connections. She dragged in her brothers, Wilfred, Earl, and Tom, who had large circles of friends that included singers, dancers, and cultural people. Yvonne, Rosemary's sister, came from the friendship centre in Toronto and she was a great help. She could read situations and suggest solutions to problems. Her husband, Paul McCrae, volunteered for any job that needed workers. As Rosemary started to advertise the event during the week of the August civic holiday, a lot of people, mainly from Toronto, wanted to be part of it. People asked to bring concessions to assemble at the site.

Rosemary had a drum that she was prepared to lend to people for the event. However, she wanted the Wiky people to know that the drum belonged to them. Local women sewed moccasins specifically for dancing. Other artists and craftspeople from the reserve made souvenirs of feathers for sale to the tourists. And the people came. They came from all over the island, from Sault Ste Marie, Toronto, and Michigan.

Singers came from Fort Qu'Appelle. They were old men who could sing and dance. Dancers came from other reserves, bringing new styles and songs, and inspired the local drum groups. This first powwow started a tradition of westerners coming to the Wiky powwow to show their stuff.

The first powwow was a week long. People came by boat, mobile home, and tent trailer. People put up tents everywhere along the shore. We filled the village with visitors' cars. We had a success!!!!

The chief and council were not the only ones that saw the powwow as a threatening thing. The Church had worked for 300 years to rid us of our traditional dances and ceremonies and to instil in us a fear of damnation if we went against its wishes. Father Flaherty reminded the community that the Church did not support the powwow. However, as we got more support and it became evident that the powwow was going to happen, Father Flaherty changed his opposition, saying that the powwow could go ahead but that the money raised should be contributed to the Church!

That's what happened. Margaret Pitwanakwat, who acted as our treasurer, presented Father Flaherty with the profits from the gate receipts, and in the end everyone was happy, even the Church.

All that was left was the garbage. We had not thought of the fact that so many people would make so much garbage.

●●●

My life revolved around teaching during the school year. However, I didn't have a wide peer group because most of the Ojibwe teachers were women. Mary Lou had an advantage that way. She was immersed in a community of women teachers including her mother, aunt, and sister. Mary Lou's mother had been the first Indian teacher in Espanola. Another mentor of Mary Lou was Stella Kinoshameg. She sought Mary Lou out as a colleague, relative, and friend. Stella was very articulate in English and expressed her ideas with ease. She was very experienced and confident in speaking her ideas in public. Since Mary Lou and I discussed issues in Indian education regularly, I was privileged to gain from the knowledge and experience of Mary Lou's female teacher network.

One of the things that Mary Lou and I discussed was the importance of keeping our teenagers motivated to finish high school. Mary Lou was interested in working with teenagers since she had experienced personally how difficult it was for them to adjust into new integrated high schools. She knew that white teachers found it hard to motivate reserve children. The majority of these shy kids were funnelled into special education, a dead-end two-year program. They could not qualify to attend university if they were streamed into this program.

Mary Lou and I believed that these students needed teachers who could speak their language, teach them about their own history and culture, and instil in them pride in their Indian identity. The students would receive caring counselling to help them adjust not only to the new situation but also to racial prejudice that they were experiencing, often for the first time in their lives.

We knew that all things were not good with the schooling of Indian students on Manitoulin Island. We had a drop-out problem—fewer and fewer students were graduating from high school. What was wrong? What was happening to our kids? Why were they dropping out? What needed to be done? Indian Affairs responded to the concern and I ended up as what they called a counsellor. The job was to convince students to go on to high school. I dealt with elementary-level students and worked to encourage them. It worked out well and I liked the job, but it meant travelling around to the reserves.

During this time, Mary Lou Fox and I were involved in trying to get the Ojibwe language approved for teaching in elementary schools. We succeeded in this and saw the Ojibwe language program offered at the elementary levels in northern Ontario federal schools and accepted as an option at the secondary level with a course developed from the original course outlined for elementary schools. In 1965 Virginia and I welcomed another daughter, Alanis, into the world.

I became very interested in the development of Native languages for inclusion in regular school curricula. To do this I recognized the importance of developing a teaching

The King family, December 1969. Left to right: Alanis, Cecil, Anna-Leah, Denise, Virginia (née Pitawanakwat), and Daryl.

methodology program for the instructors of Native languages. It became apparent that standardizing the written Ojibwe language was a necessary step in establishing a province-wide Ojibwe language teaching program. Here we ran into the debate over the appropriate orthography. Now we realized that to teach the language in the school we needed to have a written language and material for the children to read.

The idea of using media to teach Ojibwe seemed an interesting new approach. As I said, Estelle Shawana from Cutler had been working on materials, and others had programs that they had developed for their own classrooms. Success in teaching Native languages in schools would be dependent on a teacher-training program specifically for teachers of Indian languages.

This resurgence of interest in teaching Ojibwe in schools resulted in a course for teachers being offered at Trent University in the summer of 1970. I was the instructor chosen to deliver this course to a group of non-Indian teachers. I introduced them to the Ojibwe language. We sang. We laughed. We learned. During the six weeks, the teachers learned the basics of listening and speaking. They enthusiastically became confident in simple conversations. For me, it was an affirmation and it was empowering to see a classroom of "white" teachers eager to learn Ojibwe. It seemed that, at last, the educators were showing respect for our culture. No longer would our children have to sacrifice their Indianness for their schooling. This course proved to be very popular. Teachers wanted to know Ojibwe and I taught it for two more years. After the first stint in the fall of 1970, my youngest child, Shoo-Shoo (Tanya) was born.

There was a movement among the First Nations teachers in the province to work together. We came from our various schools on- and off-reserve. Iroquois and Ojibwe, status and non-status, we all were committed to promoting the success of our students. We met to discuss our concerns and our successes. We got a chance to exchange ideas and realized that we were not alone in the way that we were seeing the cultural gap between the schooling that our children were receiving and what we as Indian teachers believed that our children needed.

It was a time when issues related to human rights were being discussed in a variety of grassroots organizations. These organizations were awakening to the fact that Canada's Indian people were not treated the same as other Canadians. From October 27 to 29, 1967, a weekend conference, Universal Human Rights and the

Indian in Northern Ontario, was held at the Centre of Continuing Education in Elliot Lake. The conference was to draw attention to the twentieth anniversary of the United Nations' Universal Declaration of Human Rights and the problems confronting citizens of Indian ancestry in Northern Ontario. I was conference chairman, and guest speakers at the conference led the 200 Indians in attendance in gathering information, analyzing the current situation, and discussing pertinent issues. Speakers included Alban Daigle, director of the Human Rights Commission; Omer Peters, president of the Ontario Indian Council; Basil Johnston, teacher at Earl Haig Collegiate, Toronto; and Elmer Sopha, MLA for Sudbury.

Sopha's speech was entitled, "Human Rights and the Law." He said there was one law for the rich and one for the poor and that Indians failed to realize their rights because they were among the poor. He said a major problem of Indians was alcohol, which "they can't handle because of their mental and physical make-up." He said that motivation to deal with the addictions problem had to begin on the reserve and with the next generation. I reminded Sopha that it was the white man who had brought alcohol to the Indian.

Sopha went on to point out the words of the original treaties and their abuse. He used the Manitoulin example. The question arose as to why Indians would not move from the reservations to the cities and towns in which they worked. Omer Peters responded sharply to the question. He said the reserve was home to the Indians away from prejudice and discrimination. He concluded, "You have to be an Indian to understand, and anyway, why should we move to the city when the reserve is our home and community?"

Basil Johnston pointed out that the values and initiative of the Indians had been stifled by white men in Canada. Johnston said that the white men "chose to keep the Indian a beggar and a dependant." He claimed that the 220,000 Indians in Canada had had to operate in a "dehumanized, degrading system which has robbed Indian people of their will and self-confidence and that when a people have been betrayed, they can no longer count on their rights being inviolate."

The Indian delegates reported Indian women crowded into Northern Ontario jails; underpaid and overworked Indians in lumber mills, camps, and mines; and near-starvation conditions on some reserves. Delegates identified the "built-in prejudices" of white people against Indians. They asked for programs to educate white people, government assistance in making reserves self-sufficient, and the expropriation of productive lands adjacent to poor reserves for the use of Indians. They requested the banning of inferior handicrafts and souvenirs. They objected to the practice of identifying Indians by race in reporting court cases (*Sudbury Star*, October 30, 1967).

The conference ended with resolutions to be forwarded eventually to all Indian bands, government agencies, and legislative assemblies. They included:

—that government establish larger reserves and expropriate crown land for this purpose in areas where hardship is felt because of reserve location or poor economic standing;

—that representatives from Indian reserves be invited to sit on local school boards that have Indian children enrolled;

—that all individuals, especially Indians, be informed of their rights under the law;

—that abuses under the minimum wage act, especially in remote areas, be investigated;

—that a crash program to educate white people and accustom them to Indian problems be implemented; and,

—that the status of Indians should not be adversely affected by the use of the word "Indian" in certain newspaper headlines.

(*Sudbury Star*, October 30, 1967)

On November 4, 1967, I was on the executive of the Nickel Belt Indian Club when we held the sixth annual banquet. In recognition of the centennial year, we had decided that our presence in Canada should be recognized. To ensure this, the planners, Margaret Jackson, Stella Kinoshameg, Ken Alexander, and I, invited the guests to come in traditional Indian dress.

We were in changing times. In 1960, Prime Minister John Diefenbaker ensured that Indians in Canada were given the legal right to vote in Canada's elections. My reserve happened to be in the riding of Algoma East, and when we received the vote, our Member of Parliament happened to be Lester B. Pearson, the leader of the Opposition in the Canadian Parliament. Pearson was an active constituency man who made it his business to visit reserves and to encourage us to become involved in politics. He made sure that the citizens of the reserves in his riding were informed of their rights as Canadian citizens. He gathered many Liberals on these visits.

On June 24, 1966, Art Nahwegahbow, Fred Shawanda, Philip Pitawanakwat, and I met with Prime Minister Lester B. Pearson, seeking the reinstatement of Gerald McCaffrey, a school superintendent, and Maurice Curtin, principal of the Wikwemikong School. We told the prime minister that these two men were largely responsible for programs that decreased the juvenile delinquency problems on the reserve and that their efforts also cut down on the number of school dropouts. We blamed the removal of these men on education director R.F. Davey. There had been constant friction and frustration under Davey's administration, created by the failure of the Indian agents to provide suitable living conditions for teachers by making required repairs to roofs, windows, furnaces, and sump pumps. Curtin and McCaffrey had spent hours trying to remedy the conditions to keep the teachers from resigning because of the facilities.

Our delegation also presented the prime minister with a letter containing a resolution expressing to government officials our concern about the role of religion in education that had passed overwhelmingly. On July 8, we released our letter to him from the Manitoulin Unceded Band's education committee asking for his assistance. This was reported by the *Sudbury Star* under the heading "Manitoulin Indians Protest School Policy" with an accompanying picture of Art Nahwegahbow, Fred Shawanda, Philip Pitawanakwat, and me with Prime Minister Pearson.

When Pearson was prime minister, he never forgot his voters, and we were energized by his encouragement. We took our problems to him and he looked for answers. He convinced our elders of our right to participate in Canadian democracy to such an extent that, when he was to be replaced as MP when he retired, the elders of my community chose me to run for nomination as Liberal candidate in the riding. The *Globe and Mail,* May 9, 1968, had the headline, "Two Indians Seek Liberal Backing in Pearson's Old Seat." I was described as a thirty-four-year-old Indian who had been employed by the provincial and federal governments for more than ten years, and Tom Pelletier, thirty-two, as the publisher of an Indian newspaper in Ottawa. Since there were four men running for the nomination, we represented half of the men seeking the position. In the new redistributed Algoma riding, more than 8,000 Indians living on fourteen reserves accounted for one out of every five electors.

For me, running for the nomination and entering a race for a job that had always been occupied by a white person was a scary experience. It goes without saying that I did not win. I was never so glad to lose anything in my life. I did, however, become a delegate to the convention that elected Pierre Elliott Trudeau as Liberal leader. I was thrust into the excitement of a leadership convention for one of the two major parties in the country. Although I didn't catch the bug to dive into federal politics, this preliminary foray into the politics of a Canadian election, after only eight years of the franchise, opened a new world to our people.

Tom Pelletier, my Indian competitor for the nomination, questioned a restrictive clause in the constitution of the new riding. He argued that it discriminated against the rank and file membership being able to make their own choice and was biased towards candidates from larger centres because of the large size of the new riding. Earlier elections did not have any Indian participation due to the lack of the right to vote; now it was felt Indigenous communities were being marginalized due to gerrymandering. Pelletier said that the system in place was put in the riding constitution to prevent packing of the meeting with people from any one part of the large riding. However, he said that the restrictive clause based on the Liberal vote in the last election could result in packing from large communities. Pelletier sought a change that would give each member of the riding association one vote for the nomination meeting. Tom showed that we were prepared to become full participants in the business of the riding association.

Our efforts were praised, despite our defeat, in a May 24, 1968, letter to the editor of the *Sudbury Star* entitled, "Indians Learning Technique to Gain Political Results." The writer observed that, although there was no victory at the nomination, victory comes in various ways: first, we focused attention on a minority; second, we learned many things. The Indian commentator wrote that one way that Indians could make their voices heard was through the political arena—a peaceful, lawful way. The Indian portion of the vote was about 10 percent of the delegates. Despite the loss of Indian candidates, it was observed that the Indian block of votes eventually appeared solid and it was believed to have gone to the winning nominee. Those Indian delegates learned what power a small minority can exert if it stays together—10 percent represents bargaining power. The writer said that the result boded well for the next time.

The letter recommended that Indian leaders preach the gospel of getting out the vote with the aim of earning greater representation at the next nomination meeting. The writer suggested that potential nominees demonstrate their leadership qualities early in the race and not only concentrate on Indian support but on the populace as a whole. For the Indian there was only one issue, the right of recognition and a place in Canada. It was acknowledged that the calibre of the Indian candidates was good. The writer stated that even if the Indian candidates fell by the way, it was to inferior men!

Former Prime Minister Lester B. Pearson, known by the honorary title we had bestowed on him—Chief Ogimabenisse—was not a local resident, even though he had served the constituency of Algoma-East since 1948. He continued to tour our communities after stepping down as leader, spending time touring, in particular, educational institutions, including the Elliot Lake Centre for Continuing Education and an addition to West Bay School that he had helped to establish in the riding. At Wikwemikong he spoke to more than 200 students and teachers. He visited schools at Spanish, Birch Island, Little Current, and Manitowaning. He had a special appeal for the children at each school, who gathered around him to shake his hand and get his autograph. He was so convinced of the potential of our people that he told the students at West Bay that Canada might one day have an Indian prime minister. His comment was reported in both the *Toronto Telegram* and the *Ottawa Journal* on August 31, 1968. He said that the government was concerned with improving housing and education for Indians. Leonard Marchand, first Indian MP to be elected, credited the Pearson administration with doing more than any other government to raise the status of Indians.

Now Canada was changing. We had a visit from the old warriors of Parliament with familiar names like Dr. Maurice Foster and John Diefenbaker. So a new era had hit Buzwah, and Northern Ontario blossomed. Mr. Trudeau became a household name. Dr. Foster referred to the regional economic disparities. And thus, the aim of the Liberal

Party's Just Society became the buzzword of the time and was about to change our First Nation forever.

The Old Ones began to leave us. Madeline, Mama's sister, went first. Then old Peter Tekummah died. Mama passed away, and Pa died in Little Current Hospital. He took a spell at home, and when I went to see him in the hospital, he had already passed away. Again, I felt alone and deserted, as I had when Kohkwehns left me.

My work in the Manitoulin District Office developing the Guidance Counselling Program for the Department of Indian Affairs in the district's federal schools, combined with my Specialist Guidance Certificate, resulted in 1969 in an offer of a job in the Guidance Counselling Program for Native students entering urban life in Ottawa.

Our counselling unit was in the same building as the headquarters of the Department of Indian Affairs, but we were not really part of the headquarters. We were actually part of the Kingston District Office. It did give me a good vantage point from which to observe the activities of the federal department that controlled so much of the life of Canada's Indian people. I learned about the importance of being promoted to a window office. I soon knew who had been promoted to Ottawa because they had been trouble in the field. I was one of these. While the job seemed a promotion since my contributions in setting up student guidance departments was being recognized, what was being unsaid was in fact that federal employees were strongly discouraged from running for public office—I was being reprimanded for my political activity. I also saw that many who ended up in HQ were those at the end of their careers who had little energy and few new ideas! And I noted, I was one of a handful of Indian people with jobs anywhere in the building.

I soon became aware of the hierarchy within the department. It reminded me of the tight authority structure of the residential school. Everyone was acutely aware of the role of everyone working in the building and the lines of communication between them. This reality of Canada's governmental system was so far removed from the relationship that then-Prime Minister Lester B. Pearson had had with our people when he visited the reserves, was flocked to by the children, and joined in community activities. I had thought that would be how Ottawa functioned. Sadly, it was not. It was an alienating place for Indians, and especially for the young people sent there from small northern communities. It was part of my job as counsellor to these young people to provide some welcoming kind face they could turn to.

I was labelled a receiving counsellor. This meant that I was responsible for welcoming students, mainly from the north, to Ottawa and finding accommodation and programs so that they could continue their education. Students came from feeder schools from such diverse areas as Moosonee, Attawapiskat, and other James Bay communities, and my own reserve. These students did not come with a program or personal determination to get a certain career. It was our job to find something for them in the city.

My work began when I received a telephone call from a school official in the communities telling me that they were sending some students to Ottawa. My job was varied, but the first requirement of our students was shelter, meaning I had to find a boarding home for them. Most landlords I found were grumps and they saw no good in boarders. Unfortunately, sometimes the boarders lived up to the landlords' low expectations of them and left, sometimes with damage behind them. The system for paying the rent to the landlords created problems. The department, in its wisdom, did not pay the landlords directly; the cheques were made out to the students and it was up to them to pay their rent. If the landlord didn't get the payment exactly on the day it was due, I heard about it. I often had to question the student, only to find that the money had been spent. The landlord still needed to get paid and frequently refused to let the student remain there. This made it even more difficult for me to find a place for the next boarder looking for shelter.

After the students arrived at the airport or bus depot, they came to my office by taxi. Many were not prepared for the coming changing weather in Ottawa, as they essentially arrived with just the clothes on their backs. Many didn't bring parkas or mitts. I would ask them about their travel and if they had any documents from their advisor in the community. From the documents I would get the information I needed to assign them to a boarding home and begin the process of getting them settled in the city. I took them to find suitable clothes for their new life.

An urgent requirement was to ensure that the students were given TB X-rays. At the time, there was still active TB in some of the northern communities and the boarding homes and the schools did not want to accept students without the reassurance of knowing that they did not carry the disease. If the students were found to have lice or any other health issues, we were not expected to treat them and they were sent back home.

Their next need was transportation. Having found the boarding home, I had to locate the bus route and instruct the uninitiated student how to use the bus. However, this involved having to know what school the student would be attending. Since the students rarely came with career knowledge or test results from aptitude or interest inventories, I had to assess them, establish their interests and abilities, and then match them with the array of programs that we used in the Ottawa school system.

A number of schools had been working with the department for years and the schools determined the program that the student would fit into. Some schools had a specific counsellor, but in most cases I took the student to the school and the principal took over from there. Principals were a funny lot. Some were happy that we had tested the students and found out their interests and abilities. However, some of the principals were quick to inform us that they would make the decisions about the student and weren't interested in what the counselling unit had to say or in our recommendations.

Jim McTavish and I ran the counselling unit. We soon found that the system was not set up to respond to the unanticipated needs of the students. There was a moral aspect to every decision that was made by our superiors. The answer to our requests for assistance for the students was always, "No." We had to set up a contingency fund to access money when the students had an urgent need—as they often did. They would lose things. Glasses were often left on the bus or dropped somewhere. The student would come to our office on Bank Street to tell us that they could not see the blackboard or read their textbooks. We would requisition a new pair of glasses, only to be told that we could not give a student another pair of glasses because only one pair was approved. The student would be labelled and called irresponsible and we would be told that we couldn't keep giving these students everything they asked for. The students had to learn a lesson. The problems would not be dealt with by the department.

It didn't take long before my wife and I became acquainted with other Indian people working in the city. There were certain places, the Beacon Arms (which we called the Broken Arms), the Blind Pig (the Blind Swine), and the Traviatta, where the Indian employees met after work. Someone said that I couldn't talk about Ottawa at that time without talking about these places. We made a subculture within the civil service. It was not unlike the way that the residential school had functioned. We were educated Indians from different parts of the country, but the fact that we found ourselves working in Ottawa gave us a common identity. The core group included Ken and Jean Goodwill from Standing Buffalo Reserve in the Qu'Appelle Valley. Ken was a Dakota and Jean was a Cree. Later in life, Ken was an integral part of First Nations University of Canada as a respected elder; Jean had a long and illustrious career, receiving the Order of Canada in 1992 for her contributions in the field of health. Ken and Jean both had strong family connections in Indian politics in Saskatchewan. Jean's father, John Tootoosis, was an early Indian nationalist. He had organized the New Union of Saskatchewan Indians, which eventually became the Federation of Sovereign Indigenous Nations. Jean's adopted family, the Cuthands, were strong leaders in public service through the Anglican Church and urban services to Native people. Their experience and knowledge helped me to understand how the government worked and what was important to Indians in western Canada.

Russ and Helen Moses introduced me to the culture and history of the Haudenosaunee. Helen was a nurse, as was Jean Goodwill. Having two sisters who were nurses, I was comfortable with these two women and their perspective was very helpful to me in dealing with some of the issues that the students had. Russ had been in the navy, and when he left the service, he got a job in Ottawa. He loved to go out after work and knew a great deal about what was going on in Ottawa. He worked for the Public Service Alliance of Canada (PSAC), the union of federal workers. His knowledge of the benefits that I should be aware of as a federal worker was invaluable to a new employee from the "bush."

Helen Moses had an uncle, Uncle Gib, who was the grand old man of our circle. To the rest of the Ottawa world he was Dr. Gilbert Montour, a highly decorated Mohawk, a direct descendant of Joseph Brant, and a prominent public servant. He was a World War I veteran but it was his work in World War II for which he received the Order of the British Empire (OBE). During the war, he had provided vital service as the Canadian Executive Officer of the Combined (Canadian-American-British) Production and Resources Board, helping to allocate strategic minerals for the war effort. I learned a lot from him. He fascinated me. He was so knowledgeable. He was a proud Mohawk, celebrated by his people. In 1958, he was made an honorary chief of the Six Nations. In 1967, he had become an Officer of the Order of Canada. He was someone who walked in both worlds. He always had time to give me advice and encouraged me to hang in and to continue my studies. He was passionate about education and had set up a program at Queen's University for the employment of students, a first in Canada. I was privileged to know him.

Victor Pelletier, a member of our gang, was my buddy and, like Estelle Shawana, was also from Cutler. He and his wife, Billie, moved to Ottawa after we did. They had a big family of three boys and two girls. They arrived in Ottawa in an old car with a very vague job offer and nowhere to stay. Knowing a number of landlords in the city, I helped him find a place to live big enough for the whole family.

Among our circle was Duke Redbird, who served as vice-president of the Native Council of Canada in the 1970s. He had been the editor of a Native newspaper in Toronto called *The Thunderbird* and was an active organizer of protests and a speaker on Native rights. Although he was an Ojibwe from Saugeen Reserve, he had been in the social services system and been raised mostly with non-Indian people. He experienced racism in non-Indian schools and identified with the Metis and non-status Indians.

He was in touch with the activists on the Indian political scene and kept us informed of the movement. Duke was affiliated with the Peltier or "Pelletier" siblings, Rosemary (Fisher), Wilfred (Wilf), and Tom. Wilfred was part of the rebellion among the young people of Toronto who were involved at Rochdale College. Rochdale College was an experiment in a student-run, free-expression, alternative education cooperative. It was a creative centre out of which came *This Magazine Is About Schools*, Theatre Passe Muraille, and House of Anansi Press. It epitomized the concerns of progressive politics, hippies, and idealism—with a few drugs thrown in. Wilfred Pelletier was one of the non-academic resource people who led informal discussion groups.

It was an interesting time to be in Ottawa. Indians from all across the country were coming there. There was a strong movement against the White Paper released by the Trudeau government outlining the plan to off-load Indian services to provincial schools. This was an anathema to the Indians with treaties and it went counter to the *British North America Act*, which, under section 91(24), assigned Indians and lands reserved for Indians to the federal government. The Indian Association of

Alberta responded with a document entitled *Citizens Plus*. A groundswell of opposition to the White Paper arose across the country. Indian groups descended on Ottawa to protest. The National Indian Brotherhood took the fore in organizing the national Indian reaction.

Our gathering became the place where Indians gravitated when they were in town for meetings or to lobby the politicians. This gave us new information and linked us to the forces that were communicating to others what was happening in our lives. They were demonstrating to Indians that we needed to get involved and have some influence on the laws and policies that affected our lives. People like Johnny Yesno, who was hosting and producing CBC's *Indian Magazine*, the first Canadian radio program about Indian people, was among those who joined us on occasion in our deliberations.

There was a temptation for some of the young Indians who came to Ottawa to become part of the bar scene. For some, it became their only existence, and I saw many young men with high ideals and great expectations lose their way as the clubby side of life became their total world. Unless individuals had families or a responsible job, they could easily become derailed. It would have been so easy to settle into the lifestyle as a young person and just drift through your days convincing yourself that you were doing an important job for your people.

To be honest, I didn't fit in to the Ottawa scene. It soon became evident that without more and different education I would be a receiving counsellor for the rest of my life. I liked working with the students, but the hassle with the bureaucracy when I tried to do something that would have made a big difference in the lives of the students was overwhelming. The first response to any request was "no."

Sometimes I could call on my residential school training in finding ways around the obstacles put up by the administration, but it seemed to me that there was a unit in the department devoted to finding reasons things couldn't be done and creating rules, regulations, and paperwork by the ton that would result in the request being withdrawn. I had been dedicated as a teacher to making things better for Indian students. Being within a department that could make things better but didn't, couldn't, or wouldn't went totally against all I believed in. I have to admit that I was not happy working in Indian Affairs in Ottawa. I either had to accept the fact that I was destined for a career as a low-level bureaucrat or, if I had aspirations to move up in the department to a position where I could make the department more responsive to the needs of Indian people, get more education. I decided the time had come to get the credentials that would allow me to move up in the civil service.

7. JOINING THE REVOLUTION

To increase my opportunities for advancement in the Ottawa bureaucracy, I had to upgrade my credentials. Despite the fact that I had been going to Toronto (it seemed like every summer) and amassing Department of Education courses, they did not count towards advancement in the civil service. It had become increasingly difficult to justify my lack of promotions to my wife and myself. While teaching Ojibwe in the summer of 1970 at Trent University, I met and became friends with a Shoshone professor, Dr. Art Blue. He convinced me that I would be able to tackle and succeed at university but that it would entail studying full time, not just in short spurts picking up a course at a time as I had been doing. This was disappointing news. However, in September 1971, Dr. Blue was taking a new job at the University of Saskatchewan where Father Andre Renaud had been pioneering courses designed specifically for teachers in Indian and northern communities. Dr. Blue suggested that if I could get a leave of absence from my work and come to Saskatchewan for a few terms, he would guide me through the university programming to ensure that I would receive a degree as soon as possible.

After discussions with my wife and receiving the department's approval of leave with half salary for one year, to be paid directly to my family, I departed to work on the degree that would allow me to pursue my career in the civil service. When I made the decision to go to Saskatchewan, I did not know that it was going to have a profound impact on my life. I knew nothing about Saskatchewan except what I learned from Art. I found out that he was moving to Saskatoon from the University of Western Ontario because the University of Saskatchewan was, at the time, at the forefront of the training of teachers to teach Indian children. This was one of the reasons that Art was so insistent that I should abandon my university education in Ontario and go with him to Saskatchewan. He was joining the Indian and Northern Education Program to direct its graduate program, the only such program in the country. He believed that this program was what I needed.

Neither of us knew much about the Indians in the province, but I was soon swept up with them. Just at the time that Art and I arrived in Saskatchewan, the Federation of Saskatchewan Indians (FSI) was working with the National Indian Brotherhood (NIB) on a new approach to Indian education that culminated in the publication of the *Indian Control of Indian Education* policy paper in 1972. In 1969, the FSI established a task force under the direction of Rodney Soonias, a Cree educator, to investigate issues of Indian education in Saskatchewan. The subsequent report convinced the chiefs of Saskatchewan it was time for the Indian people themselves to become involved in the education of their children. As one FSI official said at the time, "We can't do any worse."

The NIB document, *Indian Control of Indian Education*, which had been developed in close cooperation with the Federation of Saskatchewan Indians, articulated its objectives:

> The time has come for a radical change in Indian education. Our aim is to make education relevant to the philosophy and needs of Indian people. We want education to give our children a strong sense of identity with confidence in their personal worth and ability. We believe in education:
>   . . . as a preparation for total living;
>   . . . as a means of free choice of where to live and work;
>   . . . as a means of enabling us to participate fully in our own social, economic, political and educational advancement.
>   We do not regard the educational advancement as an 'either or' operation. (National Indian Brotherhood, *Indian Control of Indian Education*, 1972, pp. 3–4)

Based on the philosophy of *Indian Control of Indian Education*, they developed a master plan for all levels of Saskatchewan's Indian education. The creation of a teacher education program for Indian people was part of a bigger plan for revolutionizing education for Indian children in Saskatchewan.

The chiefs believed that having their own people as teachers was a critical part of the plan. They believed that Indian teachers were necessary for many reasons: firstly, to bridge the gap between the school and the home and community. At that time, non-Indian teachers in Indian communities lived in what was referred to as the "teacher ghetto," a cluster of teacherages around the school often surrounded by a fence separating the teachers from the community. This symbolic separation reflected the reality of the separation of the school and the community. Secondly, Indian teachers were seen as having the same experience and background as the students so that they could help students to understand concepts through examples from Indian life. Thirdly, the chiefs believed that for Indian children to succeed, they needed to have their community knowledge and experience reinforced in the school, and teachers of Indian ancestry would be able to incorporate Indian language, culture, and history into the curriculum. Fourthly, Indian teachers would be able to work with the parents and community, where necessary, in the community's first language. The chiefs saw Indian teachers as the frontline troops in the revolution.

My travels brought me to Saskatchewan just as this revolution was getting underway. I had no income but was somehow lucky enough to receive the support of the Saskatchewan Indian Cultural College, which was housed on the university campus in McLean Hall, the heart of another revolution. The Saskatchewan Indian Cultural College was tasked with collecting and preserving what is now called "Indigenous Knowledge." This entailed locating elders who had gone underground during the residential school era and had preserved the knowledge that had been passed to them through the oral tradition and the ancient ceremonies. Smith Atimoyoo, who lived with me at McLean Hall, was in charge of the elders program. So I met and was educated by many of the elders of the different communities and cultures of Saskatchewan in my life there. These men (for the men were the ones with whom I spoke) taught me so much about being proud of my own culture. They showed me that there was much knowledge available but it was in danger of dying with them. I had the opportunity to eat with the elders who came to the college to share their knowledge. The cultural college had a thorough approach to preserving the knowledge. Smith, who was an ordained minister and teacher and trilingual (English, Cree, and Saulteaux), had field workers around the province identify traditional elders. He brought the elders to Saskatoon, where they would stay at the college for a few days to talk to each other and share cultural knowledge. They spoke in their languages. Their discussions were taped and then transcribed by Ed Lavallee to be preserved as an archive of traditional knowledge.

I had the privilege of living in this environment as I was piecing together a program that would lead to a degree at the university. I had been counselled into courses that would support those that I had previously completed and count towards a degree in the most expeditious way possible. My studies kept me busy. I had to pass first-year English to get a degree from the U of S. This almost sunk me. I remember one paper that I wrote and was very proud of. When I got it back, the professor had scrawled across it that I wrote like a seventeenth-century monk! I was devastated. It wasn't until one of my friends said, "Of course you write like a seventeenth-century monk! You were taught your English writing skills by French-speaking Jesuit priests." I can now rationalize my prose at that time. Then, I was totally deflated and worried that I would fail this course and not get my degree. The way that I had been taught to write a paper was the correct way according to the Jesuits, who considered themselves to be impeccable academics, but I took the advice of the professor and managed to pass my English course.

I was honoured to meet Dr. Zenon Pohorecky, who taught the history of the Plains Indians from an archaeological perspective. Zenon, as I came to know him, brought a completely different approach to the study of Indian people than I had ever been exposed to before. Zenon was Ukrainian and very proud of his history and culture. He and his family hosted the students at their family's Ukrainian Christmas and Easter celebrations. Little did I know that part of my university course work would involve creating Ukrainian Easter eggs on my professor's pool table. I learned from Zenon that each nation has its own proud history, traditions, and beauty.

Dr. Mary Marino tried to convince me of the need for the study of linguistics to understand the dynamics of my Ojibwe language. She was very concerned with the survival of Indian languages as a valuable part of the world's knowledge. Her particular interest was the Dakota language and she worked with Sam Buffalo, who also lived at McLean Hall when he was in town. She and I did not agree on the usefulness of applying theories taken from other languages to Indian languages. I believed that we first had to study our languages from the inside before comparing them to other world languages. However, because of Mary's dedication to the need for Indian people to develop our own languages, she generously relinquished control of the Indian language teaching to the Native Studies Department when it was created, with the understanding that the language would be taught by those who spoke it.

I had settled into the life of a student, not thinking about becoming involved in the activities of the FSI. However, someone had another plan for me. Unbeknownst to me,

Rodney Soonias, whom I had gotten to know through Smith, was negotiating with the College of Education to offer a teacher training program for Indian students. I had the honour to be chosen to be part of the revolution. I say that I was chosen because, one day, Rodney, who was then director of the Saskatchewan Indian Cultural College, called and told me that I was the director of a new program at the College of Education called the Indian Teacher Education Program (ITEP). Rodney told me that in his negotiations for the program with the College of Education dean, the question of who should be the director came up in the discussions. Dean Kirkpatrick said that the university had recruited Audie Dyer, who had started Northwest Territories Teacher Education Program, the first teacher education program for Aboriginal people in Canada. The dean was confident that Mr. Dyer would be able to develop an appropriate program in Saskatchewan. Rodney said he didn't think so, saying that FSI believed that the task was too important to be undertaken by a "white man," no matter what experience he had.

Apparently the dean challenged Rodney to name an Indian who could do the job and was available. So, Rodney told me, "Your name popped into my head. So, you've got the job." I was still in a state of shock because I had come west to finish my BEd and wasn't even thinking about taking a job. Rodney misinterpreted my hesitation as a bargaining tactic. So he quickly added, "You'll get an FSI car and your own office and the job pays well." Well, what more could I say except, "When do I start?" This suited the Indian half of the negotiation, but there was some concern on the part of the dean as to my lack of academic credentials to head a teacher training program. The dean even suggested that I be awarded an honorary degree because of my unique qualifications for the job. He said such was common practice in disciplines such as art and music. In the end, the program was set up so that I was an administrator and not on faculty. This allayed the fears of the academics in the College of Education. Staying put in Saskatchewan with this new opportunity also meant that Virginia and I decided to permanently separate.

It was at that moment that I began to understand some of the differences between my Odawa background and my Cree cousins. Rodney didn't understand that, among the Odawa, you don't make life-altering decisions on the spur of the moment. In fact, we avoid making any decisions at all as long as we can. Our motto has always been, "If you don't do anything, the problem will go away." When I went back to Ontario a few years ago to set up teacher education programs for Queen's University in my own First Nations communities, I rediscovered the Odawa/Ojibwe style. The most significant decision to come out of some of the meetings was to pick a date for the next meeting. In Saskatchewan I had learned that the Cree are risk-takers and make decisions on the run, like Rodney did when he hired me. I saw this in action over the years. Whenever I gave a speech encouraging change, I had to be careful what I recommended, because as sure as can be, some one of the many Crees in the audience would take my ideas and set out to implement them—immediately!

As I found out, it was my job to develop a program that would produce graduates to fulfil the expectations of the chiefs. The chiefs put a few more guidelines in place and were adamant that the Indian graduates get the same certification as all other teachers. The graduates were under no circumstances to get a certificate stamped "Indian" that restricted them from teaching anywhere they wanted. Furthermore, the chiefs did not want the students to have to commit to teaching on the reserve for so many years after graduation. They said that the Indian students who chose the teacher education program had to able to fulfil their dreams, too.

Therefore, the new task was to design, develop, and implement a program that produced Indian teachers who received the same credentials as other Saskatchewan teachers but who were equipped to change the education of Indian children in the province in accord with the wishes of the chiefs, communities, and parents while preparing children for their place in society.

In Saskatchewan, in 1972, only the University of Saskatchewan in Saskatoon and its Regina campus had the authority from the provincial government to deliver the courses of a teacher education program. However, the content of teacher education was approved by the Board of Teacher Education (BTE), a body made up of provincial government education officials, university personnel, and Saskatchewan educators. To ensure that the Indian Teacher Education Program's students received the same certification as other teachers, it was necessary to work with the university and the Board of Teacher Education. My first task was to develop a program that contained all the elements demanded by the university and the BTE but would also produce graduates who met the expectations of the chiefs. This was challenging because, in 1972, there were no models of programs for Indian teachers in Saskatchewan. We were breaking new ground.

To prepare to go to the BTE, Rodney and I, in good teacher fashion, got all the course outlines in the Standard A program for teachers and looked at their objectives, methodology, and content. It soon became apparent that we could agree with the objectives of the courses but that we would need to change the methodologies and content to "Indianize" the program. We developed a schema that showed how we would meet all the objectives of the various courses but would do it with Indian content and learning approaches. We were very thorough. The program would be based on an equal but parallel model for teacher education that mirrored the "regular" teacher education model at the University of Saskatchewan. We showed how we would provide the learning experiences, skills, and knowledge so that our students could obtain a Standard A certificate while, at the same time, obtaining a core of understandings, knowledge, and skills to equip them to be frontline troops in the revolution of Indian education. The BTE bought it, as did the university.

Not only did we have to satisfy the BTE but we had to get the approval of the various bodies within the university—the faculty of the College of Education, the faculty of the College of Arts and Science (because teachers had to have cognate disciplines as a base), the senate and the board of governors. Here it was the work of the faculty of the Indian and Northern Education Program, Dr. Andre Renaud, Jerry Hammersmith, Dr. Art Blue, and Don York, to make the case within the university. Whenever Dr. Blue came to work with his snakeskin tie on, it was the signal that he was going to some university meeting to sell the program. It soon became clear that there was a great deal of support within the College of Education and from the dean. Dr. Blue would take me with him to Regina to meet the appropriate people in government and the Department of Education. Other professors came forward to offer their services and it was evident that many saw this as an opportunity to try out ideas and break out of the traditional ways of teaching.

The acceptance of the program for the certification of our prospective students was just the beginning of our work. The vehicle that came with the job was essential in the first months of my new employment. I had to visit all the First Nations, introduce myself to the members of community education committees, check out the schools, explain the program, and meet the teachers and hopefully enlist their support. I visited some existing Native studies and teacher education programs, such as the Brandon University Teacher Education Program (BUNTEP) and the Program for the Education of Native Teachers (PENT), and courses taught at the University of North Dakota. I corresponded with Audie Dyer about the development of the Northwest Territories Teacher Education Program (NWTEP) and with personnel in Fairbanks working with the Alaskan Native people.

The program was so embraced by the establishment that when the minister of Education, Hon. Gordon MacMurchy, came to the College of Education he took credit for it— even though there was not a cent of provincial money in the program; it was fully funded by the federal government to produce teachers for on-reserve schools. After his enthusiastic speech, he was asked why he didn't sponsor some Metis students with provincial money. He agreed and was pressed for a number. That is how the Indian Teacher Education Program admitted five Metis students with each new intake!

Rodney Soonias accompanied me to meetings with Saskatchewan chiefs and community members when it was important to explain the relationship between the FSI, the cultural college, and the university within ITEP. I remember

one of these meetings in particular. Rodney picked me
up and told me that we were going to Cowessess reserve
at the request of Mary Ann Lavallee. I was still very new
to Indian politics in Saskatchewan and did not know that
Mary Ann Lavallee was known to ask the toughest questions and demand that she be satisfied with the answers
before she gave her approval to anything. She was a member of the Saskatchewan Native Women's Association,
which was organizing Native women in Saskatchewan and
instrumental in the development of the national Native
women's group.

I was so naive that I didn't know what we were heading
into, but I noticed that Rodney was driving slower and
slower as we got closer to Mary Ann's reserve. Rodney
was quite relieved when we survived the meeting relatively
unscathed. On the way home, he announced that we had
passed the most difficult test that we were likely to meet
in the communities and we should now be able to go
forward without worrying.

One of our other priorities in visiting reserves was to look
for potential students. It would have been so embarrassing
to get all the approvals for the program, hire the staff and
professors, and then have no one want to take the courses.
Research at the time showed that most Indian students did
not achieve their grade twelve graduation, so we knew
that we had to fill our seats with people who wanted to be
teachers, who had some experience in classrooms, such as
teacher aides, were mature, or had experience working with
children or in responsible positions. They were classified
as "adult admissions."

The Indian Teacher Education Program model was
based on ten principles:

1. *Indian Involvement*
    The program was conceived by Indian people; the training model was developed by Indian people—Rodney Soonias and me. Student applications were screened and interviews conducted by a panel consisting of Indian representatives. The cultural college funded part of the program and staff were involved in all aspects of it.

2. *Orientation Principle*
    The ITEP students spent the first semester orienting themselves to city life and the university. During this period, skills in reading, mathematics, and study habits were upgraded to meet all admission standards and to prepare for regular university work as well.

3. *Equal Certification*
    Equal certification was another fundamental principle of ITEP.

4. *Continuous Field Experiences*
    Continuous field experiences were built into the program. Students began student teaching midway through their first semester. Each semester included six weeks of student teaching.

5. *Coordination Between University Courses and Field Experiences*
    Efforts were made to decrease the gap between university experiences and actual teaching experiences. Prior to each student teaching session, ITEP staff contacted pre-identified cooperating

teachers to discuss possibilities of relating what students were taking in their current university courses with what would be taught in classrooms. Semesters were organized so that students spent six weeks on campus, three weeks in schools, two weeks on campus, three more weeks in schools, and the final week of the semester back on campus.

6. *Cooperative Planning Among Course Instructors*
Instructors in the cognate disciplines were encouraged to coordinate with the instructors of the methods courses, e.g., between the English professor and the language arts methods class instruction.

7. *Relevant Course Content*
There were attempts to develop background knowledge and competencies for teaching through content relevant to Native culture.

8. *Flexibility*
The principle of flexibility was illustrated in the organization of courses and in the teaching assignments. Because the ITEP class remained an intact group during the fall and spring semesters, daily time schedules could be more easily altered than the College of Education schedule. Sequencing of courses was altered with the university department schedules and availability of various instructors.

9. *Tutorial Aspect*
   Tutoring services were available for students taking academic courses. Individual, pairing, and group sessions were offered.

10. *Counselling Aspect*
    The counselling aspect involved individual counselling, couples counselling, family counselling, and group counselling. The program encouraged the students to become more aware of themselves and their relationships with other people.

These ten aspects guided our work and our relationships with our many partners. Student recruitment began with our partner, the Indian Cultural College. Liaison officers of the college's education component who were in the field and covered all reserves in the province were the first contacts. Simultaneously, counsellors from our other partner, Indian Affairs, disseminated information to potential candidates. Other organizations like the Saskatchewan Native Women played a role in recommending candidates for ITEP.

In developing the program in the College of Education, we had to have a team and were fortunate in hiring Myrtle Aldous, an experienced counsellor of Indian students. She was able to deal with the personal crises that the students inevitably encountered either in their academic or personal lives. She had a wonderful contagious laugh that convinced the students that ITEP was a happy place. Dr. Don Barnett, experienced with academic programs and the ways of a university, was a dynamo. He was the kind of guy who appeared scatterbrained but could accomplish more in a day than two other people. He was the motor of the operation who kept us moving in the right direction. He taught some courses and helped the students with their academic development. I taught the introductory Indian education courses and took it upon myself to build the students' belief in themselves. This entailed asking them what it meant to them to be Indian or Metis and to impress upon them that they needed to be proud of who they were. Since I loved teaching and working in the schools, most of the administration (i.e., the paperwork of the program—and there was lots of it, what with the college, the Department of Education, the cultural college, and Indian Affairs to report to) was efficiently handled by very competent assistants such as Joan Drummond and Beryl McCullough.

Don, Myrtle, and I were all expected to check in on new teachers conducting practicums, and we covered the roads of Saskatchewan together, as ITEP had student teachers all over the province. We worked well together and managed to laugh a lot. At that time the teacher training was only two and a half years, with nine weeks in the schools, practising the things learned in courses inside an actual classroom environment. One time, I chartered a plane from Buffalo Narrows to visit the northern schools; however, this proved to have its drawbacks. One of the students from Patuanak found out that a plane was chartered for the use of ITEP and commandeered it for trips to visit his friends and family around the north. I used to say, "Every program should have a Marius! He makes everyone else look *so* good!"

The recruits applied by letter, accompanied by letters of reference from Native people such as chiefs, school committee chairpersons, band administrators, school personnel, or former employers. Transcripts from the Department of Education were enclosed along with a letter from the applicant and the application for university entrance was completed.

Applications were scored by weighting such variables as age, marital status, children, academic background, category, employment experience on or off reserve, work experience in education (teacher aide, school committee work, etc.), fluency in a Native language, and experiences in summer courses or university training. Scores determined whether the candidate was admitted to the program or received a letter advising them on areas for improvement so they would be considered the next year.

The open interview was conducted largely by Native people representing the Indian Cultural College, ITEP personnel, and members of the staff of the Indian and Northern Education Program at the university. For our first intake, the interview team was Father Andre Renaud, head of Indian and Northern Education; Ed Lavallee, cultural liaison from the Indian Cultural College; and me. General personality factors and fluency in their Native language was evaluated during the interview. As I recall, we admitted one student, only to find out later that the one who came to the interview was not the one that had applied. It was later recommended that he might feel more at home in another profession!

One issue that we confronted was the question of whether we should accept husbands and wives at the same time. Some argued that they might be competitive and this would detract from the success of one or both. We were also aware of the distribution of students from across the province. We had to be evenhanded in taking students from as many reserves as possible. There was some effort by friends and relatives to influence our decisions. However, for the most part these first trainees who committed themselves to the program were real pioneers. They were idealistic, ambitious, and courageous. They were the trailblazers of Indian education in Saskatchewan. Most had never been to campus before. Finding the College of Education was their first challenge. Many had not been to Saskatoon before, so finding the university was a big problem for them. Most had never lived off the reserve before and the prospect of living in the city was formidable for many.

We believed that teachers who were themselves Indian or Metis would provide the Indian and Metis students in Saskatchewan's schools a more relevant and familiar schooling. We believed that these recruits had qualifications that could not be taught to non-Indian teachers. They had grown up with the cultural knowledge of their communities, knew the languages, and were aware of the cultural norms of the communities. They would know what life was like for parents and children and would have status in the community as someone who knew ways of communicating and ways of doing that reflected the communities' ways, as well as having knowledge of the social and attitudinal conditions of Indian and Metis life in Canada. The program would be built on the pride that the students had in their Indianness. It was important that the students and the Indian communities felt that the program was theirs and reflected their reality, way of life, values, and goals.

One of the most important tasks was to elicit the support of the Saskatchewan Teachers' Federation (STF). If the program was going to work, we had to have cooperating teachers. We had decided that the students should have a longer period of time in schools than was required in the regular Standard A program, which was the basic training program for teachers at the time. We also decided that the students should experience urban, rural, reserve, and northern experiences, if possible. Although it seemed like a good idea at the time, the logistics were formidable. Enthusiastic teachers were needed throughout the province. Student teacher supervision had to be coordinated with the College of Education placement office.

Teachers' schedules and workloads really were at the pleasure of the boards of education. Critical to the operation of the program was the involvement of the Saskatchewan Trustees Association, for provincial schools, and the Department of Indian Affairs, for most reserve schools. All of this had to be in place before the program could begin. However, time to work out the arrangements was provided in the first six months of the program when the students were placed in upgrading courses.

To gain the support of teachers and boards of education, I had to present the program to countless teacher workshops and conferences around the province. The first thing that had to be explained was why a special program for Indian teachers was needed. Many believed that everyone should be treated the same. I found that when I explained the contrast between the Indian worldview and the non-Indian worldview, the teachers would have an "aha" moment. Many had never thought about the fact that there were different ways to see the world.

Through summer school courses Dr. Andre Renaud had developed a cadre of teachers who recognized the need to understand the culture of students to maximize their learning. A network of teachers working in reserve and northern Native communities bonded during these courses and were independently developing materials suited to the students in the schools where they taught. They had a newsletter describing some of their projects and the success they were having. This group was open to having our students in their classrooms.

The student recruits' academic preparation for university was often limited. I think we may have had one grade twelve graduate apply. This meant that, within the program, we had to have academic and personal supports as well as the capacity to provide upgrading classes. Two areas were of particular concern: English and math. To graduate from the university at that time, a student had to pass first-year English. Furthermore, within the teaching certification process, a person had to have grade twelve math, even to teach elementary arithmetic. We were lucky that one of the math methods professors, Dr. Jim Beamer, volunteered to offer the math upgrading. He was superb. He tailored the course to each of the students and helped them to succeed in a subject that they were terrified of. I don't remember any complaints, and the students were able to achieve the level necessary for their certification.

English was another matter. Most of our students had difficulty with English and were English-as-a-second-language speakers. The subject was almost universally hated until we added a young, bright, Mohawk woman, Mary Claus, to our staff. She was an English major who loved literature and could work with students in such a way that they saw the beauty of the language and the relevance to their lives. Mary was from Tyendinaga Mohawk Territory in Ontario with a family tradition of education. She was the daughter of two teachers and grew up in a household where English literature, particularly poetry, was part of her life. Her love of the subject was a complement to the efforts of the English professors to make their course relevant. Mary's sense of humour eased students through many difficulties.

With new programs, and particularly with "Indian" programs, there is always the question of standards. Is it as good as the regular program? For most of us working in the program, we just knew what we were doing was right, but our secretary, who had been around the college for years and was constantly asked her opinion, came up with the best answer I ever heard. When asked if the program was "watered down," she replied, "Watered down? It's not watered down. It's beefed up."

The chiefs had high expectations for our students. At this time in Saskatchewan, Indian people knew that the state of education of their children was deplorable. The situation was well documented. A study of Saskatchewan students done in 1960, less than a decade before, found that seven out of every ten Indian students failed grade one. In federal day schools, only one of every four reached grades five to eight. Two-thirds of all Indian students, whether in residential or day schools, were one or more grades displaced (terminology used at the time to describe the situation that resulted when a child was not at the appropriate grade level for his or her age.) This displacement began early and students were very discouraged. By grade three, over 75 percent of all Indian students in Saskatchewan were age–grade displaced. It was no surprise, then, that less than two out of every three students reached grade eight; only one out of every six reached grade ten and only one out of every fifteen students reached grade twelve.

In 1960, the Saskatchewan government had reported to the Joint Committee of the Senate and the House of Commons on Indian Affairs that, "at the present time, a majority of Indian children in the province achieve only a limited education" characterized by low educational achievement rates, high failure rates, so-called age–grade retardation and early school leaving. Many Indian children quit school in grade five. Commenting on this pattern, researchers William Knill and Arthur Davis reached the following conclusion:

> The manifest and intended function of Northern [Saskatchewan] schools is, of course, training children for adult roles in modern Canadian society. But the latent function—the actual unintended result—of the . . . school effect is the education of Indian and Metis children for failure. (Knill, William D., and Arthur K. Davis, "Provincial Education in Northern Saskatchewan: Progress and Bog Down, 1944-1962." In *A Northern Dilemma, Vol. 1: Reference Papers*. Eds. Arthur K. Davis et al. Bellingham, WA: Western Washington State College, 1967, p 229)

The Indian and Northern Education Program had been created as a response to the failure of the schools. This program, at first, offered a summer course for teachers in Indian and northern communities to help them understand their role in the schooling of Indian and Metis children. The program was grounded in the belief that strengthening the students' cultural identity was critical to the academic success of Indian and Metis students. It taught teachers about the cultures of the children that they were teaching. This philosophy supported the development of a program to teach Indian and Metis people as teachers.

Schools in First Nations communities quickly took hold of the idea when they realized what *Indian Control of Indian Education* could mean for them. Can we ever forget "The Louse that Roared"? That louse was responsible for one of the first and most exciting experiments in Indian control of

Indian education in the country at Saskatchewan's James Smith First Nation. The federal policy of "Indian Control of Indian Education" was accepted in 1973. That was the same year that ITEP came into being. In January/February the *Saskatchewan Indian*, published an article entitled, "The Louse that Roared." It told of an incident in a school in Kinistino, Saskatchewan, when children from James Smith Reserve in attendance in the school were pulled aside and their hair inspected for lice. As it turned out, they had none. The parents reacted by pulling their children out of the school and refusing to let them return. Instead of letting their children go back to the offending school, the community decided, in accordance with the Indian Control of Indian Education policy of Indian Affairs, that they would educate their children at home on the reserve. A school administration was established, accommodation found, and staff hired, making James Smith Reserve one of the first reserves in Canada to assume control of their children's education.

In the 1970s, what made working in Saskatchewan Indian education so stimulating and rewarding was that the milieu was full of supportive educational initiatives. The Saskatchewan Indian Cultural College had elders to advise communities. Smith Atimoyoo developed materials such as the tipi model to show how values were taught in traditional culture. I remember how upset he was when he tried to teach non-Indian teachers who believed in the "free school" movement that the "Cree way" was a disciplined approach to life and learning, not a license for children to do what they wanted. He said people confused freedom with license. He said this was not the "Indian way." As he said, "The Indian way allowed freedom of individuals because the culture was based on discipline. Everyone knew what they must do. Survival of all depended on people having self-discipline."

The Indian Cultural College developed a curriculum department because, at that time, there was no material for teachers that reflected the social, cultural, and historical reality of Indian children from the community perspective. A community liaison function was established at the Indian Cultural College to aid communities and support them in implementing Indian control. Badgered and cajoled by John McLeod, co-chair of the Task Force on Indian Education, communities took necessary steps to bring the school back to the goals of the community. John was a dear friend and feared colleague. I was reamed out by him and inspired by him. He took me with him and was my entree into communities as far-flung as Cote First Nation and Stanley Mission. The time spent driving the Saskatchewan roads with John McLeod taught me more about life than years spent in libraries. He used to be so exasperated with my views, which he saw as limited to the academic context. And so his argument would always start with "Don't they teach you anything in that place?"

In 1973, John and I went to various Cree communities throughout the province, at the expense of Indian Affairs, I might add, to find six communities to pilot the first Cree language projects in Saskatchewan schools. At that time, I witnessed the incredible duo of John and Ida McLeod at work. Ida established the Indian Language Program at the cultural college, and she and John were a tireless, dedicated pair who could convince any audience of the value of both the Cree culture and Western contemporary education.

In Saskatchewan, Indian control of Indian education in those heady days seemed so clear. We would have a system of education starting with kindergarten and extending to the post-secondary level. We would control the content, process, and product. We would define the kind of skills, knowledge, and behaviours we wanted in our graduates and set up programs to ensure that those graduates were produced. It is hard to explain the power of a singular vision for a people. Everyone—students, parents, community elders, politicians, and educators—was on side and working towards the same goal: to take control of education for First Nations people in Saskatchewan. The power, the force, the energy that was released was incredible. Just look at what was accomplished in those few years—a revolution in Indian education in Saskatchewan.

We all understood our mission. It was to take over our own education and provide an education that recognized and affirmed the Indianness of our children. It was to ensure that our traditional knowledge, our community knowledge, our worldview and values became part of the schooling experience of our students at all levels in their education. We believed that to succeed in the Western educational system, our people had to be strong in their own cultural identity. We believed that we were going to develop generations of students who were going to be bilingual and bicultural. We believed that our survival as unique peoples depended on nothing less.

Smith Atimoyoo, who was trilingual and tricultural and who had been schooled in the residential school system and in a Western theological environment, passionately believed that the education of First Nations people had to start with an education in our own cultures. It was from this grounding in a dual education that Indian people were going to feel whole. To provide this kind of education was the mission of my generation of Indian educators in Saskatchewan.

After we had chosen our first intake and they had passed the orientation period and entered their first semester of university courses, as a staff we felt that we needed to speak to other people who were operating Native teacher education programs. In mid-October 1973, we organized a conference to pool information on the working operations of these programs. We wanted to hear from others facing the same challenges day-to-day. This was the first conference of its kind in Canada.

The conference program began with presentations in a session called "Perspectives of Native Teacher Education." The three presenters represented the major stakeholders of Native teacher education in Canada. J.B. Kirkpatrick, Dean of Education, University of Saskatchewan, set the tone for the conference in a speech entitled "Parameters on Native Teacher Education." The dean, in a very blunt way, said that he assumed that all those present held a common set of convictions:

> . . . that the educational system as it has operated until now has failed miserably to meet the needs of children of Native ancestry;

> . . . that the parents of these children, like all parents, should exercise a strong and indeed a determining influence on the kind of education which their children receive. Parents are now beginning to recognize and assume this responsibility;

> . . . that we need teachers who fully understand and appreciate the cultural background of the children whom they teach. It follows that we need more teachers of Native ancestry; and,

. . . that such teachers should then become agents of change—to improve the curriculum and procedures in the schools in which they teach in such a way as to make them more attractive and more meaningful to the children whom they teach.

The dean went on to say, "If we do not believe the four 'articles of faith' which I have just enunciated, I do not know what we are doing in the business of Native teacher education."

Dean Kirkpatrick said that in the next two days there were five major questions that had to be answered in relation to Native teacher education programs. These were:

What is the best way of selecting and of screening students in the program so that we do in fact recruit and develop teachers who are able to act as change agents in the schools to which they go?

What kind of experiences, academic and professional, should be provided for these students during their period of professional preparation? How and by whom should the content and sequence of classes be determined?

What kind of certification should they receive?

What employment opportunities are open to graduates, and what can we do to place them in situations in which they can make good use of the professional preparation they have had?

How can we evaluate the success of the programs in which we are engaged, both during the professional preparation period and when our graduates are on the job?

Clive Linklater, representing the National Indian Brotherhood, laid the groundwork for the conference as seen through Indian eyes. His address was entitled "The World as It Was, The World as It Is; The World as We Want It to Be." He began by describing traditional Indian education in the following way:

In the Indian world as it was, the people performed many tasks necessary to the smooth functioning of the tribe. These tasks were taught and passed on by the observation method (watch-and-do), by indirect instruction and individual teaching . . . .

Teaching-learning was a constant ongoing requisite shared in by the young and the old—the male and the female.

In the world as it was, the Indian people had a system of education that, in today's terms, paralleled individualized instruction, tutorials, evening classes, week-end classes, daily lessons, field trips.

But, the Indian tribes did not have that strange white man's institution—a building labelled 'a school'! And the Indian tribes did not have a class of people labelled 'teachers.' It was the function of everyone to teach and learn . . . .

In the world as it was, the education of Indian people was participative and dynamic, involving the whole community, at every level of community life, every day, all day . . . .

In the world as it was, education was integrated into the fabric of the tribal community. It was not a segmented, institutionalized, and closed system operated by professionals whose allegiance is to the perpetuation of the system itself rather than to the total community which it was originally set out to serve.

In the world as it was, the education process served the people; the people did not serve the system.

Linklater went on to describe "the world as it is." He began:

In the world as it is, the present Canadian education system does not serve the Indian people, nor is their traditional system fully operative. The results of this are tragic!

He demonstrated the tragic results of the dropout rates of over 90 percent of Indian students in high schools and over 60 percent in elementary schools. Most Indian people of thirty-five years or older had little or no schooling at all. In the world as it is, lack of education compounded the problems: 58 percent of Indian people unemployed; Indian people made up 40 percent of inmates; life expectancy of adult Indians was lower than the national average; and the rate of infant mortality double the national average.

Social problems were rampant: alcoholism; family- and child-abandonment; illegitimacy; separation leading to single-parent households and female-headed households; discrimination and prejudice; personal alienation; and group disgust. Linklater added:

> The schools, instead of bridging the gap between white and Indian, are increasing it.
> In the World as it is, the education of Indian people has been termed as "education for failure."

He concluded this section of his speech saying, "What a sad commentary on the state of the civilization of this country!! The civilization that set out to civilize savages!"

Linklater concluded his remarks by looking at the "world as we want it to be." He began:

> The difficulty in producing Indian teachers for Indian schools, or white teachers for Indian schools, or Indian teachers for white schools, is not a lack in the techniques, or the "how" this can be done, but in the attitudes and beliefs that exist in the white people's minds (and have now been engendered in some Indian peoples' minds) that Indians are inherently uneducable or so pronounced in savagery as to be unredeemable.

Linklater said that the ideas persisted so strongly that teachers forgot the basic principles that were the very foundation of their own educational system: "Start where the student is," and "Go from the known to the unknown!" Education for Indian students started where the student wasn't and proceeded from the unknown to the unknown.

Then, in looking for what was wrong, instead of asking, "What is wrong with our system?" or "What is wrong with our methods?" the educators asked, "What is wrong with those damn dumb Indians?"

Linklater told of the world as the Indians wanted it to be. He said the teachers:

. . . will be of the particular tribe they are teaching;

. . . will be thoroughly knowledgeable about the past and present of the particular community in which they teach;

. . . will be thoroughly knowledgeable about the past and present of the particular tribe they teach;

. . . will be thoroughly knowledgeable about the past and present of the immigrant peoples of this country;

. . . will be knowledgeable about the peoples and cultures of other countries and other lands;

. . . will be fluently bilingual and specially trained in teaching a second language whether English or French;

. . . will use the particular community, including its people, as a daily source and resource to the school;

. . . will recognize that the school is of the community, to be used by the community.

And Linklater added:

if the teachers were white, they would think of Indian people as people, who are as educable and as thirsty for knowledge as any people can be. . . . [Teachers must think of themselves] as people whose role it is to stimulate, to agitate other people to the full use of their faculties, and not set themselves up as the accumulators and infallible purveyors of all the past wisdom of all the past ages.

According to Linklater, teachers, in the world as Indians want it to be, must recognize that "the human person is not only an intellectual being, but a spiritual being, and the school must serve the student's soul as well as his mind."

Teachers, in the world as Indians want it to be, would teach "how to learn, how to think, and how to ACT!"

Linklater had advice for the teacher training institutions. He said that in the world as we want it to be, the teacher training institutions:

. . . will immediately allow into their halls Indian people from the educational continuum of the illiterate to the possessor of a graduate degree who show the skill, ability and aptitudes to become teachers;

. . . will actively recruit such Indian people;

. . . will develop techniques to allow the Indians' own mastery of knowledge-gaining and knowledge-spreading to be used in the training of teachers;

. . . will create special agencies or work in conjunction with existing or projected Indian institutions to develop a method and philosophy of education amenable and adaptable to Indian perspectives;

. . . will, if necessary, leave teacher training of Indian people, or for Indian people, to Indian people, if the institution's existing mandates are so inflexible as to disallow experimentation, diversity and innovation;

. . . will examine their code of "professionalism" in relation to "qualifications" to allow the Indian people to make up the long years of educational lag because they were considered ineducable.

The wish of the National Indian Brotherhood was for teachers who would be taught and then teach that the purpose of schools is the pursuit of knowledge. Teachers would be taught to begin where the student is and to start from the known and move to the unknown, and to do this, the teacher of Indian students must know what is known by the Indian student. The Indian community should teach them. Community members could if community people were part of the school.

Teachers needed to recognize that Indian knowledge is oral "and the preservers of that culture are the elders. Their knowledge should be recorded in some form in order to preserve the legends, beliefs and accounts of the past, so their descendants can know who they are today, in order to survive tomorrow." Teachers must teach that the Indian students are the descendants of Tecumseh, Poundmaker, and our own tribal forefathers.

Linklater concluded by saying:

The teachers will be taught that Indian students are
of this land, Canada; not as it is, but as it was, and
as we want it to be.

The third perspective was presented by I.E. Fitzpatrick
representing the Department of Indian and Northern
Affairs, Ottawa, who thanked the organizers for allowing
him to speak at "the first national Native teacher education
conference to be held in Canada."

Mr. Fitzpatrick quoted extensively from the *Indian
Control of Indian Education* document, ending the analysis
by saying that teacher education ramifications appeared on
almost every page. He summarized the long-range teacher
education goals to be:

. . . an ever-increasing supply of native teachers,
guidance workers and paraprofessionals to serve
the Indian student population in federal schools,
provincial schools, and territorial schools;

. . . a curriculum aimed at making the schools the
"models of excellence" which Indian parents hope for;

. . . the development of appropriate instructional
media materials correlated with the improved school
curricula;

. . . in collaboration with Native parents, Native
organizations, Native educational/cultural centres,
designing and arranging for courses and programs
for the training and the development of educational
personnel, which will guarantee a constant source of

trained and certified teachers, guidance counsellors, and paraprofessionals for the future; and

. . . the production or assisting in the production of materials which would help make each Native tribe better known to the forty-nine other tribes and the other forty ethnic groups which comprise the rest of Canada. This would be a much needed service to the rapidly increasing number of non-Indian schools now providing courses in Indian studies.

Mr. Fitzpatrick described the Native teacher supply requirements. Using the last school year, there were about 30,000 Native children in federal schools and approximately 44,000 Native children in non-federal schools. Fitzpatrick used the teacher–student ratio of one teacher for every twenty children and concluded that about 3,700 Native teachers would be needed. Then, Native specialist teachers, guidance workers, administrators, supervisors, and paraprofessionals would be needed. The number of qualified Native teachers in federal schools at that time was 125. The number in provincial schools was unavailable.

It was estimated by the official that, for every eight to ten Native teachers in the classroom, at least one Native teacher trainee must be in training to offset losses to the teaching force. If all Native children were being taught by Native teachers, 350 to 400 Indian teacher trainees would be needed in the system. There were 300 in training at the time. Fitzpatrick described the support available for teacher trainees. He explained that the education branch was conducting a nationwide study into the recruitment, training, and certification of Native teachers and paraprofessionals to determine how the recommendations of the policy paper could best be implemented. He emphasized that the study was conducted for Indian people to identify Indian problems and Indian solutions to Indian problems with the assistance of those "who are competent to help."

Fitzpatrick instructed the conference on "a concatenation of that which constitutes the material, formal, efficient and final causes of Indian education in federal schools and joint schools" (with an accompanying chart). He emphasized the need for awareness of all the linkages in Indian education. He suggested one solution would be the inauguration of a modern Indian educational communication system.

The official from the Education Branch, Department of Indian and Northern Affairs, Ottawa, described the new Canadian cultural commonwealth, "*a most exciting, a most refreshing juncture in our national life.*" He suggested this new iteration of Canada was reminiscent of the idea of "confederacy" of many tribes in the olden days. He concluded that the pivotal question for the future would certainly be:

> How can the perennial values of our first citizens be enshrined, defended and perpetuated in the newer concept of national life and national unity?

In answering his own question, he said, "It could be that what we are doing here, our concern for Native teacher education in Canada will be more than just a little help!"

These three statements by the most important stakeholders in Indian education in Canada established the context for the discussion of individual programs that followed. Nine programs sent delegates, including the University of Alaska, University of Alberta, Brandon University, University of Calgary, Université du Québec à Chicoutimi, Teacher

Education Program of Northwest Territories, University of Saskatchewan, University of South Dakota, and the Winnipeg Centre Project. The programs presented their contact people, program objectives, funding sources, course descriptions, unique aspects of the program, impact on Native education, and written comments from students.

Father Andre Renaud gave a conference closing statement. The first purpose of the conference was to establish precisely what was going on in Indian teacher training in North America and to allow people from various agencies to meet one another. He said the conference had attained its objective.

In reviewing the major achievements of the conference, he identified the following:

. . . hearing from the major stakeholders (the university, National Indian Brotherhood, and the Department of Indian Affairs) on the state of things in Indian Education from their perspective;

. . . beginning the dialogue among institutions, agencies and programs for Native teacher education—listening to the descriptions of programs;

. . . learning from each other—recognizing problems and solutions;

. . . identifying the need for the Indian people to join the dialogue;

. . . acknowledging the need for current students to be in the dialogue, "Our programs are really their program";

. . . flexibility at the universities to meet the diverse needs of different Indian people;

. . . the importance of advocates within the institutions, "program friends," who can do a certain amount of "pulling and pushing" so that the necessary accommodations take place;

. . . need for university professors who are advocates for Native teacher education programs to get together to discuss "how" to make things happen internally in the institutions;

. . . program flexibility so that things can be changed or added as the needs of the Indian people are identified;

. . . every bit of knowledge that has been taken out from Indian communities in the past, whether by linguists, archaeologists, anthropologists, etc. as well as everything learned from other people all over the world and accumulated in the university library and other departments, all this knowledge, plus all the skills to be found there anywhere in the world is the property of all people; and

. . . all of the knowledge collected and studied by the university must be open and available to the Indian people. Most of the information on the history, traditions and languages of Indians has been written just for university people to understand. It is time to give back to the Indian people what has been borrowed or taken out by university people over the years.

I was very proud of what we had accomplished. My staff had organized this one-of-a-kind gathering. The participation was outstanding. Government representatives came from the Ministry of Education, Ontario; the Department of Indian and Northern Affairs, Regina; the government of the Yukon Territory; the Education Branch, Department of Indian and Northern Affairs; the Department of Indian and Northern Affairs, British Columbia; and the Department of Colleges and University Affairs, Manitoba. University representatives came from the University of Saskatchewan, the University of Alaska, the University of South Dakota, Brandon University, Université du Québec à Chicoutimi, the University of Manitoba, the University of British Columbia, the University of Calgary, the University of Alberta, University College of the North, and Simon Fraser University.

Programs in attendance, some that made presentations, included: Indian and Northern Education Program, University of Saskatchewan; Winnipeg Centre Project; Institute for Northern Studies, University of Saskatchewan; IMPACTE, Brandon University; Centre Satellite Program, University of South Dakota; ARTTC, University of Alaska; Intercultural Education Program, University of Alberta; Bilingual Education Program, University of South Dakota; Teacher Education Program, Chesterfield Inlet, Northwest Territories; and Indian Students' University Program, University of Calgary. Indian organizations involved were: National Indian Brotherhood, Ottawa; Quebec Indian Association, Village Huron, Quebec; and Sagkeeng Education Authority, Pine Falls, Manitoba.

This was the beginning of an exciting collaboration among people and institutions engaging in training Indian and Metis teachers. We had the same goal: improving the education of Native children. We followed this conference with the creation of the Canadian Indian Teacher Education Program (CITEP), an organization that met annually in different centres. It was a powerful network that allowed us to examine what we were doing alongside people who were involved in the same enterprise. We were energized and faced the future with enthusiasm.

8. WORKING FOR CHANGE

I n 1975, my son Daryl came to live with me and stayed three years. That same year I received my masters of education degree in Indian and Northern Education from the University of Saskatchewan. Dr. Art Blue, a psychologist interested in psycholinguistics, guided my research into the limits of animate/inanimate verb usage in Ojibwe. This primary research peeled away the English-based definitions of the terms that had been used to define the internal dynamics of Ojibwe. I was interested in learning how Ojibwe worked from within the language. As a speaker, I wanted to make a contribution to the study of the Ojibwe language that a non-speaker could not make. I had studied linguistics in my BEd program and knew the theories of language and the terminology used by linguists.

I concluded that within the Ojibwe language the dichotomy that dictated what verb was used was not animate versus inanimate. For any inanimate noun could, at some times, under certain circumstances, be animate. For example, a growing tree is animate. When the tree is cut down, it is inanimate. When it is carved, it becomes animate again.

An Ojibwe speaker makes this adjustment naturally. I found that children acquire these nuances in a developmental way, with older children being more correct in their verb usage.

After completing my MEd, I realized that without more education, I was not going to advance at the university. ITEP was firmly established. We had had our first graduates. The program staff was strong and the Indian communities had taken ownership. I decided the time was right to pursue my PhD. Finding a university was tricky, as Indian and Northern Education was not a discipline recognized in other universities. Searching through various university calendars, I thought that the Comparative Education Program at the University of Calgary was the best fit. I applied and was accepted to begin my advanced studies in the fall term of 1975.

My major had been anthropology at Saskatoon, but since the Comparative Education Program did not have an anthropology stream, I became a sociologist. This was not a comfortable discipline for me because it stressed the "problem approach" and my people always came out as deviations from the norm, which was never interpreted as a positive! It reminded me of my IQ score in teachers' college. My studies in Saskatchewan had emphasized the cultural strengths of my people and the basis of ITEP had been to build up the pride of my students in their language, culture, and history. While at Calgary, through the sociological approach, I was studying the failures of my people.

The Red Lodge was the one place on campus where I felt that Indians were seen as people with potential. Evelyn Moore, whom I had met at our first national conference on Indian teacher training, watched over the Red Lodge with motherly eyes. She immediately invited me to join her staff. Everyone who worked there was bubbly and cheerful, the perfect antidote to the cold, unfriendly atmosphere of the closed doors and dark corridors on the ninth floor of the education tower. The Red Lodge was my refuge during my two years at the University of Calgary.

One of my classes was taught by Dr. Matthew Zachariah. This class looked at issues of sociology in a global context. One of the major papers that I wrote, entitled "The Indian and Equality," allowed me to develop the context to issues of Indian and human rights in northern Ontario. The research took me back to the first encounters of Europeans and Indians of the Americas. I found that, since the days of Columbus reaching the shores of North America, European philosophers and great thinkers were tasked with defining who we were, how we were to be treated, whether we were human beings, and what rights we had. What I found was that the same questions were being raised in Canada in 1977.

The paper I wrote was a seminal document for me. I analyzed intellectual debates in Indian education and arguments about our human rights that I had been thinking about since the "Human Rights and the Indians of Northern Ontario" conference. I concluded that to evaluate the concept of equality in relation to the Indian people of Canada "it was imperative to have an understanding of the historical development of the status of the Indian people."

Previously in my education, what I learned of our history came from the whispers I heard in the community and from the other boys. What I had learned of our international relationships I had learned from the Jesuits, where a strong emphasis had been placed on our people's barbarism in relation to dealings with the Roman Catholic priests. As an experienced teacher in Ontario schools, I had never been called upon to study the place of our people in the

Canadian mosaic (as I had been taught that Canada was in my sociology courses). Furthermore, I had not been called upon to teach our students about the relationship. This paper helped me to study our people's experience within the context of these larger philosophical and theological questions, as well as the historical, legal, and political questions related to my own experience.

Europeans brought to the Americas their views of how societies were and should be structured. They did not acknowledge that we saw the world in a different but equally valid way. They justified their view of the world with theological and philosophical treatises. They tried to fit our existence into their worldview. The cynic might say that our people received equal treatment when we were needed allies in economic pursuits or in times of war. The Europeans, regardless of their religious or philosophical opinions of Indians, quickly delegated equality to us when it was expedient for them.

Surprisingly, the first question that the Europeans tackled was: "Are these creatures people in the sight of God?" A search of the Bible by eminent theologians of Portugal and Spain found no reference to a "red" race of people. Hence Pope Paul III issued an edict, the *Bull Sublimus Deus*, in 1537, stating that, in fact, my people were human beings. How incredible!

Even though our status as members of the human race was settled, the question remained: "How are members of the red race to be treated?" It was the Spaniards who tackled this one. To justify the bloody conquests of the Conquistadores and to clear the conscience of the Christian Spaniards, Juan Ginés de Sepúlveda called on Aristotle's theory of equality, which stated that there were natural slaves and natural masters, and Thomas Aquinas's argument in favour of "just wars" being fought by Christians against infidels. Sepúlveda applied these two theories to the Indigenous peoples of the New World.

On the other hand, theologian Bartolomé de las Casas passionately argued that, as human beings, our people had to be treated with love, gentleness, and kindness. Las Casas argued that the way to civilize any people was not by the use of force but by bringing religion and education to them. Las Casas declared that "God" would not allow any nation to exist that might not "be persuaded and brought to a good order and way of life and made domestic, mild and tractable provided the method that is proper and natural to men is used" (Las Casas, *Apologética historia sumaria*, ca. 1550).

I found that European nations approached our humanity differently. The Jesuit missionaries to the Indians in Brazil were sskeptical of the ability of those Indians to become true members of the faith. This was the experience on which the missionaries landing in Quebec based their behaviour towards our people when they arrived. The Jesuit mandate in New France was to Christianize and civilize the Indians and to establish the Catholic Church and the French nation as powers within New France. (S.R. Mealing, ed. *The Jesuit Relations and Allied Documents: A Selection*, Toronto: McClelland and Stewart, 1963, pp. viii–ix)

The Jesuits judged Indians by their own Christian values and the lifestyle of France at the time. What I read in the *Jesuit Relations* gave me a new understanding of the Jesuits and their history with my people. Recruits were given the following instructions in 1637:

> leaving a highly civilized community, you fall into the hands of barbarous people who care but little for your philosophy or your theology. All the fine

qualities which might make you loved and respected
in France are like pearls trampled under the feet of
swine, or rather mules, which utterly despise you
when they see you are not as good pack animals
as they are. If you could go naked, and carry the
load of a horse upon your back you would be wise
according to their doctrine, and would be recognized
as a great man, otherwise not. (Mealing, *The Jesuit
Relations*, p. 50)

The Jesuits at Spanish, Ontario, carried this attitude into
our education in the twentieth century. In annual retreats
at residential school, we were upbraided for our barbarism.
We were told that we could never aspire to the level of the
priests. We were admonished for the sins of our ancestors.
One would have thought that the attitudes would have
changed in the intervening more than three centuries,
but they hadn't. The Jesuits perpetuated them with us at
Garnier Residential School and, I am sure, taught the same
attitudes to the non-Indian students in their other schools.

Our people passed from the tutelage of the French to
the "protection" of the British. The Royal Proclamation
of 1763 recognized us as separate and sovereign people
ruled by our own laws and capable of making alliances
and treaties with other sovereign nations, while at the
same time restricting our ability to make decisions about
our own lands. So, within the Royal Proclamation, the
British did not consider our nations as equal nations but as
nations that needed the protection of a benevolent power
to maintain our own independence.

This was a time of confusion for our people. Not only
were our allies, the French, no longer in the picture but
our relationships with the British were ambiguous. At first

we were regarded as allies in the wars with the Americans. Then, as the settlers came and wanted land, we were asked to sign treaties giving up ownership to our lands. My own history was tied to this development. In 1836, in negotiations between my people and Sir Francis Bond Head, Lieutenant Governor of Upper Canada, Bond Head explained how the British felt towards us and our rights:

> In all parts of the world farmers seek for uncultivated land as eagerly as you, my red children, hunt in your forest for game. If you would cultivate your land then it would be considered your own property, in the same way as your dogs are considered among yourselves to belong to those who have reared them, but uncultivated land is like wild animals and your Great Father who has hitherto protected you, has now great difficulty in securing it for you from the whites who are hunting to cultivate. (J.L. Morris, *Indians of Ontario*, Toronto: Ontario, Department of Lands and Forests, 1943, pp. 27–28)

For me, this explained much about the relationship of my people with the Crown. Bond Head demonstrated an ignorance of our history. We had practised agriculture for several hundred years, producing corn to trade with the fur trade companies. Subsequently, the corn and maple sugar that we produced were shipped by the shipload to big American cities such as Chicago. We were no longer respectfully addressed as the most "faithful" ally. Now the tone of the negotiations had changed to the tone used with small children. We were chastised like children for not living up to the parental expectations. We were no longer seen as "equals." Bond Head's tone reminded me of the tone that an Indian Affairs official had used to me when I was implementing the Indian Teacher Education Program. In response to a question, the official would talk down to me like I was a child, even though I was asking as an educator employed at the university. More painfully, it reminded me of the way that Kohkwehns was treated by the Indian agent when she asked for the support that she was entitled to. It had always made me sad to see my beloved elder/teacher treated like she didn't know anything.

I found that pre-Confederation legislation eroded our rights based on the moral judgment of legislators that we were "uncivilized" if we chose to live in our traditional manner. It was determined that, because of our differences from other British citizens, we required special legislation: one, to protect us from others; two, to restrain our vices; and three, to regulate our passage from uncivilized to civilized state. This was all new to me because, in Buzwah Day School and in the Jesuit Residential School, I learned nothing of my people's history and, suffice it to say, nothing about the relationship of Canada's various governing nations with our people.

The treaties and post-Confederation legislation answered the question, "Who are these creatures?" The legislation defined who we were, what rights we had, where we could go, who we could marry, and a myriad of things governing the minutiae of our lives. We became even less "equal." We learned about these things when we experienced the power of the Indian agent on our lives. Although very low in the hierarchy of the Department of Indian Affairs, as the local representative of the law, the Indian agent had a repressive effect on our lives.

One of the issues I discussed in the paper had direct impact on my own family. My first cousin was Jeannette Corbiere

Lavell; her father was my mother's brother, my Uncle Adam. In 1970, Jeannette married David Lavell, a non-Indian, and received notification from the Department of Indian Affairs and Northern Development that she was no longer considered an Indian according to section 12(1)(b) of the *Indian Act*, which stated: "12(1) The following persons are not entitled to be registered, namely . . . (b) a woman who married a person who is not an Indian unless that woman is subsequently the wife or widow of a person described in section 11" (*Indian Act*, RSC 1970, c 1-6). This would mean that her children would not be "Indian." They could not live on the reserve, own land, or inherit family property. They could not receive treaty benefits or participate in band councils and political or social affairs of the community and could not be buried in cemeteries with their ancestors.

In 1960, the *Canadian Bill of Rights* spelled out the basic human rights of Canadian citizens by virtue of their Canadian citizenship. It clearly established one's civil rights without distinction of race, colour, creed, or sex. On the strength of the *Canadian Bill of Rights*, Jeannette took her case to county court. In June 1971, she lost. In October 1971, the Lavell case was heard in the Federal Court of Appeal, which ruled unanimously in Jeannette's favour. This decision was appealed to the Supreme Court of Canada. On August 27, 1973, the Supreme Court, in a five to four ruling, held that while both the *Indian Act* and the *Canadian Bill of Rights* are acts of Parliament and that, while the *Canadian Bill of Rights* does assure one's human rights, to change the *Indian Act* would require an act of Parliament and therefore as such it would supersede the *Canadian Bill of Rights*. I concluded that any human rights that Canadian Indians may have were only those defined and contained in the *Indian Act*.

Speaking in Vancouver in 1969, Prime Minister Trudeau provided his view of the human rights of our people:

You're at a crossroad—the time is now to decide whether the Indians will be a race apart in Canada or whether they will be Canadians of full status. And this is a difficult choice. It must be a very agonizing choice to the Indian people themselves because, on the one hand they realize that if they come into the society as total citizens they will be equal under the law but they risk losing certain of their traditions, certain aspects of culture, and perhaps even certain of their basic rights. This is a very difficult choice for them to make, and I don't think we want to try and force the pace on them any more than we can force it on the rest of Canadians. But here again is a choice which is in our minds: Whether Canadians as a whole want to continue treating the Indian populations as something outside, a group of Canadians with which we have treaties, a group of Canadians who have, as many Indians claim, aboriginal rights, or whether we will say forget the past and begin today . . . ."

The Prime Minister continued,

It's inconceivable, I think, that in a given society one section of the society have a treaty with the other section of the society. We must be all equal under the laws, and we must not sign treaties amongst ourselves. (Pierre Elliott Trudeau, part of speech delivered in 1969 in Vancouver. In Bowles et al., *The Indian*, pp. 71–72)

Thus, in 1969, Pierre Elliott Trudeau articulated his discomfort with the concept of "special status." For him the only road to "equality" for us was to remove our "special status." Our Indian leaders did not agree with this belief. In 1970, the chiefs of Alberta said, in part:

> We reject this policy. We say that recognition of Indian status is essential for justice. Retaining the legal status of Indians is necessary if Indians are to be treated justly. Justice requires that the special history, rights and circumstances of Indian people be recognized. (Bowles et al., *The Indian*, p. 219)

Most of Canada's Indians supported the Alberta chiefs. The platform of the regional Indian organizations was: "We have special rights vested in the land by our ancestors and is our heritage to keep, remove it and we end up with nothing. Our special rights must be protected and maintained" (Ibid.). At that time, for Indian people in Canada, the road to equality lay in the maintenance of our inequality.

Indian people believed that equal opportunity and equal access to the benefits of society was the equality that really mattered to them. Education was seen as the most urgent area of concern. This is why the National Indian Brotherhood published the *Indian Control of Indian Education* policy paper in 1972. It was accepted as policy by the federal government. Finally, Indian parents and local communities were allowed by the federal government to become part of the process of educating our children. It was this change that led to the development of the Indian Teacher Education Program and my career as a teacher of teachers.

I pointed out that, for our people, education was a weapon in the new nationalism, a unifying force for all Indian communities and individuals, but at the same time a "consciousness raiser." An awareness of our heritage, a new pride and identity, a belief in a fulfilling philosophy on life and values unchanged by time, was brought into the modern society. A new generation of Indian people would then set a new definition for our equality.

A review of my people's relationships with Europeans and legislation showed a concerted effort by the newcomers to determine for us our place within society. The legislation crafted by the Europeans was founded on the Darwinian assumption that societies were on a continuum from "uncivilized" to "civilized," with Europeans being the most civilized. Our people were assumed to be less civilized than the Europeans and the legislation was formulated to bring our people to the same level of civilization as the Europeans. The underlying attitude led to more and more laws made on behalf of our people, for the protection of our people, which left us fewer and fewer areas of life which we could decide for ourselves. In the name of protecting us, the legislators divested us of our human rights until, within the *Indian Act,* an "Indian" became a "legal entity" subjected to all the legal restrictions contained in the act.

I pointed out that we had always wanted to be recognized for our own reasons. In 1977, our people had a different interpretation of the equality we wanted for ourselves. We wanted equal opportunity and equal access to the benefits of the larger society, but at the same time we wanted to retain our special status within the Canadian context.

My assessment of the Indian and equality was that maybe it would have been more desirable for our people to be declared natural slaves because the slaves received their freedom over 100 years ago while, over that same 100 years, our freedom as Indian people had been systematically eroded!

After two years at the University of Calgary, I had finished all my course work and candidacy exams. It was time to get back to work. I applied for a position with the Indian and Northern Education Program at the University of Saskatchewan and was accepted. Life on faculty began. Although I was not finished my dissertation, I was regarded as a colleague by the other faculty members. I was an accepted member of the "fraternity." I had always loved teaching and working with graduate students was just an extension of that.

During my absence, negotiations to become an affiliated college between the Saskatchewan Indian Cultural College and the University of Saskatchewan had broken down. In the meantime, Dr. Lloyd Barber had moved from the University of Saskatchewan to the newly established University of Regina (formerly the University of Saskatchewan's Regina campus) as president. He had worked with the Indian leadership while at the University of Saskatchewan and as Treaty Commissioner. He invited the Saskatchewan Indian Cultural College to come to the University of Regina as a federated college. In 1976, the Saskatchewan Indian Federated College opened its doors at the University of Regina. The cultural college moved off the University of Saskatchewan campus and left a very large hole in Indian resources on campus. I missed the camaraderie and stimulation of meeting, talking, joking, and delving into the meaning of our lives with other Indians. It also left a big gap in the resources available on campus to support Indian students.

254 THE BOY FROM BUZWAH

Teacher education programs for Indian and Metis people were expanding. The Northern Teacher Education
Program (NORTEP) had developed. Students from northern
communities were employed by the school board in the
north, spending their time in the schools, except when they
went to La Ronge for classes in intensive one-week sessions.
This model brokered classes from both of the provincial
universities. Instructors travelled to La Ronge and received
accommodation and payments for travel and sustenance
from NORTEP. As the Indian and Northern Education classes
were part of the program, I was one of the first instructors
to teach in the program. Travelling the north, to a part of
the province that looked a lot like the part of the shield I
came from, was very exciting for me. The students were
not jaded by city life and were strong, passionate advocates
for providing northern children with the best education
they could. The members of the NORTEP staff were eager
to discuss, debate, and challenge current ideas about Indian
and Metis education. A trip to NORTEP was invigorating.
In addition to NORTEP, I taught in northern communities
such as Montreal Lake Cree Nation for the Saskatchewan
Indian Federated College and had meetings with northern
superintendents about Indian and Northern Education
Program courses for northern teachers.

My support of the Federation of Saskatchewan Indians
(Federation of Saskatchewan Indian Nations after 1982, and
Federation of Sovereign Indigenous Nations in 2016) had
started when I was hired for ITEP. The same year that ITEP
had come into existence, the FSI had decided that there was
also a need for Indian social workers. The Indian Social
Work Education Program (ISWEP) was offered in Saskatoon,
even though the School of Social Work was in Regina. I
soon became part of the instructing staff for ISWEP. These

students were just the opposite of the northerners. For the most part, they were coming into social work because they had had personal experience with the child welfare system or social services. They wanted to use their own experience to make things better for Indians who came in contact with these systems. As students, they were talkative and forceful in their opinions. The biggest challenge I had was to keep them focused on what I was trying to teach them because they had so much they wanted to teach me!

When I returned from Calgary, I found that my role as a faculty member was very different from the role I had as the head of ITEP. I was now the institutional advocate for Indian and Metis students and programs within the university. NORTEP needed a great deal of support and development within the College of Education. The Saskatchewan Urban Native Teacher Education Program (SUNTEP) was in the development stage and needed a voice within the faculty and committees. At the same time, I had the support of my colleagues in the Indian and Northern Education Program. Del Koenig had taught and consulted in the far north. She had been in Pelly Bay in the Northwest Territories (today's Kugaaruk in Nunavut) when the inhabitants still lived off the land. She was a wealth of knowledge and a font of new exciting ideas. Audie Dyer had experience in the Northwest Territories, too. He had been the director of the Northwest Territories Teacher Education Program, the first Aboriginal teacher education program in the country. He attracted northern students and teachers to the program. His style was combative, seasoned with humour. He was the best supporter the teacher education programs in Saskatchewan could hope to have. We were a formidable team eager to work with the communities—hard workers always there for graduate students.

With my added educational experience, I was immediately thrust into working with graduate students. When
we had started ITEP we had had to say no to the use of our
students as a convenient Indian and Metis sample population
for every sociology professor and grad student on campus.
Many have criticized us for not doing research on the program when we had the chance. As a staff, and in keeping
with the wishes of the FSI, we felt that we had to avoid
making our students the "red" objects of academic study.
They had enough to deal with. However, as a supervisor
of grad students, there were many topics to which I could
steer non-Indian students without overwhelming our
students or communities.

I had the opportunity to teach students at ITEP, which
was, by then, an integral part of the College of Education.
The systems of support for the students were firmly in place.
The students were becoming familiar with the university
and city because others had gone before them. I was starting
to see the children of former students, nieces and nephews,
and family groupings, to say nothing of community clusters.
This way there was a student and community support system
that blanketed the students and shielded them from many
of the concerns of earlier cohorts.

When in Calgary, I had become involved in research
conducted by the Canadian Institute for Research (CIR). In
the next few years, I was part of the CIR evaluation team
when the evaluation was related to work with First Nations
or Metis people. In 1978, we evaluated the work of the
Centre for Training, Research and Development (CENRAD)
Corporation, Prince Albert. I was also part of the CIR
team evaluating the Centre for Training Research for the
Department of Indian Affairs and Northern Development
and the Industrial and Training Research Corporation,

Rivers, Manitoba, in 1980 and the development of research instruments for the study "Native Integration in the Oil Sands Region" in 1980–81.

• • •

Back home on Manitoulin Island, changes were coming. All high-school students from the island were integrated into a single high school. Indian and non-Indian students were going to be schooled together in the same facility for the first time in the history of Manitoulin Island. In this new era of the Indian Control of Indian Education policy, the United Chiefs and Councils of Manitoulin wanted to ensure that the Indian students were successful in the schools they were attending. I was principal researcher for the United Chiefs and Councils of Manitoulin in secondary school education of Indian children of the Manitoulin District and in a study of the elementary schooling for children from the six reserves of the Manitoulin District. The reports showed areas where students were not successful and where they were. The recommendations were far-reaching and the chiefs passed a resolution to accept all of them.

As mentioned, the conference that we had initiated in the fall of 1973 had grown into the Canadian Indian Teacher Education Program (CITEP) conference. It met every year in a different location. Teacher education program administrators, teachers, and students got to see another program in operation and, in most cases, another Canadian Indian cultural community hosted. In 1979, after being absent from it for a few years, I was asked to speak. I looked at where we had come from and what was left to do. As a teacher, I had always been aware that my grandmother, Mama, was trained as a teacher. Even as her beloved grandson, I was chastised and upbraided as if I were her student. Her view of what was appropriate behaviour, what was appropriate discipline, and the tone of her conversations with me came from a Victorian schoolmarm. I did not go to her with my fears or little problems. I did not bring her my tears; crying was not acceptable.

I had Kohkwehns (literally translated as "Little Grandmother") to dry my tears, listen to my fears, and teach me the things of the heart. At the conference, I tried to explain to the audience that we have different models of teaching and that we needed to examine what each could bring to our own teaching. My grandmother was all about academic teaching. She was working with my head. Kohkwehns was appealing to my heart and helping me to deal with the emotional side of life. I also had my grandfather, who taught me to work with my hands. All were essential in my education. Each wanted me to succeed. Each taught me about life in a different way. Mama believed that I would need English to get along in the world, so she was adamant that I not speak Ojibwe at home. Kohkwehns was concerned that I become a good human being, as the Creator intended. Pa wanted me to be able to work and provide for a family. Each was willing to teach me the lessons that they could to ensure that I succeeded in life. The paper struck a chord for many of the listeners. Many of them had people in their lives that could provide them with models for their life.

When I returned to Saskatchewan from Alberta, I found that the whole educational community was transforming. When we had started the Indian Teacher Education Program, there was concern that the graduates would not be hired. However, the Provincial Human Rights Commission studied the situation of Indian and Metis students in integrated schools in the province and concluded that all boards of education serving Native students should have the same proportion of Native teachers to Native students in the student body. To ensure that boards were recruiting Native teachers, boards were obliged to report each year on their student population and the number of Native teachers in the board's schools.

Within the city itself, Councillor Helen Hughes set up a Saskatoon city community liaison committee that met biweekly at city hall to investigate the conditions of Native people in the city. I was a member of the task force on education preparing recommendations for the city boards of education on Indian schooling. I remember being asked by Mrs. Hughes to present my views to the task force on what I felt Saskatoon's Indian high-school students needed. I had heard all the statistics about Indian students not graduating from high school and the dropout rates from the urban high schools. I had read about the push-out theories. These theories were explanations for why Indian students dropped out of school. They maintained that it was not the student who left their education voluntarily but the structure and processes of the school that pushed the students out.

When I looked at Saskatoon's urban high schools and the structure of them, I did not see the answers there for our students. I always liked to leave audiences with something to think about, something to jar them out of their normal perception of an issue. So, on September 19, 1979, I made a presentation. I entitled it "Separate Schooling for Indians in the Saskatoon City System," saying that, as Indian people, we needed our own school.

I had always believed that a strong sense of identity as Indians and a firm grounding in history, culture, and, hopefully, language was an important factor in Indian students' academic success. It did not seem that there was any opportunity for Indian students to receive that knowledge within Saskatoon's high schools as they existed. Therefore, in this era of growing Indian control of Indian education, the logical conclusion had to be local Indian control of the education of Indian students in the city. There was stunned silence as I sat down after my presentation. However, this stimulated action. The (Saskatoon) Native Survival School Committee was formed and I was appointed chairman.

Vicki Wilson and I worked on a proposal for an Indian school. The public school board turned the proposal down because their philosophy was that their schools could educate anyone who came through the doors. We approached the separate school board, which believed that their children needed a different kind of education based in the teaching of the Roman Catholic Church. Our proposal was accepted. Negotiations for provincial funding ensued, and a three-way contract was signed between the parents' council, the separate school board, and the provincial government, outlining the roles and responsibilities for the operation of the school. The old St. Joseph's School on Broadway Avenue was offered as a location.

Beyond the work in the city, I was involved in meetings with Walter Currie, an Ontario Indian educator employed by the Gabriel Dumont Institute, concerning Native studies programming for Saskatchewan Indians. I had worked with him in Ontario, and when he came to see me about Native studies courses, I could introduce him to the process of course development in Saskatchewan universities. I had meetings with Mr. Gary Wouters, Department of Education, regarding affirmative action and the involvement of the Indian and Northern Education Program in the establishment of the STEP (Saskatchewan Teacher Education Program) urban Native teacher training program. This program became the Saskatchewan Urban Native Teacher Education Program (SUNTEP). I met with Lyle Mueller, a Saskatchewan Metis teacher, on the Dumont College proposal. This was an exciting time of development and change in Indian and Metis education in Saskatchewan.

When the Indian Teacher Education Program came into existence, the history of Indian people was taught through the anthropology department. There were no Indian or Metis history classes anywhere at the university. However, it soon became evident that the schools expected the Indian and Metis teacher trainees to deliver this material when they were in the schools. It was assumed that the Indian or Metis practice teachers knew everything there was to know about their people, and the schools were excited to have the opportunity to add this content. ITEP Metis students John Dorion, Lyle Mueller, Verna St. Denis, and Brian Aubichon, members of Local #126 of the Association of Metis and Non-Status Indians of Saskatchewan, met with Dean Douglas Cherry of the College of Arts and Science about their concerns regarding the lack of courses on the Metis. Without a discipline base in arts and science, the students could not get credit for being teachers of Native studies.

The dean established a working committee that included arts and science staff members who either taught about Native people or were interested in developing the new discipline, which already existed at some Canadian and several American universities. Following the lead of the Metis students, the Gabriel Dumont Institute (GDI) spearheaded the push for a Native studies component somewhere in the College of Arts and Science. GDI sponsored

Dr. Catherine Littlejohn, who I was fortunate to marry in 1991, to undertake a tour of existing Native studies or Native American programs at universities in Canada and the United States. Her report explored the diverse ways that Indian and Metis content had been brought into the university context. The committee reporting to Dean Cherry recommended creating a Native studies department. The concept was accepted by the University of Saskatchewan and the search began for a department head.

I re-established my relationships with the other FSI educational institutions. The Saskatchewan Indian Cultural College directors, Smith Atimoyoo, Myrna Yuzacapi, and John McLeod, invited me to be involved in consultations on a new direction for cultural college programming. Rodney Soonias and I reviewed a draft position paper on administrative coordination between the Saskatchewan Indian Federated College, the Saskatchewan Indian Cultural College, and the Saskatchewan Indian Community College.

I spoke in a number of classes for my colleagues in the College of Education on the "Indian worldview." Further, I conducted workshops with teachers, staff, and students at the Riverview Alternative School; the Native Urban Orientation Program at the Saskatchewan Institute of Applied Science and Technology, Kelsey (now Saskatchewan Polytechnic); St. Mary's School; the Saskatchewan Indian Education Commission of the Federation of Saskatchewan Indians; and separate schools teachers' in-services. Teachers have "in-service workshops": specific subject workshops, conferences, curriculum workshops, and others too numerous to name. These take place annually, in some cases, and as needed or requested at other times. Initially, these were easy, because all they wanted to learn about was the Indian Teacher Education Program. As time went on and teachers got to know me, I became the person to invite to talk about Indians. Often, I was the one they invited when the expert they had invited informed them at the last minute that he or she wasn't going to show up. This happened most often when they had invited a Native politician. I was the last resort to save face for the Indian people of Saskatchewan! What I resented was being asked at the last minute to fill in for a high-powered, high-paid consultant that they were flying in from California to tell them how to handle their Indian students. I usually tried to give them something to think about, even at short notice. I usually ended my presentation with a challenge. I always tried to push them on to the next level in their understanding and practise of Indian education.

While my daughter Anna-Leah had stayed with me the summer before in Calgary, it was a great joy when she and another daughter, Alanis, came to live with us in Saskatoon from 1980 to 1985. During this time I also consulted with the La Ronge Band. I spent time in Stanley Mission studying the implementation of the Indian Control of Indian Education policy as part of my research for my dissertation. I had the opportunity to live in the community in the household of Tom and Betsy McKenzie. Tom was the perfect person to introduce me to the community because he had the reputation of being the community historian. I was very comfortable in Stanley Mission, and when I came home I didn't know how I could write about it objectively because it was so much like other First Nations communities. I had to remind myself that I was there in a role of an anthropologist.

In 1981, the Saskatchewan Department of Education established the Curriculum and Instruction Review Committee, which undertook a large study of education in Saskatchewan to make recommendations to meet evolving needs of students and the public. The resulting report, presented in 1984, was entitled *Directions*. In response to the *Directions* recommendations, the Department of Education launched the Curriculum and Instruction Review, a complete examination of the provincial curriculum from kindergarten to grade twelve. A revision was recommended, an enormous task in scope and dynamic in nature. The public consultation impressed upon the provincial government that Native content had to be part of the core curriculum of a province that had a very important Indian, Metis and non–status Indian history.

In 1982, in the midst of the evolution of Indian and Metis education in Saskatchewan, the provincial election was called. With the new self-confidence of Indian and Metis individuals, a number of us decided that it was time to create a party that placed an Aboriginal platform before the voters and ran a slate of candidates in the election. The Aboriginal People's Party of Saskatchewan came into being. We ran candidates in ten constituencies: John Dorion, Saskatoon Fairview; Joe Gallagher, Saskatoon Riversdale; Cecil King, Saskatoon Sutherland; Freda Moosehunter, Saskatoon Westmount; Harry Bird, Melville; Olga Flesjer, Kelsey-Tisdale; John McLeod, Prince Albert-Duck Lake; Garry Standing, Shellbrook-Torch River; Vital Morin, Athabasca; and Leon McAuley, Cumberland. I received less than 100 votes, but I considered that a success.

We believed in what we were doing and stood up to be counted. We had a platform that looked at resource development issues in northern Saskatchewan. As I think about our platform now, I realize that we were ahead of our time! None of our candidates got elected, but Roy Romanow, Attorney General in the NDP government, lost his seat, probably as a result of our candidate running. This made us realize the power that we had been playing with.

The election was a rout of the NDP province-wide. This was scary for those of us who had gotten used to the ways of the NDP government and had many initiatives that were in their infancy and vulnerable to political interference. There were few Conservatives among the Indian and Metis leadership at the federal or provincial levels. Most were recognized, card-carrying Liberals at the federal level and NDPers at the provincial level. With the status of many programs tentative, we held our respective breaths until we could figure out the new provincial government. All we knew was that the Conservatives did not like special status for anyone. It was a surprise to us all that things remained pretty much as they were, despite the fact that many of the familiar and sympathetic members of the bureaucracy had moved on.

I graduated with my Doctorate in Philosophy (PhD) in education from the University of Calgary in 1983. It was announced at the convocation that I was the first Native Canadian to receive a PhD from the university. It was at that point that I believe my mother was proud of me. She and other family members were in attendance. My mother and Rosie Fox, one of my old teachers from Buzwah Indian Day School, had come from Sudbury on the train. Up until this time, my mother had had trouble understanding why, at my age, I was still in school. I am convinced that, sitting in the auditorium in Calgary among the thousands of spectators, when my name was announced and they acknowledged my accomplishment, my mother was proud.

A number of issues in the 1980s led to the redirection of Native curriculum. The urbanization of an increasing number

Dr. Cecil King with his mother
Adeline King (née Corbiere)
at his convocation ceremony in
1983. He was the first "Native
Canadian" to receive a PhD
from the University of Calgary.

of Indian students meant
that more emphasis was
placed on urban educa-
tion for Native children.
Urban teachers and
boards asked for help in
meeting their needs. The
Community Education
Branch was created to
oversee the development of community schools in areas
of high Native population. Part of the philosophy of these
schools was to provide children with relevant and appropriate curriculum. At this time, the Federation of Saskatchewan
Indian Nations initiated the Saskatchewan Indian Education
Commission and a Curriculum Department within the
Saskatchewan Indian Cultural College. The Association of
Metis and Non-Status Indians of Saskatchewan (AMNSIS), in
cooperation with the provincial government, implemented
the Gabriel Dumont Institute of Native Studies and Applied
Research and the Saskatchewan Urban Teacher Education
Program. For the latter two programs, the development of
accurate curriculum materials concerning the history and
culture of Metis and non-Status Indians in Saskatchewan
was a high priority.

With all of these agencies involved in the creation of
Indian, Metis and non-status Indian materials for schools in

the province, the provincial government recognized a need for a body to provide guiding principles to the curriculum development for Saskatchewan schools and coordination of activities. The Native Curriculum Review Committee was established to advise the Minister of Education and facilitate the development, production, and implementation of Native-oriented curriculum.

Membership on the original Minister's Advisory Committee on Native Curriculum Review was primarily Indian and Metis educators: Gail Bear, Saskatchewan Indian Cultural College; Rita Bouvier, Saskatchewan Urban Native Teacher Education Program; Earl Cook, Northern Teacher Education Program; Sydney Davis, Saskatchewan Indian Federated College; Angus Esperance, Saskatchewan Indian Languages Program; Keith Goulet, Member at Large; Caroline Krentz, Development Division, Department of Education; Harry Lafond, Indian Native Education Council; Sherry Farrell Racette, Community Education Branch; Harold Schultz, Saskatchewan Teachers' Federation; Martin Shulman, Gabriel Dumont Institute of Native Studies and Applied Research; Myrna Turner, Member at Large; and Myrna Yuzacapi, Saskatoon Native Survival School. I was the chairman of the committee.

In March 1984, I presented our report, *A Five-Year Action Plan for Native Curriculum Development* to Hon. Patricia Smith, Minister of Education. The provincial government had asked that we recommend a process for integrating Native content into the curriculum for all Saskatchewan students. We recommended a curriculum development process for Saskatchewan Education and spelled out the role of various groups in Native curriculum development. Integral to the incorporation of Native content to the curriculum was embedding Indian and Metis employees into the curriculum development process going on in various grades in separate disciplines at any particular time within the Department of Education. Curriculum revision was continuous.

The 1984–85 annual report for the committee, which was then called the Indian and Metis Curriculum Advisory Committee, included an introduction that described the Indian and Metis Curriculum Advisory Committee, the Indian and Metis Curriculum Development Team, and the Principles and Guidelines for Indian and Metis Curriculum Development. The report documented the core curriculum development in the following areas: social studies, English/ language arts, health–lifestyles, aesthetic education, Indian language development, Native studies, northern materials, as well as the northern education unit and the Indian and Metis awareness in-service program.

The committee encouraged the development of materials by Indian and Metis individuals and organizations. During the year, Saskatchewan Education partnered with Gabriel Dumont Institute and separately with the Saskatchewan Indian Federated College in joint projects to commemorate 1885. Other Indian and Metis materials were developed to support the English/language arts program. Future projects were included in plans for 1985 to 1986. We worked well together and in cooperation with the Indian and Metis Curriculum Development Team, we were directing the inclusion of relevant and appropriate Indian and Metis content in the curriculum for all students in Saskatchewan.

During the 1980s, I was asked to be head of the Indian and Northern Education Program. This involved fighting for the program in an environment of fiscal restraint and efforts to rationalize our existence in an era of consolidation and reorganization. As far as I was concerned, my most important contribution to the management of the College of Education was as student advocate. First Nations, Metis, and Inuit students brought a lot of unique problems with them to university. While they struggled in an unfamiliar environment, often personal, family, and other issues engulfed them. I sat on the Committee on Studies, where decisions about students' marks, performance, and tenure in classes were made. In some cases students were asked to leave the university. The cases of many Aboriginal students were not straightforward and I was able to argue that the student could, in fact, do the work if given another chance. As in all human endeavours, the committee members had a variety of opinions. There was the "by the book" professor. There was the "up by the boot straps" advocate and the "I didn't get any special treatment" one. Of course, I would have been called the "bleeding heart liberal." However, I found that we worked well together and the committee as a whole was supportive of students who deserved a second chance. Usually, we could agree when someone was not cut out to be a teacher. As for the Indian, Metis, and Inuit students who were asked to leave the university for one year, a surprising number returned with renewed commitment and finished their degrees.

•••

Throughout this period, I was researching the history of an Odawa hero to some and a traitor to others. J.B. Assiginack was a name I knew growing up on Wikwemikong First Nation, Manitoulin Island, Canada. In my youth, his name was spoken in hushed tones. He was buried in the churchyard. Try as I might, as a curious youngster I could not find out who he was or why people scorned him. As

I had become interested in history, I decided to seek the answers for myself. I began to find reference to Assiginack in the treaty negotiations between my people and the British Crown. I found other references in the records of the Indian Department at Manitowaning, Ontario. Paul Kane painted his picture and Mrs. Anna Jamieson wrote about him. Government officials mentioned him in their correspondence. Roman Catholic priests wrote glowing accounts of his work for the Church in the 1830s and reviled him in the 1850s. I continued to ask, "Who was this man? Why were the documents so contradictory on who he was and what he had done?"

A colleague, John Lyons, aware of my research, invited me to give a presentation on my work at the conference of the International Society for Educational Biography in San Antonio, Texas, in April 1985. I entitled my paper, "Problems Involved in Researching Indian Heroes." By this time in my research, I had found nothing but problems and contradictory reports on Assiginack. I was trying to figure out who he was and I was not getting a clear picture of him from the sources. I hoped that other people who were writing historical biographies could help me in the analysis of the sources.

I told the audience that on my reserve, in one of the cemeteries, is a grave marker that is different from all the rest, as compared to the usual small wooden crosses. This one is a tall sandstone pillar. It particularly stands out not only in its stature but also in its composition of stone, carefully fashioned by someone. The inscription reads, "Jean-Baptiste Assiginack, died November 3, 1866."

While I had submitted the topic of my presentation as "Problems Involved in Researching North American Indian Heroes: The Assiginack Case," in the agenda for the conference it appeared as "American Indian Heroes." I pointed out that this alteration demonstrated my point that problems can arise in meaning when merely passing the written word from one person to another. I explained that, while using my research of J.B. Assiginack, an Indian hero, as the example, my discussion would really analyze the processes of history as a discipline and the obvious (or perhaps not so obvious) pitfalls that plague the historian, the biographer, the chronicler of Indian lives. My presentation was given from my perspective as a North American Indian.

I began by acknowledging the fact that all peoples have a worldview. I proceeded to explain that Indians had a worldview different from the "Western intellectual tradition." These worldviews contrast, and I examined that contrast in relation to "history" as a discipline using my own Odawa perspective:

> In the Odawa worldview, historical truth is told. History is subjective while in the Western intellectual tradition, history is documented and assumed to be a completely objective reality. Historical truth then is perceived in two different ways. The documents of the white world are written from the worldview of the white world and the documents, coloured by self-aggrandizement or xenophobia of the writer from a particular perch in historical time, will be as far from the "historical truth" as the "tibah-djimowinan" related from another worldview. And so we have the story as the Indians perceived it, placed beside the "truth" as the others saw it.

I continued telling the listeners that, while the written word is the primary source of information for contemporary historians, for historical figures in Indian communities, their stories are primarily orally preserved. When written accounts are left, they reflect the worldview of the Western intellectual tradition, with the biases and motivations that the writer had. I was faced with the question, "So where do we look for the history of our Indian heroes if their story is no longer preserved in the Indian memory?"

I returned to the International Society for Educational Biography Conference in Chicago the next year, 1986, with a paper documenting the life events of J.B. Assiginack that I had discovered over the year of research. Much of what I had found came from the records of the Indian Affairs departments of the United States and Canada. From what I gleaned from these sources, I titled the paper "J.B. Assiginack: Arbiter of Two Worlds." I had come to see that Assiginack was a key cultural broker between the American government and my people, and then an interpreter and intermediary between the British government and the Canadian government and my people. I explained to the listeners:

Jean-Baptiste Assiginack was an arbiter of different worlds. He was an Odawa who lived, it is said, between 1768 and 1866, a period of crisis and unprecedented change for his people. Assiginack both shaped and was shaped by the forces engulfing his people's existence. Guiding the Odawak beyond the surety of the Sacred Circle upon the perilous unknown road to the future, he tried to find the straightest path for his people to walk. He was the arbiter between the two different worlds: one, a sacred mystery, immutable; and the other a conundrum, ever changing in its nature, continually shedding its past blinded by its confidence in the future.

My presentation in 1985 had spoken in general about the problems involved in researching the life of an Indian. My presentation in 1986 gave specific examples of J.B. Assiginack's life which showed how difficult this task was. The Odawak had been negotiating coexistence with the Europeans for 160 years before Assiginack was born. They had been allies of the French. The French language was the court language of New France. They had fought wars for the French against the British and their Iroquoian allies. The fall of New France in 1759, where the Odawak had fought with the French, turned the world of Assiginack's people upside down. The British took ownership, they believed, of the lands of the French territories. Fort Michilimackinac was within the territory that the Odawak claimed. Assiginack was born just as the British took possession of the fort. Documentation of the activities of his people was now in English in the reports of the military and business activities of the British.

Very soon, the British and the Americans were in conflict. By 1800, the Americans were in possession of the fort at Mackinac, about twenty miles from L'Arbre Croche where Assiginack was born. The Americans had been the enemies of the Odawak in many battles with the English. The Odawak had been part of the confederacy of nations refusing to make treaty with the Americans. The Americans denied the Odawak claim to any land that the Americans had taken from the British.

This short account of the context of Assiginack's people's history showed the incredible task for the researcher trying to uncover the story of one Indian individual. Three sets of government documents had to be searched. The role of the Odawak was defined and redefined based on whether they were a "trusted ally" or "the enemy."

I explained the need for researchers to be careful about the interpretation placed on the government and military records where the encounters with Indians, whose names were either written phonetically or in a translation, may or may not be correct. This created incredible confusion for the researcher, particularly if they did not know the Indian language. Many Indians had the same English name and this involved identifying Indian characters from the different translations and spelling of their names and sorting out the correct individual's history from the other Indians with the same English name.

I cautioned that care be taken in working with reports produced by the missionaries working among the Indians. The missionaries from New France who would have still been at L'Arbre Croche at the time of Assiginack's birth wrote about their experiences in *Les Annales de l'Association de la Propogation de la Foi*. In Assiginack's case, as a Roman Catholic throughout his life, a French record of his work with the Church during his lifetime can be found. In these record, he is referred to by four different French translations of Assiginack: *le Sansonnet, le Merle, L'Étourneau*, and even *L'Oiseau Noir*. Ironically, the story of his early life is documented most fully by David Bacon, a Congregationalist minister who Assiginack lived with to learn English so he could be the spokesperson for his people who could not speak English. In Bacon's letters to superiors, he wrote Assiginack's name as "Signoc." Bacon and his family were learning Ojibwe from Assiginack and it follows that his written Ojibwe would be phonetic.

Many of the other biographers at the conference admitted that they had not considered the additional problems for those trying to tell the Indian story working from the documentary perspective.

Beyond my research and teaching, when other professors were involved in the evaluation of an educational program on a First Nation or in a school with a high First Nation and Metis student population, I was often asked to join the team. I consulted with the Assembly of First Nations on research instruments for a national study on Indian education. In 1987, I was consultant to the Saskatchewan Indian Languages Institute on a provincial Indian languages needs assessment project and special resource person to Laurentian University in the development of an Indian social work program.

In 1988, I learned of the Newberry Library in Chicago, purported to be the most complete collection of materials related to Native Americans in the world. I needed to do some research as part of my commitment to the University of Saskatchewan. This was the time when the contribution of instructors at the university was judged not by their contribution to the community and students around them but to the world of scholarship. I was being pressured to "publish or perish."

I obtained an application for a post-doctoral fellowship to the Newberry Library and sent it off with very little confidence that I would receive a positive reply. To my surprise, I was offered a Senior Rockefeller Fellowship and was invited to join the American Indian Center for six months from September 1988 to April 1989. I had proposed a study of Jean-Baptiste Assiginack. I knew that I had to look for the answers to the questions I had about him.

I am indebted to the people who I met there in my quest, with whose guidance and direction I gained the courage to believe that I could write the history of my people. A stalwart in North American Indian history and a woman who understood the importance of helping our people to tell our own stories, Helen Hornbeck Tanner, gave me the confidence to challenge the conventional interpretations of my people's past and to look for the answers to the riddle of Assiginack within myself.

John Aubrey, librarian of the Ayer Collection at the Newberry, was my guide to navigating through the vast collection and finding the specific references that I had come to look for. Then, when I had exhausted the obvious resources, he unearthed more reading for me to do. I was amazed at the array of places and sources where J.B. Assiginack's name was mentioned.

It was during my stint at the Newberry that I met one John Sugden. Basically, I feel that destiny kind of threw us together, the result of our individual pursuits. It must have been the Creator that put a novice Odawa researcher next door to a world-renowned North American Indian historian for a glorious six months of studying. A truer friend than John would be hard to find. A Yorkshire man, he is what we call a workaholic, and for me, I needed that kind of role model to keep going.

Our day started when the library doors opened to the fellows. We would go to our assigned cubicles and begin to read the books or documents that had been delivered to us the day before. Promptly at ten o'clock, John would come to my carrel and say, "Shall we go for breakfast?" Of course the answer was always yes. We went to our lockers, retrieved our coats, and headed out the front door. Breakfast for us was served at the Oak Street Restaurant, where we sat down and were immediately served our usual "bacon and eggs." Thus, another day of research had begun at the Newberry Library in Chicago.

Life in Chicago was amazing to the newcomer from Two Clock, by way of Saskatoon. It was not an unfamiliar city to the Indian people from Manitoulin Island. In fact, in the 1950s many of our neighbours had travelled to Chicago to get work. Work, I found out from some of those who were employed there, was gotten by paying a fee (one might call it a bribe) to the person you encountered in the employment office of a company. Chicago was known for being just a little different from the way business was usually conducted in our part of the country. When we were there in 1988, it was revealed that the police officers who arrived at an accident scene were paid $100 for every cadaver they sent to a certain funeral home.

What do I remember of Chicago? I remember the smell of the sewer coming up through the manhole at the centre of the street when crossing. I remember the constant sounds of sirens and horns. I remember the sight of cabs, cabs, cabs, and flashing lights that are supposed to alert people to imminent danger but that have long since become just another feature of the city scenery. I remember the impatient, aggressive, and hectic pace on the streets. This contrasted with the slow-paced, laid-back manner in the businesses and shops. Everyone expected to wait in line for things. So they came prepared. People played Trivial Pursuit at their restaurant table while waiting the forty-five minutes for their made-from-scratch pizza. People waiting for seating at the Original Pancake House read the paper, did a crossword puzzle, or just visited. People were advised to bring a book and they did. Waiting was done cheerfully.

To the pedestrian in downtown Chicago, the streets were a major concern. The first rule of the road: everyone behaved in his or her best interest. The speed was fast and anyone taking turns, giving up the right of way, or letting the other car go first only disrupted the flow of traffic and became a hazard. The second rule of the road was that horns were placed on cars to be used. Horn-blowing was the automatic reaction of most drivers in Chicago, even when it was perfectly clear what was holding up the traffic and that it was completely unavoidable.

Drivers had to know a number of basic things about Chicago. The roads were rough. There were potholes, and while I was there, a few cars fell into them. The streets in Chicago followed or veered towards the lake. There were some strange intersections where a number of streets would all come together. There were five-cornered corners and six-cornered corners, which added more challenge to the novice city driver.

Parking was a nightmare and double parking was the norm. Delivery people and carry-out customers parked in the middle of the street, put on their hazard lights, and leapt out of their cars to do their business. The drivers following them had to find a way to avoid both them and the oncoming traffic or sit and honk their horn until the double-parked driver finished business. Despite signs posted indicating times and places where one could park on the street, few Chicagoans paid any attention. Few paid attention to the parking tickets duly given out; city hall issued a statement that only about 10 percent of parking tickets were ever paid.

Some Chicago streets were more than streets. They were frontiers. Newcomers soon learned about safe territories, dangerous territories, territories where you could go in daylight only, territories where you did not go at all, "white" territories, "black" territories, gang territories, and so on and so on. I soon found myself defining my own territory, which was bordered by Chicago Avenue in the south, Division Street in the north, Clark Street on the west, and Lake Michigan on the east. The borderlands throbbed with activity. Bag people pushed their shopping carts full of treasures retrieved from what the more well-to-do threw away. This was the closest thing that Chicago had to a recycling system.

In the midst of this brash, raw, vibrant city was the Newberry Library, where researchers could while away their days immersed in times long gone. This only happened, though, after you had passed the various tests to prove that you were a legitimate scholar, with your appropriate identification, specific project, and a friend in the establishment! Security was tight, so tight that when the Governor of Illinois was being handed scissors to cut the ribbon to open the Lincoln exhibit, his secret service man tackled the Newberry employee who was handling the scissors. In my case, there was intense scrutiny of my car. Despite the fact that I had a legitimate parking pass hanging from the mirror of the car, the weekend relief security man would not believe that a car with a Saskatchewan licence plate could be parked in the Newberry parking area.

However, when I was recognized on sight by security and I knew the names of colleagues within the library, my days of delightful reading and studying could begin. I was lucky to have arrived at the Newberry when Helen Hornbeck Tanner was still to be found in her special place at the library. She was a woman who had been working on the history and contemporary issues of the Great Lakes Indians since the 1950s. The Odawa, my people, were of particular interest to her. She owned a summer place among the Odawak of Michigan. Her knowledge of sources was invaluable to me, and she took me under her wing. Between her and John Sugden, I was introduced to the documentary history of my people. They both pushed me to interpret my people's history through the values and perceptions of the Odawak. I needed that kind of validation. Helen Hornbeck Tanner stewarded John and me on our scholarly journeys. At an institution like the Newberry you needed an advocate and Helen was certainly ours.

I began to put Assiginack's story together. Little written information was available about his early years; the paper trail began when he was in his twenties and lived with a Congregationalist family in Mackinac. His life was documented through the War of 1812. However, even then, controversy existed over his contribution. He was called "Blackbird" in English and American writings, which is one translation of his name and in the record of events he was often mistaken for one of the other "Blackbirds" of the same era. So his story went, mired in confusion.

An important aspect of Assiginack's life was the War of 1812 or, according to the Odawak, *Gee meegaading kitchi gindaaswan a pee* (the War of the Big Numbers). The documents available at the Newberry added to my understanding of the war from the American perspective. The Odawak lived in the American territory in much of our history. However, the information that I found in the Chicago Historical Society Library was very disturbing. It blamed Assiginack for the Fort Dearborn Massacre in which they said "over half a hundred" settlers were killed. I was stunned because the source was quoted as the great-grandson of Assiginack in Wikwemikong. There was no evidence in any of the documents that indicated that Assiginack was

anywhere near Chicago at the time. Evidence from wit-
nesses stated that the attack was under the direction of Black
Partridge, a Potawatomi. It appeared that the problem was
a mistake in the translation of the leader's name!

The Newberry hosted fellows' seminars, open to scholars
from Northwestern and Loyola universities. The discussion
was sometimes polite and interesting, and on other occasions the fellow was attacked viciously by outside scholars.
The latter kind of seminar took place the week before I
was scheduled. Dr. Sharon O'Brien, a professor in Indian
Government from Notre Dame, was raked over the coals
by the visitors. In preparation for my presentation, I realized that I had to go on the offensive with these professors,
so I borrowed a war club from one of the people from
Manitoulin Island who had invited me to supper and had
shown me his.

I retrieved the war club from my friend and carried it
with me to the library. I thought I would have trouble
getting the club past security, but I didn't. Then I remembered that security wasn't concerned about the weapons
you brought into the library, only the documents that
you were taking out. When it was time for the seminar
to begin, I methodically took my war club out and placed
it ceremoniously on the oak table in front of me. Before
I started my presentation, I explained that in my culture
we had rules, and one of them was that when one person
was speaking, no one interrupted or disrupted him. If they
did, we had ways of ensuring that the behaviour was not
repeated and I dramatically raised the war club. Needless
to say my seminar was one of the polite ones!

As a result of contacts that I made at the Newberry
Library, I was asked to speak to the eighty-eighth annual
meeting of the American Anthropological Association in

Washington, DC, in November 1989. The meeting was looking at the ethics of doing research on Indian reservations. I approached the topic using Floyd Westerman's song, "Here Come the Anthros." The song expressed the anger of Indian communities at the researchers who came from universities to "study" them and gave nothing back to the people or the communities. I began my presentation by saying:

> We, as Indian people, have welcomed strangers into our midst. We have welcomed all who have come with intellectual curiosity or even in the guise of the informed student. We have honoured those whom we have seen grow in their knowledge and understanding of our ways. But as has been known to happen, many times we have been betrayed. Our honoured guests have shown themselves to be "peeping toms" or rank opportunists, merely interested in furthering their own careers by trading in our honoured traditions. Our people have felt anger at the way that our communities have been cheated, held up in ridicule and our customs, sensationalized.
>
> We have been observed, noted, taped, videotaped and our behaviours recorded in every possible way known to man, and I suppose we could learn to like this, if we did not feel imprisoned in your words. The language that you use to explain us traps us in linguistic cages. It seems we must explain our ways through your hypothetical constructs. Our Ezhwabezewin must be described as material culture, economics or religion. We must segment, fragment, fracture and pigeon-hole those things that we hold sacred. The pipe, our Opwahgan becomes a sacred

artifact, a religious symbol, a political instrument or an icon. We have to describe our essence, our Ojechaugwun to fit your conceptual packages. And we have become prisoners of what you have "done to our words" to verify "your words." We want to be given the time, money and the luxury and security of academic credibility to define our own constructs from within our languages and our worlds in our own time, I might add.

I continued:

Having to first define ourselves with inappropriate English terms is not sufficient. It is confining and it is wrong. But it seems that we must defend ourselves against your categories. We must find a way to break out of these cages, but that process takes a lot of unnecessary, unproductive time and energy, it seems to me. In the last twenty years, Indian, Metis and Inuit people have moved from reserves and isolated communities into greater visibility but they are seen through the images built out of anthropological studies of them. We have been defined as "poor folks," members of a minority, tribal, underdeveloped, nomadic, less sophisticated and less fully evolved. Therefore, real Indians are poor. We have cop-outs: Indian time, if we are late; "It's not the Indian way" if we don't want to do something.

I concluded:

We do acknowledge, with gratitude, the attempts of the National Endowment for the Humanities and the American Anthropological Association to regulate researchers by guidelines or Codes of Ethics. However, for most of us, these efforts are yet part of the problem. For we ask, "Whose Ethics?" In this era of aboriginal self-government, it is not for the outsider to set the rules of conduct on our lands and in our communities. It is our right and responsibility as aboriginal nations to do that. It is the right and responsibility of researchers to respect and comply with our standards. The dictates of Western Science and the standards of behaviour demanded by associations of researchers dedicated to the advancement of your science may or may not be compatible with the Code of Ethics of our aboriginal communities.

Creative approaches must be discussed and debated by aboriginal communities, academic institutions and individual researchers to reach a working relationship which neither constricts the advancement of knowledge nor denigrates the aboriginal communities' legitimate authority over the integrity of their own intellectual traditions.

This speech was published as a chapter, "Here Come the Anthros," in Thomas Biolsi and Larry Zimmerman, *Indians and Anthropologists* (Tucson: University of Arizona Press, 1997).

One of the most challenging things I became involved in was the investigation of Indigenous languages in the delivery of justice in Manitoba for the Public Inquiry into the Administration of Justice and Aboriginal People in 1990. Freda Ahenakew, a former ITEP student, Cree scholar, and writer, and I worked together. Justice Murray Sinclair asked us to translate a list of 100 legal terms into Cree and Ojibwe. Since many were Latin terms, an Aboriginal lawyer had to translate the terms into "lay English" for us. Then, Freda and I translated the lay English terms into Cree and Ojibwe. The problems inherent in translating words that have a culture-based meaning into languages that do not have the cultural framework for those words were immediately apparent.

We reviewed all previous studies of interaction between the justice system and Indian clients and communities. Although some of the contemporary literature spoke to the culture and values of Aboriginal peoples, they did not connect these to our languages and worldview. Even the specific evidence at the Donald Marshall Jr. Prosecution Inquiry and the Manitoba Justice Inquiry demonstrated that only some of the individuals in various roles in the justice system were aware that problems of meaning, not just words, existed between the Canadian legal system and its operation and Aboriginal people and communities.

We also examined some of the concepts key to the Canadian legal system such as "truth," "time," "distance," and "knowledge." These were explored within the Ojibwe language and worldview. Cultural behaviours were presented that showed that courtroom behaviour is not necessarily a reaction to or against the Canadian legal system but emanated from a set of "appropriate, respectful behaviours learned from childhood."

It was found that, even within the Public Inquiry into the Administration of Justice and Aboriginal People, the continuing and long-standing delegitimization of the Indian languages was evident. It was found that the transcript did not contain the actual evidence provided by elders speaking in their languages to the inquiry. The analysis of the views of the true representatives of the traditional cultural peoples was, as a result, censored from the written record of the evidence from the communities. It became evident that one of the problems was that, although making provision for translators, the legal system did not schedule appropriate time for the translators or interpreters to do their work. This devalued their role in the process.

Most upsetting was to find in the transcripts the simple statement "speaks in Cree." This seemed to be a generic comment for any witness who spoke an Indian language, because some of the communities where this statement was entered in the record were not Cree. However, this is an assumption and could not be concluded from the transcript. Many of the examples, comments, and recommendations made by Freda and myself were included in the final report of the inquiry.

Although I worked on university committees and graduate committees and was teaching classes on and off campus, the spirit in the College of Education was becoming less open to ideas and more confining. The days of challenging conventional ways of teaching were over. Many of the staff that had supported the introduction of the Teacher Education Programs of Saskatchewan had gone. Father Andre Renaud had died; Audie Dyer was sick with Parkinson's and leukemia. The new faculty had not fought the fights for programs and were working to establish themselves as academics. I increasingly found that the interesting proposals were coming from outside the University of Saskatchewan and even outside education. I was visiting lecturer in social sciences for Aboriginal peoples for the National Native Access to Nursing Program with the College of Nursing, University of Saskatchewan. I worked with the Metis National Council on the structure and content of consultations on archaeology legislation and regulation for Metis people. During 1990–91, I was a consultant to the Ontario Historical Foundation for Resource Development for Aboriginal content. I was involved in two different evaluations: Se-Se-Wa-Hum School Evaluation, for Big River Band, Debden, Saskatchewan, and was external evaluator of the Saskatchewan Indian Cultural College.

Changes were coming in the way that the Indian and Northern Education Program served the Indian and Metis students. I could not understand the changes in relation to the very real needs of the province or the Indian and Metis people of the province. It was the end of an era!

9. MOVING ON

n 1991, I realized that I had reached the glass ceiling for an Indian professor at the University of Saskatchewan at that time. I had applied for full professor and was turned down. Furthermore, the Indian and Northern Education Program, for administrative reasons, had been collapsed into the Department of Educational Foundations. In a time when the demand for courses and the need in the communities was at its height, the University of Saskatchewan decided that, instead of making our small unit into a department, we would be subsumed under a department with a very different mandate and raison d'être. I was not promoted to head this combined department, despite the fact that my PhD was through the Educational Foundations Department at the University of Calgary.

At this time, because of my national reputation in Indian education, Queen's University offered me a position as full professor and director responsible for implementing the plan to deliver teacher education in Ontario's First Nations communities, including my own home community. Whereas the University of Saskatchewan penalized me for working almost exclusively with communities and not writing for my peers in academia, Queen's University considered my community work to be exactly the background that they wanted. Again, as I had found at other times in my career, I had advanced as far as I could at the institution I was part of, and to move forward I had to leave the institution. One of my colleagues said that he would have thought he had died and gone to heaven if he had gotten an offer to go to Queen's.

I felt a lot of emotions moving to Queen's. First and foremost, it meant moving back to Ontario—back to family, back to a familiar place, back to a place where I would be able to speak my language and be among my own people. It meant working for the same goals as I had been in Saskatchewan—the success of our children in schools—only in my own communities. Bringing my knowledge of what was needed in classrooms, schools, and universities to provide our kids with academic success and the confidence to dream big dreams motivated me.

I had always viewed Queen's as the bastion of the old white, Anglo-Saxon, Protestant culture of Upper Canada. The new universities of Ontario, like Trent, had been free to work on the fringes of conventional academia and develop Native studies programs, but such had not been the case at the old bulwarks of what was considered legitimate knowledge at traditional institutions such as Queen's. When I returned to Ontario in 1992, there was a new openness to diversity in the province. I wondered whether this was the result of the summer of 1990 when the Oka crisis had propelled our presence in the territory to the forefront of Canadian minds. It had crystallized the feeling of many of our people that our reality was not on the agenda of Canada. It demonstrated the ignorance that most average Canadians had about the issue that was paramount to our people—traditional lands. This was the first time that Canadians were exposed to the Haudenosaunee governmental system that had been in continuous existence since about the time of the signing of the *Magna Carta*. This was the first time that many Canadians knew of the Clan Mothers, the Longhouse, the Tree of Peace, and the Warrior Society and the way that these ancient respected political institutions functioned in contemporary Canada. Kingston is in Haudenosaunee territory. The territory around Kingston still is the home to Haudenosaunee. Perhaps Queen's no longer could ignore that reality.

Kingston was not my territory. I had had a short stint there when I was living in Ottawa and had been involved in a project to develop a cadre of Indian prison guards. For many of our people, Kingston is known only for its prisons. When I went there, five major penal institutions were in the area. The notorious P4W women's prison was the view I had from my office window. The decision to close P4W had been made, but at the time more and more horror stories were coming out about the lives some of our women had lived in that institution.

The correctional staffs were a large subculture of the community, as were the families of inmates. While I was in Kingston I think I only met one prison employee socially, and that was our next-door neighbour. As a university professor, my social group and the corrections subculture never met. The closest we came to the inmates was that our house was about two blocks from Kingston Penitentiary. The Catholic Church that I attended was called "The Church of the Good Thief" and seemed to be the gathering place for former prisoners. Everyone's background was irrelevant and the church welcomed us all. The local Friendship Centre was run by ex-cons. The meetings that I attended were more raucous and obscene than anything I had experienced before.

Another self-contained group in the community was the military. The military had been part of the history of the place since Frontenac established Fort Frontenac on the site of Katarokwi in 1673. The fortress was built to protect the territory of New France from invaders, and to be a symbol to all the inhabitants of the territory that the French had arrived. Kingston was a naval centre for the British in the War of 1812. It has always had a military presence. I had no contact with members of the military.

Kingston was the home of Sir John A. Macdonald. A statue of Canada's first prime minister dominates the corner of one of the city's parks. Everyone knows where his law office was located and his home with its tower was one street from our home. "John A.," as he is affectionately referred to in Kingston, is buried in the Cataraqui Cemetery, which is a national historic site of Canada. It was ironic that I was moving from the homeland of the Metis and the Battle of Batoche to a place where the man who is still reviled by the Metis was the local hero. For some of my Metis friends, the disconnect between the east and the west of our country could not have been clearer. My first Metis visitor told me he was going to show his disdain for Macdonald by urinating on his grave. I kept him under close surveillance the whole time he was visiting us.

When I arrived in January 1992, the planning and development phase of the Aboriginal Teacher Education Program (ATEP) was complete. When I took over, our staff members were already in place. Lucky for me, Jan Hill, a Mohawk woman from Tyendinaga Mohawk Territory, about forty miles down Highway 2 from Kingston, was one of my staff. She finessed the local and Haudenosaunee politics. Beyond this, she set up the complex schedules and travel arrangements to meet with local groups in the communities. She was an efficient administrator, liked by everyone, and she made sure that I met the appropriate people in each community. She was very supportive of the students. If a student needed anything, Jan would find it.

Kate Freeman knew every corner of the campus. She knew where everything was and whom to talk to to get what we needed. Her father, Mac Freeman, was a professor, and she had literally grown up on campus. She was always sunny and filled our classrooms with laughter and joy. She was involved in student counselling, but she was first and foremost a teacher. Also, she herself was a student working on her PhD with the Ontario Institute for Studies in Education (OISE). She could speak to students as "one of them."

Jeff McDonald was the enigma on staff. He identified with the Aboriginal students as one of them, but was somewhat vague on his Aboriginal ancestry. He had spent time out west and had connections to the Sioux reservations in the Dakotas. He was my male assistant and brought that perspective to working with the students. Jeff was a free spirit and had his own way of doing things.

The program was organized around teaching centres off-campus, with the students coming to campus for summer classes. I had not understood that it was an off-campus program when I had arrived in Kingston. I was so used to seeing hundreds of Aboriginal students on the campuses of Saskatchewan universities I was surprised that there was no such body of students at Queen's. Tongue in cheek, I made the comment that Queen's was supportive of Aboriginal students as long as they stayed off-campus.

Our off-campus programs were offered in cooperation with Six Nations of the Grand River, North Shore Tribal Council, United Chiefs and Councils of Manitoulin, Kiskinnohamakaywi Weecheehitowin, Kasibonika Lake Band Council, and the Grand Council of Treaty Three. I travelled Ontario from north to south and east to west. This was a very enjoyable part of the job. I got to meet individuals in far-flung Indian communities who were as committed as I to ensuring that our young people were successful in school. It was exciting to be involved again in creating a new initiative that had the potential to impact thousands of Indian children. I had seen how a program could change the futures of the program's students who in turn would have a positive influence on a generation of Indian children.

Needless to say, the Indian communities were enthusiastic about hosting the program. There was no shortage of students who wanted to be in the program and there was an obvious need for Indian teachers in Ontario. Negotiations with communities were sometimes difficult because some communities wanted the funds for the program to be transferred to them. However, that was not the way the program was set up and Queen's was not prepared to carry local control that far. An institution that had been operating for 150 years had its ways of doing things. Kate used her institutional knowledge to accomplish magic in getting things we needed through the maze of university red tape.

The people in the First Nations communities saw the potential of ATEP. They understood the importance of having people from their communities taking the places of authority in their children's schools. For too many years all the individuals who worked in the institutions in their communities had been outsiders. The elders saw the teacher trainees as those who could bring their language, history, and culture into the schools as a natural part of the students' education. Many saw the hiring of their own people as teachers in the community as economic development. They anticipated that these young people would become self-sufficient members of the community employed in good paying jobs. Others saw the program as contributing to the local control of education. Teachers supported the program and were willing partners in the process.

Visiting the communities and working in local schools was a very rewarding aspect of my work. I found that the ATEP students who came from the north and were fluent in the community's language had a different impact on the learning experience in their classrooms. They used Cree or Ojibwe to deliver certain content, as I had in Northwest Bay and Dokis Bay. They used humour to defuse situations. I remember one classroom where one of my Cree-speaking teachers said to the class that he was going to say all their names backwards. The students were incredulous. They challenged him to do it. He rose to the challenge. He took a chair to the front of the room and sat with his back to the students and recited all their names!

The value of the Indian languages was always an issue. Queen's allowed the fluent speakers of a First Nation language to receive university credit for a second language. I tested the fluency of all the Ojibwe speakers. My judgement was needed for them to receive their credit. I had many interesting academic conversations about the education of Indian students with my students during these fluency tests.

On the other hand, there was concern from the English department that the students did not have adequate fluency in English to deserve to receive a passing mark. I argued that these students were better teachers for their communities because they were fluent Cree speakers and that their English skills would improve as they were involved in more classes and had greater exposure to the university. It reminded me that such efforts by schools to rank English as more important than our Native tongues had almost resulted in the disappearance of our languages.

I did not teach very often, but my areas of specialization were curriculum development for First Nations schools, First Nations language teaching, research, and methodology, and Ojibwe culture, language, and history. I found it hard to find a group of kindred spirits with whom to talk about Indian education. Saskatoon had always had a lively group of professors who were ready and eager to talk ideas. They might not always agree with you, in fact they were very likely to challenge you, but it was an interesting intellectual dialogue about things that mattered. Queen's reminded me more of Calgary, where when professors were on campus they were behind closed doors doing research, one presumed. However, more often they were not there. It would be said that they were away "doing research." As a person who was a teacher first and who believed in the community-of-scholars approach to academia, I must admit that I was lonesome for the give and take, rough and tumble of professors wrestling with academic problems as they related to the real world of Indian children's success in school. I missed the challenging collegiality of people from the other TEPS in Saskatchewan and the professors in the College of Education at the University of Saskatchewan who would pose a question that revealed their concern for what I did.

My staff was good, but I found a deference to my position that kept them from pushing me. To them, I was in a role, and they were too polite to challenge me. I was not used to this. Twenty years in Saskatchewan had changed me. I expected to be challenged and I believed everyone was equal when it came to decision-making. My name might be on the memo explaining the decision, but the process of coming to that decision would be a free-for-all pooling of our views and coming to a consensus. I found it difficult operating in such a strict hierarchy. And the whole institution ran in that fashion. For that matter, the whole province did.

Ontario was going through a process of evolution. What had happened in Saskatchewan as a revolution was seeping into the institutions of Ontario in a more measured way. Soon after I arrived, I was invited to be on an education forum at one of the reserves. I was on a panel with Walter Currie and Basil Johnston. As I looked down the table it struck me that we were the same people who had been on education panels thirty years ago. I wondered where the young educators were. Where was the next generation of Indian teachers? It hit me that this was why my program at Queen's had to succeed. We had to produce a new generation of Indian teachers for Ontario's schools.

The educational institutions were being restructured to be more inclusive. In May 1993, I presented a paper entitled "Towards a More Inclusive Curriculum" to the Council of Ontario Universities/Ontario Council on Graduate Studies Conference on Educational Equity in Ontario Universities. I began by telling the audience that I was going to take them on a journey into the world of my people, the Odawak, and that I hoped that by seeing the world through my people's perceptions that they would see the curriculum of our institutions in a new light. I prayed, as my grandfather would have, in Ojibwe, asking the Creator to give me the wisdom so that my mere words could be as a medicine to all who heard them.

I started, as I began this book, with the basic foundation of the Odawa worldview. I described the *Enendagwad*, the Law of the Orders, which we believe was given to us by the Creator. *Enendagwad* is the philosophical underpinning of the Odawa belief system. I explained that, in contrast to the Christian view of the world, human beings were not next to the Creator. In fact, the order was quite different. The Creator and Mother Earth joined to bring forth the Plant World. Then the Animalkind was brought into existence, and finally Humankind, which was the least necessary and the most dependent of all the orders. Human beings are totally dependent on the benevolence on those with whom they must coexist. Human beings are last in the order of things.

I pointed out that this view of the world had profound ramifications. The awareness of our dependency made us look at the other orders as our parents, siblings, and kin. We had to be acutely aware of the health and well-being of the Earth, the plants, and the animals, for our health and well-being was intimately tied to their condition. Our reality was grounded in good relationships. It is interrelationships that give meaning to the whole. We are all part of the whole. Our behaviour affects the other orders, as actions in the other orders affect us. Our interdependence is reflected in the structure of our language. We had a system of knowledge that gave our existence meaning. I explained,

This was the framework of existence that governed my people until the newcomers came. It is into this world then that the newcomers intruded, bringing with them a new way of defining and describing the world, the relationship with the Earth, the plants, the animals, and the original peoples, my people. The newcomers' wisdom was grounded on the perception of the primacy of humankind over all things and the primacy of European humankind over North American humankind. The Western intellectual tradition soon relegated my people to the position of "red objects" to be exploited with the flora and the fauna in pursuit of the European view of progress. ("Towards a More Inclusive Curriculum," presented to the Council of Ontario Universities/Ontario Council on Graduate Studies Conference on Educational Equity in Ontario Universities, May 1993, p.5).

I challenged the scholars to engage their faculty and university communities in a discussion of what was defined as legitimate knowledge in the institution and who made the determination. I said that scholars must be open and respectful of other forms of knowledge and share time, space, and status in the institution with bearers of other views of what constitutes legitimate knowledge. I directed the audience to leaders in the North American intellectual tradition, to the philosophers and visionaries who had proposed better ways of living together. I asked how many of them taught about our thinkers in their philosophy courses, our military leaders in their history classes, or our great leaders in their political science courses.

I said that before we started to talk about moving towards a more inclusive curriculum, each and every one of us in these institutions needed to determine what the end product would be. What kind of educated person was to be produced? What was the purpose of developing a more inclusive curriculum in an institution? Were institutions including Indian, Black, and Chinese knowledge in the institutions to have a place for these students to see themselves and find a home in the institution? I said that the institutions not only had an obligation to our people to provide curriculum that was aimed at our students but that the institutions had an obligation to all their students to educate them to live in contemporary Canadian society. I went on to say:

> How well does your curriculum prepare your graduates to understand Canada from its Aboriginal beginnings? How well equipped are your graduates to work in policy formation or governance in the Canada of the 1990s where one of the major challenges is finding informed solutions to the difficult issues surrounding the relationships between Canadian society and the Aboriginal peoples in their homeland? ("Towards a More Inclusive Curriculum," p.8)

At Queen's there were some professors who came to me to learn about Indian people. In 1993 I gave a paper entitled "Ethics and Research in Aboriginal Communities." I explained that ethics entered research at every stage, from the researcher's choice of the topic to be studied to the final interpretation of the results. More specifically, in doing research in Ojibwe communities, I asked how much knowledge of Ojibwe people researchers could take with them to an Ojibwe community where they wanted to do their research. Would they know whether what they were asking people to do was appropriate or inappropriate in the culture? Would they know how to find out whether it was appropriate? Could they communicate with the elders in Ojibwe? Would they be able to create a research instrument that could convey the reality of the Ojibwe people? What techniques had they learned for interviewing people whose first language is not English? How have they been taught to interact with Aboriginal clients, informants, and communities? How do the researchers validate research that is designed to explain my people to other Canadians? How do the researchers know that the meaning being attributed to the results represents a true reflection of the reality of their Aboriginal informants? How prepared are researchers to deal with results that contradict the conventional theories of the Western intellectual tradition?

I emphasized that ethics are as important in the interpretations of the results as in the practice of the research. I pointed out that my people have been defined by researchers within the categories from Western intellectual theory based on the researchers' own background. Once we have been defined as undereducated or marginal or poor, then our "problems" have been attributed to our undereducation, marginality, or our poverty. These conditions are then attributed to our personal attributes, which have served as the accepted analyses for our failure to become like other Canadians. I stated categorically that we have never accepted these analyses, but rarely are we allowed to present our interpretation of the situation. I cautioned the researchers that "until researchers recognize the obligation they have to validate their results in the communities, the more Okas there will be, the less we will understand each other despite the valiant efforts of another generation of non-Aboriginal researchers to impose meaning on our reality."

I concluded by saying:

We want other Canadians to begin to know us for our essence, for who we really are, not only as those who do not measure up to standards set by the newcomers to this our land. We want respect for the knowledge in our Indian, Metis and Inuit communities, respect for the perceptions, insights and ways of knowing which have evolved over thousands of years on the North American continent and which spring from a foundation very different from the Greco-Roman base familiar to most Canadians. (Dr. Cecil King, "Ethics and Research in Aboriginal Communities," Queen's University, November 29, 1993)

I was asked to present the Odawa spiritual world to a theology class at Queen's looking at the contemporary pluralist world. I addressed the Creator in the prayer of my grandfather and led the students in a journey into the world of the Odawa in hopes of bringing the students to an understanding of issues of theology and spirituality through my people's eyes. Throughout my career I have found that when people acknowledged that there was another way of seeing the world, they understood why it was important to have special courses for Aboriginal peoples. This is the first time many have looked at their own views as only one way to explain reality. They tend to learn a lot about themselves from my lectures on my people's view of the world. I remember this lecture because, when I had completed my presentation and opened the floor to questions, one of the students asked, "How can I help Indian people?" This was so often the question of people in the helping professions. My answer was always tempered by the field that the individual represented. Since this was a theology class, most of these students were practising Christians, I assumed. I responded, "If you worked, approached, and communicated with us as a Christian should, as Christ would instruct you to, that would really help."

I was invited to work with the Royal Commission on Aboriginal Peoples (RCAP). I accepted a position on the

Research Advisory Committee, which reviewed all the research that was being done under the auspices of RCAP. The committee was comprised of the research director and senior researchers from across the country with a variety of areas of expertise. It was while serving on this committee that I was personally confronted with the most incredible insensitivity to our people's ways. I was asked to pray at the meeting one day. Since I never present myself as a spiritual leader, I pray when asked, but not as a ceremonial leader. When I had finished praying in my language, one of the renowned researchers took me aside to tell me that he was "offended" by having to sit through a prayer in my language. He didn't believe that we should be allowed to push our religion on him at these meetings.

I was shocked. I could not get my head around the fact that this individual would take it upon himself to show disrespect for our language and spirituality while he was serving on this committee. To me, it represented the very worst of what we had to face in trying to educate Canadians about us. A man who was making his living off our people didn't understand us at all and obviously had no respect for us. I was also disappointed with the research agenda of RCAP. I wrote a response. After reviewing all the proposed research, I concluded:

> One of the most exciting aspects of the Royal Commission on Aboriginal Peoples was the oppor-tunity it afforded Aboriginal peoples to express their concerns. Aboriginal peoples' knowledge has not been enhanced or developed because no one has given Aboriginal peoples the purpose or resources to express their own ideas except in private. Academics have for the most part examined issues which came

out of their personal or scholastic experience not out of the Aboriginal community experience. The old boys network in the Social Sciences and Humanities Research Council (SSHRC), and the granting agencies have sponsored ideas with which they are familiar. The Royal Commission appeared to afford us both the purpose and resources to develop our own intellectual systems, recapturing and describing for other Canadians traditional knowledge, our different ways of looking at the same world and of conceptualizing the same events. Our people are not academics but I have had some of the most scholarly discussions with some of the most learned people I have met, in Ojibwe, in my community. These individuals can talk philosophy in the manner of Socrates or analyze contemporary events with the finesse of a political scientist. Our language is replete with concepts and abstractions. We can describe our reality in the most precise descriptors. We can debate, defend and manipulate ideas in a most scholarly fashion. It is a shame that most academics in Aboriginal studies cannot talk ideas in the manner of the Aboriginal people about whom they speak and write. In this enterprise at least, the Royal Commission on Aboriginal Peoples, let's give the traditional scholars in our communities the chance to engage in scholarly discourse on issues that concern them. Let's give them the first word and the last word. Let the research agenda be guided by their words. (Response to the Research Agenda of the Royal Commission on Aboriginal Peoples, 1993)

At the provincial and institutional levels there were efforts being made to bring the voices of the diverse populations into the institutions of the province. Multicultural committees were formed. I was a member of these. I found this very dysfunctional. I found it hard to get my voice heard because the way that others spoke to each other didn't always leave space for people to speak. The way that I was raised to wait my turn and respect the person speaking often resulted in me being left out of the conversation.

I remember one conference where I was asked to speak. Each of us was to have twenty minutes. I prepared a speech, which was my way of ensuring that I explained the Indian perspective. The others ahead of me spoke over their time, each of them, and when it was my turn, I was told I had five minutes. This was totally inadequate to put our position on the record. I could talk extemporaneously, but it was not giving our people the respect that our position demanded. That is what I resented about these gatherings. I did not feel that respect was shown equally to our point of view because we could not shout as loud as the others. At one provincial gathering, Isaac Pitawanakwat, one of the Ojibwe elders who was there, summed up his frustration by saying, "*Gi zhagodwewe goh mi!*" which encapsulated the idea that we, too, had come to the event with a voice and ideas but because the other people spoke louder than we did, our ideas were not heard. Isaac worked with the Native Canadian Centre in Toronto and had wanted to discuss ways to expand their facilities and programs, but didn't get a chance.

Over the years I have seen and been involved in many attempts to create a more inclusive curriculum. There are many ways that this has been attempted: classroom teachers modifying what is taught in the school to reflect the child's reality; cultural institutions of Indian, Metis and Inuit communities developing curriculum materials that indigenize the content of particular courses; books published to reveal certain cultural events or practices; province-wide efforts to integrate Indian, Metis, or Inuit content across the curriculum; and universities adopting departments devoted to teaching and researching Indian, Metis, and Inuit material. These efforts have been going on for at least fifty years that I know of. Still, I am told that Indian people talking to a new bureaucrat in a position to make a difference in the lives of Indian, Metis, and Inuit people have to educate that person on the history, culture, and reality of our peoples. How is it that so many Canadians are still ignorant of our existence?

To those speaking about changing the institutions, I have offered a simple way to see how our peoples' knowledge is legitimized in their schools. I ask: "Are any of our languages taught in your program? If so, are these languages housed in the modern language area? Or are they hived off from the more 'recognized' modern languages into the anthropology department or the Native studies unit? Think about how the location of my language in your institution conveys a message about how interested you are in the knowledge of my people. Think about how where you locate the Aboriginal materials in the classroom sends a message to the Aboriginal students."

Is the law of the Iroquois taught with Roman law and English jurisprudence? Where can a student learn more about the animism of the Algonquian languages or the Orenda of the Mohawk? Who instructs about the concepts of land ownership that the Crees practise on their traditional lands? What about the myriad of Aboriginal philosophers, military leaders, diplomats, and treaty negotiators, and the host of arbiters of two worlds. Where can Aboriginal scholars feel the respect accorded to the Greco-Roman tradition bestowed on their people's wisdom? It is not enough to have white scholars dredge the archives to put brown faces in the otherwise white story. Aboriginal peoples must feel that their knowledge is respected and deemed legitimate, worthy knowledge, and not shoved in an out-of-the-way corner.

I tell those embarking on indigenizing the curriculum of their institutions, if you are serious about braiding Indian content into the curriculum or weaving a Metis sash of knowledge into your institutions, do it wholeheartedly, under the direction of our people. I have found that each generation of scholars redefines the process, renames it as relevant curriculum, integrated content, indigenized, and decolonized. Each of these words brings a judgment from a different worldview.

The elders taught me that they wanted Canadians to know us for our essence, for who we really are. The elders believed that we understood the land on which we live better than those who recently arrived. They believed that the knowledge gained by our people, the perceptions, insights and ways of knowing which have evolved over forty thousand years on the North American continent deserved a place of honour in the country's institutions of learning. They believed that these institutions should respect the knowledge in our Indian, Metis and Inuit communities.

My concern has always been that in a more inclusive curriculum we should not judge the success of its inclusiveness by the number of "sweats" offered per semester, the number of linguists who study our languages but have yet to carry on a conversation with one of us, or the length of the list of Aboriginal guest speakers to attend the class while the worldview and value system of the classes in no way reflects that which we are saying we are teaching. I am concerned that we too often have taken a material culture and have forgotten a spiritual and cognitive culture, that we can have "Indian Days," that we can bring out the pretty pictures, play Indian songs, eat bannock in the hallways, or even bring in an elder or two without our own students ever knowing that they have a separate way of dealing with the world, a mode of communication for expressing their thoughts that is the gift of the Creator and a body of knowledge that will be lost forever if they do not take it to themselves to value and protect it.

In 1995, my old professor and friend Dr. Art Blue, a Shoshone psychologist, contacted me to see what I knew about suicide in traditional Ojibwe teachings. He was preparing for a workshop for Health Canada on suicide prevention. I said that I didn't know anything but that I would ask people and find out for him. As a result I started to investigate the historical context of suicide among my people. I found that the *Gete anishnabemnanik* (our elders) tell us that suicide was not our way before contact with the Europeans.

Looking at the reports of those who came to our traditional territories and lived among us, it is evident that suicide was a very infrequent occurrence in traditional societies. In fact, it was not considered as normal behaviour. On the contrary, health and long life represented the highest good, and those who had knowledge that promoted that were highly esteemed.

I found that there is no word in Ojibwe equivalent to "suicide" or "taking one's own life." Elders struggled for words when speaking of a suicide. According to Edward Rogers in his study of Round Lake (now Weagamow Lake) in northwestern Ontario, suicide was thought of as the most upsetting type of death for the survivors to bear. In explaining the death, it might be attributed to a "witch" because attributing the death to the intervention of other-than-human forces was more culturally acceptable than an individual ending his or her own life. Life was seen as a gift of the Creator. Its beginning and ending were predetermined. Life was not taken lightly by my people. Natural death was seen as part of the cycle of life.

All Anishnabek philosophy, worldview, and concepts reinforced and celebrated life—not only the life of the individual, but the life of the community. I had to conclude that suicide came to my people with contact. Prior to contact, the Anishnabek lived with the profound belief that each Anishnabe had a necessary place in the community with a unique path to walk. Life was a journey taken in the company of the Creator, the other-than-human forces that guided you, the plants and animals on whom your life depended, and other Anishnabek who taught, cared for, and protected you with their recognition of your special place in their lives.

In the traditional way, a person had his or her own path to follow through to its predetermined end. This journey was taken in company with elders and community people as well as guardian spirits. It was a covenant between the person and other-than-human forces that were stronger than he or she and that could be called on for aid in times of distress. The person was committed to follow his or her path to the predestined end. To take one's own life was unthinkable. Life was given to us. We do not have the power to terminate it in front of the Creator.

I am convinced that answers to many of the complicated issues that our communities face, like suicide, could be aided by an understanding of the ways that our ancestors understood the issues. For example, with suicide: "Do our young

Cecil and Catherine at First Nations University of Canada's Saskatoon campus.

people feel that they have a place of value in the community?" "Are they assured that they are an important and necessary part of the community?" "Do they have elders and community members who help them along the path that they walk?" "Are they instructed that their life was predestined and that they have an obligation to live the life that they have been given?" We must look to the wisdom of our ancestors for the answers we seek.

In 1997, I hit sixty-five years of age, retirement age. I retired from Queen's and the title professor emeritus was bestowed on me. I felt lost. I did not know what would become of me. For me, teaching was more than a career; it was my life. Since all my connections were in Saskatchewan, my wife Catherine and I decided to move back to the west.

One of my old students who was the director of the Yukon Teacher Education Program said he had seen an advertisement for the deanship at the First Nations University campus in Saskatoon. He said I should apply. I did. Pretty well everyone at the Saskatoon campus knew me and were keen to have me work with them.

I remembered the excitement that the Saskatchewan Indians had had when the plan was created for a complete Indian-controlled education system. I had been involved in the development of the plan, as the Indian Teacher Education Program was an integral part of it. I expected that First Nations University of Canada would be the institution to preserve and disseminate the knowledge of the Saskatchewan Indians as the elders had envisaged in the 1970's. The Saskatchewan Indian Federated College had become the First Nations University of Canada (FNUC). I was surprised to find that, in fact, the FNUC was still a college federated to the University of Regina. The University of Regina approved the instructors, the courses, the registration, and the granting of degrees. I had assumed that, having hired a president with international credentials, at least the approval of instructors would be under his control and thus Indian control.

FNUC was a university in name only. It did not have a charter and the authority to grant degrees independent of the University of Regina. I had assumed that, with the name First Nation University of Canada, FNUC would have pursued a national charter. There was a precedent in Saskatchewan. In 1883, the first University of Saskatchewan in Prince Albert had a charter granted by the federal government. This university served the First Nations and Metis population. It was a Church of England institution that taught First Nations languages and had students from all over western Canada. When the University of Saskatchewan was given a provincial charter in 1907, the clergy at the original university said that they would surrender the name and set aside their charter if the provincial University of Saskatchewan was located in Saskatoon. They also provided sixty students in the first class. It had been assumed by many of us that it was only a matter of time until the Saskatchewan Indian Federated College would become a First Nations university, totally independent and Indian controlled with its own charter and degree granting powers. This had not happened. The university remained a university in name only. (The primary source on the creation of the University of Saskatchewan [1883] is Jean E. Murray in two articles in *Saskatchewan History*: "The Early History of Emmanuel College," *Saskatchewan History* 9 [1959]: pp. 81–102, and "The Context of the University of Saskatchewan," *Saskatchewan History* 12 [1959]: pp. 1–23. See as well, Catherine I. Littlejohn, "The Historical Background of the Indian and Northern Education Program," PhD dissertation, University of Calgary, 1983.)

When I took over as dean of the Saskatoon campus, the students were great. Like every other institution that I had taught at, the students were the same. They had their lives outside the school. Our students were more likely than the average university students to be older and have families. Students juggled classes with child care, picking up and dropping off children, family crises, and housing which had little space, time, and quiet places to write papers and study for exams. It was all familiar to me. And with all their responsibilities, they still had their senses of humour and took the time to drop in on the dean and make him laugh.

I was surrounded by people who I had worked with before when I taught for the Indian Social Work Education Program, such as Wes Heber and Louise McCallum. Stan Cuthand and I had similar approaches. We both respected the traditional ways while having university backgrounds and professional careers. Stan knew the old stories of the Cree. He was fluent in Cree and was translating books of the Bible into Cree. He was a graduate of Emmanuel-St. Chad's and had been an Anglican clergyman on many of Saskatchewan's reserves. I turned to him for advice

Dr. Cecil King and Reverend Stan Cuthand being honoured at an Awâsis Inter-agency Aboriginal Education Conference in Saskatoon.

and backup on many occasions.

Danny Musqua was a Saulteaux elder. He and I were very much in tune. We could joke with each other in Ojibwe and I could consult him on cultural appropriateness when necessary. We became so close that Danny was convinced that his people had migrated west from my home territory and there was a real possibility that we were related. I vehemently denied that I could have any relationship to him.

I soon discovered, however, that the faculty and staff were not a happy bunch. The university had had a large number of labour board complaints, lawsuits, and the release of many who had long served the Saskatchewan Indian Federated College. There was a lot of disappointment and frustration on the part of traditional people who had worked to implement Indian control and now saw the direction of the institution moving towards replicating the structure and content of the mainstream programs. I was caught off guard when Dr. Ahab Spence, one of the early educated Indians in Saskatchewan who was involved with SIFC, got up at one of the first gatherings I attended and said that

FNUC was "sick, sick, sick." However, I found out that this was a view held by many of the people who had had high hopes for SIFC becoming a special place that would honour the knowledge of the North American intellectual tradition. So far, the hope was not the reality.

I found myself reminding people of the vision of the elders for the institution. I soon realized that I was one of the few people who had been involved with the creators of the plan for Indian Control of Indian Education. Since the history of the time, thirty years ago, was not written and the actors were no longer around, I felt that I had to provide the current staff and students with the story as I knew it. I had to challenge them to carry on the vision, to live the vision of the elders.

As the keynote speaker at the graduation in 2005, I entitled my speech "*Aneesh Enadjimohnguk!*" ("What It Is All About!") I explained that the title was because the students being there and having entered the university and going into the professions "was dreamed of, struggled for, and achieved by a number of people who are no longer with us. They would tell you 'what it was all about' if they could." I pointed out that the graduates were the ones many people spoke of in their prayers. I told them that they personified the history of our people:

> When I look at you I see courage, persistence, risk-tak-ing and beating the odds. For too many, our history is the history of a conquered people, an oppressed people, people who have been downtrodden, a story of lost battles and lost cultures. This has never been the history of our people as I know it. For me our story is one of survival, of overcoming adversity. It is about victory and overcoming the might of

stronger nations that have tried to eliminate us. I believe that those of us who remain are the strongest, and I might say, the meanest, of our people. We are the inheritors of our history, culture, language and knowledge. We are the ones with the responsibility of living our lives for those who made the sacrifices so that we could survive. ("*Aneesh Enadjimohnguk!*" October 20, 2005, p.2)

I took the audience back to 1960, when only one in fifteen Indian students in Saskatchewan reached grade twelve. The education of Indian kids in Saskatchewan had been labelled by researchers as "schooling for failure." In 1969, the Federation of Saskatchewan Indians established the Education Task Force to see how bad the educational situation of their children was. The report, overseen by Rodney Soonias, convinced the chiefs that it was time for the Indian people themselves to become involved in the education of their children.

I pointed out that this was the moment when the graduation we were attending had become the dream of Saskatchewan's Indian people. A plan was formulated. The work of the Saskatchewan Indian Cultural College was to underlie everything done in First Nations education. For 100 years, our traditional knowledge (the North American intellectual tradition) had been left out of the education of our children. Our elders had been made to feel that what they had to say was not respected or accepted. Under Smith Atimoyoo, the elders of all the cultural communities of Saskatchewan were recognized and acknowledged for the knowledge that they had protected, which had been passed to them by their ancestors. Their traditional knowledge was to be preserved and incorporated into the schooling of our children and our professionals.

Looking at the communities, the planners acknowledged that until our people had control of the jobs in the communities that impacted the lives of people, we would stay uneducated, with others making the decisions. The decision makers in the communities were the teachers and the social workers. It was decided that these were the professions that needed to be filled in communities by our own people. This was the dream.

The reality was setting up programs to train people to fill these positions. ITEP, established in 1973, was the first program to be set up and implemented. Its success brought about the decision to establish the Indian Social Work Education Program (ISWEP) in 1974. At the request of the Federation of Saskatchewan Indians and Saskatchewan Indian Cultural College (SICC), the School of Social Work in Regina, in collaboration with the cultural experts at SICC, developed ISWEP. The FSI believed that good social workers in First Nations communities could be effective only if they respected the elders and had a genuine interest in the well-being of the people with whom they worked.

In 1976, when the Saskatchewan Indian Federated College (the forerunner of the First Nations University of Canada) was created, its mandate was to build on the work of SICC.

The mission of the Saskatchewan Indian Federated College (SIFC) is to enhance the quality of life, and preserve, protect and interpret the history, language, culture and artistic heritage of the Indian people. The college will acquire and expand its base of knowledge and understanding in the best interests of the Indian

people and for the benefit of society by providing
bi-lingual, bi-cultural education under the mandate
and control of the Indian Nations of Saskatchewan.
(SIFC Calendar, 1989–90)

I pointed out that it was obvious that the creators of
SIFC intended that SIFC was to be founded on our own
intellectual tradition. Enhancing our people's lives was tied
to our preserving, protecting, and interpreting our own
histories, languages, cultures, and artistic heritage. At the
same time we were not to present these things as "museum
cultures." We were to acquire and expand our knowledge
base. This mission recognized that our knowledge came
from our land and that it was different from the pathway
to knowledge taken by the "Western intellectual tradition"
that formed the foundation of knowledge at conventional
universities. It reinforced the idea that it was the Indian
people and communities that had kept this knowledge and
it was the mandate of SIFC to carry it forward for future
generations.

I told the graduands that they would face an ever-changing
world but so did their ancestors, and it was now their time
to stand up in the world because the dreams and visions
of their ancestors were vested in each of them. For FNUC,
each graduation renewed the hope of the dreamers.

FNUC went through an administrative restructuring
and the position of dean was changed from an academic
position to an administrative position: campus manager.
My first love was teaching, and this change freed me to
take on more classes and to work with students more. It
is amazing how easy it is to make decisions to follow your
passion when you are retired and not trying to climb the

academic ladder, and I happily returned to the classroom as an instructor.

The ideal job for me was teaching my language. This was the opportunity that opened to me. I became a sessional lecturer teaching Saulteaux students. This was perfect. I had a lighter load and had the direct contact with students. This lasted until Dr. Shauneen Pete, one of my old ITEP students, handed me a letter in the parking lot, telling me that "*my services were no longer required.*" I was very hurt. It was so unnecessary. Since I was now a sessional instructor, all that needed to happen was that I not be offered another class to teach. There was no reason given. However, as I was well beyond retirement age, I can only assume I was dispensable.

In retrospect, it freed me to go to the University of Saskatchewan's College of Education, where I had always felt respected and did not have to fight and get dragged into political conflicts. I was able to work with students, not as a cultural elder but as an academic elder. I believe that, at the university, this is the kind of support the students need. At the universities, the gatekeepers have been at every level. Indian, Metis, and Inuit students need role models at each step in their university journey. I now became involved with students taking on their PhDs. This was the last chance for the gatekeepers to keep the Indians out. The problem stemmed from a lack of general education about Indian people among those who would guide them through postgraduate studies, and the breadth of unconscious suppression of Indigenous knowledge being deeply embedded. For example, an Aboriginal student who wished to write their thesis in agriculture might not have received support for their vision to express the Aboriginal view of food sustainability. My role was to be on committees and advocate for the students on research topics related to their nations. I was able to give the students confidence that the topic they had chosen was worthy of academic study at this level and validate the content where the university members on the committee did not have the knowledge to guide the student.

I served as a volunteer on many Aboriginal student's PhDs at the University of Saskatchewan. I was even working with someone doing their master of law. Working with Aboriginal graduate students usually entailed a lot of time because the students often came to me when they did not think that their university supervisor "got" what they were trying to do. In many cases, it was a lack of confidence on the part of the student. I would reassure them that their study had merit and help them to massage their statement of the problem until they believed that they could do it. However, even though they were well able to handle the research, we met frequently during the time they were working on their project. These were good times. I loved watching the students "catch fire." I was usually at their oral defence to advocate if necessary and to let the student know that it mattered to me whether they were successful.

Beyond the University of Saskatchewan, I served as an external examiner on dissertations for the Ontario Institute for Studies in Education, Queen's University, the University of Regina, the University of Calgary, the University of Alberta, and the University of Victoria.

While I was engaged in these things, I was also working on the research that I had started at the Newberry Library. Every holiday was spent travelling to libraries and historic sites looking for more fragments of J.B. Assiginack's life. We had travelled to Dublin to look at an archival collection of de Peyster's time in Mackinac, as well as another collection in Liverpool. We visited libraries, including the Library of Congress in Washington, DC; Library Archives Canada in Ottawa; and the Provincial Archives of Ontario. Perhaps the most exciting and unexpected were the resources we found in local libraries in small towns in Michigan. Each had a Michigan Room. Here we found early reports, manuscripts, and journals of pioneers, traders, and local historians that had not been copied and do not exist anywhere else. They gave local flavour to historical events.

Finally, I had run out of excuses not to start writing Assiginack's story. Writing does not come easy to me. I am an orator. It wasn't until I realized that I had to write about him from the Odawa perspective that I was able to start the task.

By weaving my writing in while working on other things, the project continued over almost a quarter century. At one point I commented that the next time I wrote about one of our heroes, I wasn't going to pick a person who lived almost 100 years. J.B. Assiginack was born just as our people's existence was changing. The British defeated the French in 1759 and the country was governed by the British, the old enemies of the Odawak. Shortly after that, the American colonies rebelled against the British. The Americans took over the area around Mackinac where J.B. Assiginack was growing up. Another colonizer took over. Just as the Odawak were getting used to the Americans, the War of 1812 broke out and the Odawak decided to fight for the British. Our people helped the British repossess territory previously lost to the Americans. Unfortunately in the peace talks, the British gave the area around the Odawaks' homeland back to the Americans. Since living under the Americans was not acceptable, J.B. Assiginack followed the British to their new fort, and when that fort was also returned to the Americans, he decided to go back to his birthplace to live.

However, as the American government passed laws which might result in our people being forced to move off the Michigan land to Oklahoma, J.B. Assiginack moved with his family to be under the protection of the British. He encouraged many of the Michigan Indians to move with him to make Manitoulin Island their new home. Assiginack worked for the British in their settlement. At times he worked for the Catholic Church and at other times he was blunt in his criticism of the priests. He worked for the Indian Department for years after the government had reported that he had retired. He was an interpreter for treaty negotiations in 1836 and 1862. In his support of the 1862 treaty he went against many of his own people's leaders. For this he was called a traitor. When he died in 1866 he had lost much of the support of his people that he had had for most of his ninety-eight years.

My book was a first in Canada. It told the history of Canada through Odawa eyes. I sent the manuscript to the University of Toronto Press. I received promises of publication for four years. Since I was eighty years of age by then, I did not feel that I could wait for the academic press to act. I had given names of international scholars in Indian history to the editor and he had had two of them peer review the document. They told him it needed to be published. This did not have any impact. I requested the book back and self-published the book because I believed that it was an important book that should be available.

The work that had taken almost a quarter century entailed collecting, reading, and analyzing sources in French, English, and Ojibwe (Assiginack's own letters). Most events in his life were commented upon by recorders who disagreed with each other. British, American, and Canadian documents had to be located and researched to uncover the narrative of Assiginack's life. Turning the sources upside down to shake out the story of my ancestors took more time than when the sources report on the events from the perspective of the actor you are researching. Telling the story as an Odawa narrative was a new approach. This involved using our language at particular places in order to bring the readers into the worldview of our ancestors.

I have encountered many barriers in my career. I have often bumped up against walls in attempting to bring my people's knowledge and that of other Aboriginal peoples into the knowledge base that all Canadians will learn and know. The bias that I have found against my book in the publishing community and the agencies such as the Canada Council for the Arts is just the latest wall to breach. Hopefully, my effort will change things for those who follow me.

We had the book launch at the Native Law Centre at the University of Saskatchewan. Surrounded by my family, old friends, and students, the book was eagerly received. In particular, there have been a lot of sales among lawyers. I am surprised that educators have not embraced it, as educators have been pushing for decolonizing the curriculum and indigenizing the experience in our postsecondary institutions. I am hopeful that my book will open the door for scholars to rewrite Canadian history in the Cree voice, the Dene voice, the Metis voice, and the voice of every other nation in Canada. When that happens, reconciliation may be possible. Then we will be able to see Canada through each other's eyes.

10. SOME OF WHAT I HAVE LEARNED

I have been an educator for more than sixty years and have seen many changes in the education of Aboriginal students. In a memoir, I think it is incumbent on the writer to look at the lessons learned in a lifetime and remember the mentors who strongly influenced their life. I will try to fulfil that requirement. I guess it is time to summarize my life and what I have learned!

In my home, I lived with three old people. I was lucky because there was no one telling me that I couldn't do something. Each in his or her own way supported me, providing the foundation for me to find out what my strengths were and encouraging me to become the person I could be. My grandmother used discipline to encourage correct behaviour. My grandfather showed me how something should be done. Kohkwehns listened to me and taught me how to be a "good" Odawa.

My formal education began at the Buzwah Indian Day School. All my teachers were First Nations women. I was influenced by the many First Nations teachers in my young life. My grandmother was a teacher. My first teachers at Buzwah School were Christine Wakegejig, Clara Trudeau, Rita Corbiere (Mrs. Adam Corbiere), and Eliza Jane Pelletier (Mrs. Lawrence Pelletier). I learned a lot from Stella Kinoshameg and Rosie Fox, two more First Nations teachers of the older generation. They taught me that First Nations people could be teachers.

My teachers expected us to be able to do whatever was asked of us. They created the conditions for each of us to succeed. Like all kids, I went to school eager to learn. No student comes to school to fail. Our teachers prepared us to pass the Ontario provincial entrance exams at the completion of grade eight. Those of us who attempted the entrance exam were successful. Our teachers gave us the basic skills and knowledge and confidence to succeed. And we did!

My residential school experience had the same characteristics that have been described by others. We were taught that our language, history, and stories were quaint and would not help us in the modern world. We were taught that our ancestors were brutal savages. We could never aspire, according to the priests, to their level. It was only later that I realized that I had internalized these lessons.

I was encouraged to consider becoming a teacher by the provincial inspector who visited Garnier Residential School. Without his suggestion I don't know if I would have thought of doing it. Jobs for young Indian boys, high-school graduates or not, were few and far between when I was ready to join the ranks of the employed.

In training as a teacher, I was placed in Indian day schools to practise teaching. After six weeks of training, I found myself in complete charge of a school. I learned much in these First Nations communities. I learned that by using Ojibwe with my students in these culturally strong communities, the children learned English faster and the parents became involved in their children's and their own education. If I explained new concepts first in Ojibwe, everyone learned better than if I tried to introduce the concept in English. I saw that rather than our language being a detriment to learning school-based knowledge, it was an immense advantage.

I learned that a child brings special gifts, skills, knowledge, and aptitudes to school. As teachers we need to help the children we meet to find and develop their unique gifts. We need to believe and make them believe that they can succeed. We need to understand the vision that each child has for his or her future. We need to provide the support and encouragement that each individual needs to succeed in reaching that vision. Too often, as teachers, we focus on what is wrong with the child, on areas of weakness, without promoting strengths. I believe that as teachers we have a huge responsibility to take the extra step with students. It is *our* responsibility as professionals to set up the conditions for success for our students. Students come to *us* looking for success. No child comes to school to fail.

I have seen that we can inspire First Nations children when we build their sense of identity, when we teach them that to be First Nations is important, significant, and unique. We begin with our languages and impress on them that they are the inheritors of a gift from the Creator and they must be the stewards of that gift because, if we let our languages die, they are dead to the world forever.

We must teach our children that having two languages makes them special. They will know twice as much as those without a second language. We must teach our children our history, our heroes, and the heroes of other Aboriginal nations. We know stories of this land reaching back thousands of years. I had the opportunity to see how culturally stronger communities functioned. I saw how living in our culture in our language was possible in the modern world.

In all I taught for eighteen years in elementary schools. I moved to Ottawa and was an intake counsellor for Indian Affairs. From there I moved to Saskatchewan in 1971 to finish my BEd in Indian and Northern Education. The University of Saskatchewan was the first university in Canada to have a course for teachers teaching First Nations, Metis and Inuit children. I knew of the work done at the University of Saskatchewan because Father Andre Renaud, director of the Indian and Northern Education Program, spoke all over Canada, to conferences of teachers teaching in Indian and northern communities. What he talked about was revolutionary thinking in Indian education.

My re-education began in the Indian and Northern Education Program. Fr. Renaud believed that Indian education had to be an "education from within." He taught teachers that we had to start with the child's previous knowledge, the knowledge he or she had already been taught by his or her mother, father, grandmother, and grandfather and his or her community.

Fr. Renaud's ideas were exciting. Teachers, like me, who were Indians ourselves were especially excited because during much of our schooling, especially in residential school, we had been told that we had to "leave our Indianness at the door," put aside the teachings of our ancestors, leave our communities, and not speak our language because it would hold us back in learning the things that we needed to survive in the "modern" world.

Arriving in Saskatoon, I found students and faculty who came to the university every day looking for ways to help

Indian, Inuit, and Metis students to succeed in school. I found people who were passionate about providing a better education for these kids. I was a qualified teacher from Ontario, but the Ontario teacher training was no different for teachers of Indian children than other children. My experience in working in Wikwemikong and then in Ottawa had disillusioned me. I had come to question the commitment of Indian schools and Indian Affairs to providing Indian students with success in school. I wanted to learn more about how to teach our students and ensure that they succeeded in school.

The Indian and Northern Education Program offered a master's program. This was what brought Dr. Arthur Blue to Saskatoon. He was the first Native American university professor I had ever met. He was a clinical psychologist who believed that a person's cultural background was an essential part of their being. He pushed the Indian students like me to acknowledge our cultural selves and bring them into our teaching. He buttressed his beliefs with literature and research from psycholinguistics, cross-cultural cognitive studies, and experience in clinical settings working with Native Americans.

Dr. Blue was my supervisor. He prodded me to delve into my language in my research. At first I resisted, because all through my residential school days I had been told that the knowledge of my people and the stories told by my elders were "primitive." They were "quaint" and filled with "superstition." Art wanted to know about my language and the ways of my people. I found, for the first time in my education, a learning environment established to support who I was as an "Odawa" person.

I was privileged to be welcomed into the company of Saskatchewan's Indian people who were working to have the knowledge of the ancestors incorporated into the university. The Saskatchewan Indian Cultural College, housed on campus in McLean Hall at Emmanuel-St. Chad's Anglican College, was the heart of Indian cultural research for the Indian people of Saskatchewan. From the Cultural College, Smith Atimoyoo searched for those people who still held dear and protected the history, philosophy, spirituality, and cultural ways of each of the nations indigenous to Saskatchewan. The Cultural College had the facilities to record, transcribe, house, and care for the knowledge of these cultural caretakers. Groups of elders came to the college to be recorded in their languages, building a library of cultural knowledge.

Being around people who believed that there was urgency and importance in preserving the knowledge of our people had a powerful effect on me. This was the milieu that brought me back to my culture after having it educated out of me. With the help of the people I met at the University of Saskatchewan, I began to look to my own Odawa heritage. I completed my MEd under Art Blue, analyzing the concept of "animism" within the Ojibwe language. I was encouraged to study my language as part of my academic program at the University of Saskatchewan. Dr. Blue strongly believed that a person's cognitive ability was tied to his or her perceptions of the world. He pushed me to look at the values and worldview underlying the words of my language. That way of looking at First Nations languages became a fundamental part of my approach to my students and to the research I undertook.

I came to see that the words of our language came from a different view of the world. We cannot know the world of our ancestors without knowing our languages because the worldview is embedded in our languages. My language divides the world into animate and inanimate things, and the way we speak of things is reflected in the grammar of my language. My people learn from our language that we are the most dependent of all Creation. Our view of our place in the universe is not the same as the Judeo-Christian view, which puts human beings next to God. Our language contains the teachings of our culture. When we have to describe our teachings in English, we are limited to the words that are available in English. In many cases English is inadequate. We need our languages to tell us who we are!

The Federation of Saskatchewan Indians decided to start a teacher education program for First Nations students. I was asked to be the first director of the Indian Teacher Education Program. Rodney Soonias and I were both educated. Rodney was associated with the Indian and Northern Education Program. He and I believed that we had to have Indian teachers for our Indian students because strengthening their "Indianness" was an essential ingredient in their success at school.

In consultation with Rodney Soonias, himself a teacher and director of the Saskatchewan Indian Cultural College, and elders such as Smith Atimoyoo, a teacher and Anglican clergyman, we developed the program that was accepted by the Saskatchewan Board of Teacher Education in the fall of 1972. In January 1973 we started the program with twenty First Nations students and five Metis students. Since then, the program has graduated over 2,000 qualified Aboriginal teachers. During this time I received my BEd and MEd and decided to pursue my PhD. After my studies, I was hired onto faculty of the College of Education at the University of Saskatchewan, in the Indian and Northern Education Program. I was on staff there until 1991, when I left Saskatoon for Kingston to be the first director of the Aboriginal Teacher

Cecil and his daughter Anna-Leah King at an Indian Teacher Education Program (ITEP) graduation banquet in Saskatoon a few years after his retirement from Queen's.

Education Program (ATEP) at Queen's. At Queen's I was a full professor in the Faculty of Education. When I retired in 1997, the university conferred the title of professor emeritus on me.

Until about twenty years ago, the Canadian education establishment did not deem Indian languages and cultural knowledge and skills relevant to the education of Canadian students—Indian or not. The goal of Canadian education systems had nothing to do with producing graduates who were fluent in Ojibwe, Odawa, Cree, or Mohawk, or graduates who knew the oral traditions, the stories of Nanabush, the botanical classification systems of the medicine people, or the songs of our ancestors. The Aboriginal students who succeeded in the Canadian education system were those who learned that there were two systems of knowledge, one back home and one in the school; that there were two modes of communication, the language of their home and community and the language of school and Canadian society. Successful Aboriginal students knew when and where to express themselves in the appropriate language and learned what knowledge and skills were acceptable in each situation. These Aboriginal students lived in two separate worlds, negotiating meaning through two totally unrelated intellectual systems. Unfortunately, many Aboriginal students who were the most knowledgeable and competent in their Aboriginal language and knowledge system failed to be able to accomplish the dual identity necessary to succeed in Canada's educational institutions.

I have learned that to teach teachers about our people means not only giving them the opportunity to learn the history, culture, and relationships of the Indian, Metis and Inuit peoples with others, but giving them the opportunity to try to view the world through our eyes. This comes from having them study the language and worldview of our peoples.

For many Indian, Metis, and Inuit people, language retention is synonymous with survival. Worldview and language are tied. The languages express the structure of how the world is viewed. The grammatical structures themselves reconceptualize reality. The Algonquian languages such as Cree and Ojibwe classify nouns as animate or more animate. This dichotomy imposes on the world different relational conditions between speaker and object. To open and reveal the Indian, Metis, or Inuit world is to first hear it spoken in its own tongue. The foundation of the disciplines of Indian, Metis, and Inuit education or studies is in the words of the communities. We are not contributing to the reality of these communities when we study them as aberrations of the Euro-Canadian worldview. Primary research from inside the language and culture of the communities is essential to bringing understanding. There is so much work to be done for us to begin to know the complexity of our own ancestors' ways of being in the world.

Language is not only word lists and structures. It is meaning. It is communication. It is communication styles, sociocultural rules of discourse, values placed on silence and speaking in a community, forms of oratory, and knowing the "power of words."

To quote my daughter Anna-Leah, "We must sing ourselves in!" We must teach our children through *jingbadamwin* (songs), *mizin be giwin* (art), *neemidwin* (dance), and *mizin-akowendmowin* (poetry), the aesthetic side of their beings.

We acknowledge that the Creator had a plan for each of us. Each of our students has a pre-planned purpose. It is our job as teachers and community members to help our children find their "vision" and then live that vision.

We need to look at our past and acknowledge that the teachings of our ancestors excelled in maintaining and developing intact, surviving communities. We were sustained by the *Midewewin* (Lodge of Life), *Enendagwad* (Law of Orders), *Kendaaswin* (Knowledge), *Atsokan* (legends; ancient stories), *Kina Kitchina Nishnabeg Inendaamowinan* (all the elders practise serious thinking at all times).

We must find a way to take our foundational principles that sustained our cultures since time immemorial and interpret them into today's context. *Values are timeless.* Being brave is as important to young people today as at any time in our history. We must help our children to define how they can use the traditional ways of being to be First Nations men and women in the twenty-first century.

When the question what does it mean to be a First Nation, Metis, or Inuit person is asked, our children need to know. They need to know how to tell people who they are. Being First Nation, Metis, or Inuit cannot be defined for our children by the media or academics, it must come from them. It must be in their hearts and souls.

First Nations, Metis, and Inuit kids come to school with a mind, a heart, and a spirit. I have found that whether they are in grade one, high school, taking undergraduate classes, or are at the PhD level, there are successful ways to teach First Nations, Inuit, and Metis students. This is what I have learned:

- Treat each as an individual with her or his own culture and experiences.

- Develop a personal connection with each student.

- Use examples from First Nations, Metis, or Inuit traditional cultures—the tipi, which has been called the most perfect architectural design; the kayak; the medicine wheels designed to be aligned with the solar systems; the pyramids of Central America, built without the aid of contemporary earth-moving equipment; the mathematical systems of the First Nations people, with different counting systems, different mathematical foundations; the Red River Cart, made with perfect dimensions for moving heavy loads across the prairie but able to keep from sinking in the mud.

- Maintain high expectations for each student.

- Examine ways of talking about things that include a variety of messages and are based in multiple experiences.

- Be firm and fair.

- Make the students confident that they can succeed.

I have spent my career in education. This was not just the education of Indian children but also educating other Canadians about my people. We have seen how the lack of understanding of the perceptions of Aboriginal peoples can impact Canadian history. The confrontation at Oka was a confrontation of values and philosophy as much as a confrontation of peoples. This confrontation occurred as much because Canada's institutions of learning have excluded the Aboriginal reality as because an expansion of a golf course was to be built.

The Euro-Canadian journalists and academics continually attempt to analyze the interactions between the Aboriginal peoples and Canadian society through the prevailing theories from the various disciplines of the Western intellectual tradition. We have been defined as minority groups, colonized groups, tribal groups, ethnic groups, and primitive groups. Our problems are attributed to our colonized state, our undereducation, our unemployment, or our poverty. Our personal attributes are listed as a lack of motivation, ignorance, disadvantage, or cultural deprivation, and these have also served as the accepted analyses for our failure to become like other Canadians. We have never accepted these analyses, but rarely are we allowed to offer our interpretation of the situation.

The land that is called Canada has always been the land of our forebears, as long as our memories go back—anthropologists tell us we have been there for 20,000 to 30,000, maybe 50,000 years, but our people tell us we have been there forever. Meanwhile, the descendants of the newcomers celebrate 528 years since a lost Italian, who had the audacity to proclaim the world was round, stumbled on the continent in his quest to find India. They celebrate a mere 528 years, while my ancestors can claim continuous occupancy for perhaps 100 times that. We would be happy to celebrate life on our land by having the newcomers acknowledge their youthful existence on our continent. We would appreciate their respect for our knowledge as the wisdom of old age in relation to the ways of the North American continent.

The Aboriginal peoples of Canada are the founding peoples of this land. Our cultures, our languages, our ways of relating to each other have come from the land. What makes us either Odawa or Cree or Inuit or Mohawk is not the statistics of how many suicides are in our communities or of how poor we are—but is our different way of seeing the world around us—our relationships with our Manitou, Mother Earth, the Plants, Animalkind, and other Human Beings. This is our essence. This is our soul.

I believe we are in exciting times; significant institutional change is underway. As an Aboriginal person who has worked for over twenty years in postsecondary institutions, generally on the fringes, I am finally starting to see some real efforts being made to incorporate my people's perspective sincerely and honestly into the echelons of higher learning.

I believe that Canadian institutions of higher learning should embrace our knowledge. If they really are committed to the preservation and dissemination of knowledge, the North American intellectual tradition should be the core of these institutions. If these institutions really want to be world-class institutions, shouldn't they ensure that the knowledge from the North American intellectual tradition and that North American heroes are honoured in their institutions? This is an area where they can teach other world-class institutions. They can offer the wisdom of our ancestors to offer new ways to look at old problems in the world.

Cecil King with his daughters Alanis (far left), Anna-Leah (second from left), and Shoo-Shoo "Tanya" (far right), at the 2009 National Aboriginal Achievement Awards in Winnipeg. Dr. King was recognized for his outstanding lifelong contributions in education.

I am an orator. For me, the spoken word has always been more comfortable than the written word. In the days when our languages were only oral, our peoples knew the power of the word. We knew that everything that must be remembered must be said. It is not so different today. Everything that must be remembered about our peoples, our histories, our cultures, our stories must be said. We have more than one way now, but our voices are being drowned out. Our languages are being silenced. Our worldviews are being submerged under the weight of other worldviews.

Our artists and writers, poets and singers, and all of the collective talent of our community must be geared towards making our language sing. We are the people who have been called great orators. We were known for our wordsmithing. We are the people who love to play with words. We need all of our artists and singers, our creative people to show our children the beauty of our words, the richness of our sounds, and the awe of seeing the world through the lens of a thousand years.

We need your voices. We need your songs. We need your stories. For what must be remembered must be said. Our words must reveal the flesh of our culture. Our words must reveal our worldviews. This is our legacy. This is our duty. In my grandfather's words, we must pray to the Creator that our words might be as a medicine to all those who hear them.

As First Nations, Metis and Inuit peoples, we have sometimes questioned the significance of our stories to the contemporary world. This led some of our parents and grandparents to encourage us to forget our stories and learn the stories of others. As we have seen in the long-term effects of the residential school experience in our families and communities, losing our stories hurts us and our loved ones.

I learned to speak my language, when I went to school, to play with the other more traditional children. At residential school I practised my language and learned its subtleties. At university and in libraries around the world I learned who my people were and how important they were in the history of North America.

Let's celebrate who we are. Knowing who you are and knowing what knowledge your people have is something to celebrate. Let us remember that we are the descendants of great civilizations. We are the inheritors of great knowledge of the universe and the physical world and knowledge of

Four King siblings at the Ojibwe Cultural Foundation conference, held in Sudbury, Ontario, in 2014, at which Cecil delivered the speech that ends this book. Left to right: Elizabeth (Liz), Cecil, Don, and Loretta.

the interrelationships of human beings with the rest of Creation. We are the ones that the Great Spirit has placed here to remind the world who we are!

I have worked with people of other cultures. I have found my history in their libraries, museums, and records. In telling their stories, they relayed some of our stories, and we must reclaim them. In writing the story of one of my community leaders, I have found not only his story but the story of my nation, my community, and myself. I have found the joy of knowing who I am. I intend to celebrate this until my story ends.

I will end my memoirs with the challenge I presented to the audience in the speech I gave in Sudbury, Ontario, on February 28, 2014. The title of the presentation was "Reconciling the Duality in Historical Inquiry: The Case of Jean-Baptiste Assiginack." I concluded with the following:

I want to challenge the people in the audience to carry on my work. There is *so much* to do. We have to resist the pressure from the mainstream institutions to replicate the work of mainstream academics. We must resist doing one more study on colonization. What will we tell our children? We don't know who we were but we were colonized, passive red objects that just quietly did what we were told to do and thought what we were told to think. Don't be satisfied with that!

We have our *own* work to do for *our* communities and for *our* future generations—my great grandchildren have arrived and need to know who they are. We must:

Re-mine the resources used by Canadian historians to tell the story of Canada.

Extract the words of *our* people.

Identify *our* heroes. Tell their stories as an integral part of the history of Canada but show how their lives were really lived as members of their nation—with their own actions and motivations separate from that of the newcomers.

Write a narrative in *our* way of telling a story.

Write from *our* worldview and show why *our* story is important—we had *our own* ways of believing, seeing and being in the world.

Use words from *our* languages.

Invite the reader into *our* world. Show them what Canadians have missed from their story.

Weave the stories of *our* ancestors from the oral tradition into the story that comes from the documents.

Don't apologize for stories that have a spiritual or other than human causation. These are important to who we are.

Ahow! Now go out and tell *our* stories!!

Ahow! Minwaachitodah! Let's celebrate!

This is my story.

INDEX

do things, 46; as
sustaining First Nations
communities, 332
English language, 8, 11, 49,
155–57, 165, 180, 258,
300, 321; and difficulty
of translations with
Indigenous languages, 274,
280, 285; as inadequate
to describe Indigenous
realities, 283, 285, 329; as
language of schools, 49–
50, 119, 132, 156–57, 168,
296, 325; as needed to get
along in life, 4, 7, 46, 50,
170, 205, 220, 296, 325
Ermatinger, Harvey, 123, 141
Esperance, Angus, 267
ethics, in research with
Indigenous people, 282,
300–301, *See also* research
European settlers: negotiations
with, 273; as regarding
Indigenous as less
civilized, 252; view of
progress, 299; worldview
as different from
Indigenous worldview,
244, 308, 329, 331,
See also newcomers

F

farming/agriculture, 22, 105–6,
120, 130–31, 148, 167, 247

Federation of Saskatchewan
Indian Nations, 202–3,
206–7, 211, 254, 266,
315–16, 329; Saskatchewan
Indian Education
Commission, 262
Federation of Sovereign
Indigenous Nations
(formerly New Union
of Saskatchewan
Indians), 195
First Nations University of
Canada (FNUC) (formerly
Saskatchewan Indian
Federated College),
195, 310–14, 316–17
Fisher, Don, 176–77
Fisher, Rosemary (née
Pelletier), 176–79, 197
Fitzpatrick, I.E., 234–36
*A Five-Year Action Plan
for Native Curriculum
Development,* 267
Flaherty, Father, 179–80
Flesjer, Olga, 264
Foster, Dr. Maurice, 191
Fox, David, 123
Fox, Mary Lou, 97, 150, 157,
163, 169, 176, 180–81
Fox, Rosie (née King),
157, 265, 324
Freeman, Kate, 293–94
Freeman, Mac, 293
French language, 165, 169, 321

ABOUT THE AUTHOR

DR. CECIL KING is professor emeritus at Queen's University and lives in Saskatoon. He is an Odawa from Wikwemikong Unceded Indian Reserve who served a sixty-plus-year career as an Indigenous educator. This is his memoir of that remarkable journey.

CPSIA information can be obtained
at www.ICGtesting.com
Printed in the USA
JSHW021436210723
45195JS00001B/84